GENERATION ROE

GENERATION ROE
INSIDE THE FUTURE OF THE PRO-CHOICE MOVEMENT
SARAH ERDREICH

Seven Stories Press
NEW YORK

A Seven Stories Press First Edition

Seven Stories Press
140 Watts Street
New York, NY 10013
www.sevenstories.com

College professors may order examination copies of Seven Stories Press titles for a free six-month trial period. To order, visit www.sevenstories.com/textbook or send a fax on school letterhead to (212) 226-1411.

Book design by Jon Gilbert

Library of Congress Cataloging-in-Publication Data

Erdreich, Sarah.
  Generation roe : inside the future of the pro-choice movement / Sarah Erdreich.
    pages cm
  ISBN 978-1-60980-458-9 (pbk.)
  1. Abortion--United States. 2. Pro-life movement--United States. 3. Abortion--Moral and ethical aspects--United States. I. Title.
  HQ767.5.U5E73 2013
  363.46--dc23
                                2012046132

Printed in the United States

9 8 7 6 5 4 3 2 1

To my mother, who taught me how to talk to anyone;
and to my father, who showed me how to listen to everyone

CONTENTS

Chapter One: Abortion is Not a Four-Letter Word 9

Chapter Two: Hands-Off Training 27

Chapter Three: Isolated, Stigmatized, and Romanticized 51

Chapter Four: (Mis)Representations of Reality 95

Chapter Five: The Amazing Talking Fetus of Ohio 117

Chapter Six: Defending Choice, One Generation at a Time 159

Chapter Seven: I Went to the March For Life, and
All I Got was this Fear of Choice 177

Chapter Eight: On Demand and Without Apology 209

Acknowledgments 231

Resources 233

Notes 243

About the Author 269

CHAPTER I

ABORTION IS NOT A FOUR-LETTER WORD

I am not a Nazi.

That is not a statement I ever thought I'd have to make, particularly as a Jewish woman. But if there is one thing that anti-choice activists love more than ultrasound images of fully-formed and healthy fetuses, it is equating pro-choice beliefs with Nazism. The person who called me a Nazi in a particularly nasty e-mail has no idea where I spend my days or what I look like. Others who work to protect abortion rights cannot enjoy the safety of anonymity. Luckily for me, his hatred can take no expression greater than a viral insult—one that I never want to read again, yet one that I save because it means something: it means that I can't give up.

Each pro-choice activist and abortion provider has his or her own reasons for pursuing this stigmatized work, which carries a very real threat of harassment and violence. My own reasons stem from a deep-seated desire to safeguard women's rights. I'm unwilling to stand by as a passive witness as women's rights are chipped away to the point where abortion becomes, effectively, illegal. I'm reminded of why this is important every time I meet a woman whose life was directly impacted by this larger struggle, such as when Renee Chelian, the founder and director of several abortion clinics in the Detroit area, tells me about the abortion she had as a fifteen-year-old in 1966.

"My mom was six months pregnant with my younger sister, so it was my dad that took me," she recalls about the procedure, which cost $2,000—a substantial sum today, never mind over forty years ago. "We went to a parking lot near a building; we were put in the back of a car and I remember I couldn't see where we were going because we were blindfolded, so I couldn't look out the windows. We were driven into a warehouse; it was probably a garage. There was oil spilled on the cement floor and a card table, and there were a lot of women. I was afraid if I looked up and I said anything they wouldn't give me my abortion. They gave me something, thankfully, and when I woke up my dad took me home. After my abortion my dad told me we'll never ever talk about this again, no one [will] ever marry you if they know, and we can't risk anybody going to jail. And we didn't talk about it, really, for I can't even think how many years. When I opened the clinic," she adds, "my parents were very, very proud of me, very, very supportive."[1]

As harrowing as that experience must have been, Renee was fortunate not only to have her parents' support but also not to have suffered any adverse effects following an illegal procedure. June Ayers, the director of Reproductive Health Services in Montgomery, Alabama, recalls a much more dangerous environment in her hometown. "Before there was *Roe v. Wade*, [women] knew what abortion was like when you had to stand on a street corner with your money in hand and be willing to be blindfolded, then taken to God-knows-where to have it completed on someone's kitchen table or wherever," she tells me as we sit in a small office in her clinic, our conversation punctuated by the heavy clang of the front doors as patients are buzzed into the building. "My father, who was a state trooper, remembered that in Opelika [Alabama] there was a house that they just didn't pay attention to. He knew that they did abortions there; he knew that the abortions actually were done with broom straws. Imagine a broom straw, what a risk for infection. But until someone died, nobody paid attention; I mean it would take a death for them to go in and say, 'Hey, you can't do this anymore.'"[2]

And women did die from illegal abortion in the years before *Roe*: In 1930, it was the cause of death for almost 2,700 women, or 18 percent of maternal deaths recorded that year.[3] By 1965, the number had declined to just under 200, but that still accounted for 17 percent of all childbirth- and pregnancy-related deaths that year.

Like June, Emily Lyons, a nurse who was seriously injured when Birmingham's New Woman, All Women Healthcare Clinic was bombed in 1998, grew up in a small southern town. "[I] came from a very strict Baptist house, didn't watch TV, didn't listen to music, didn't read a newspaper," she recalls as we sit at her dining room table. "Civil rights and all that, it happened when I was growing up, but not in my house. We didn't talk about anything. How I turned out like this is beyond me."[4] While she doesn't mention any experience with illegal abortion, Emily does bring up a particular case she worked on early in her nursing career.

"When I was in school, my last semester was in labor and delivery. One of my patients was a saline abortion. They really just sent her off, she did her thing, I didn't have to monitor too much of anything except for her, and once she delivered in the bed, then you cleaned up, weighed it, and et cetera. When I look back now I think man, she must have felt so alone. I think that kind of got things started. That was '77, so abortion had been legal for four years. Obviously, her doctor decided this was what she needed to do; this was what she wanted to do. Whether it's at four weeks or however many weeks on up, it's still your decision to make; it's a choice just like everything else in the world. Everything is a choice. You know people say it's not a choice, it's a child. No, it is a choice; it is a decision that you have to make.

"I'm reading a book now," Emily continues, "*The Girls Who Went Away*.[5] Talk about being ostracized. It's all the girls' fault, of course, whisked off in the middle of the night to these homes [for unwed mothers]. Golly, when did society get so judgmental?"

Hundreds of miles away, Robert Blake, a professor emeritus at the University of Missouri's School of Medicine, e-mails me about his involvement in the pre-*Roe* pro-choice movement when he was a medical student in St. Louis.

"A group of folks, including physicians, medical students, other health professionals and health professional students, and clergy was formed in the late 1960s in St. Louis to assist women in obtaining safe abortions at a time when abortion in Missouri was only legally available to save a woman's life. Several OB/GYN physicians were willing to perform the procedure for women referred through this group. I don't know who they were, and I don't know how women found out about the group—probably through clergy, counselors, etc. The role of the students was to meet with women one-on-one and 'counsel' them. This involved informing them of the nature of the procedure and medical risks but also involved assessing their social and psychological conditions. In one case that I know about, the woman actually stayed at a student's home while the process of abortion was completed.[6]

"I counseled a few women. One I particularly remember was a married graduate student who could not afford a child. She was well educated and emotionally well adjusted with a supportive husband. In fact she and her husband seemed to be very similar to my wife and me, except she was pregnant and did not want to be. I think this experience dispelled some misconceptions I had about women who sought abortion. My stereotype was that they often had significant psychological problems and were immature. I discovered that this was not valid."

The world that Robert, June, Emily, and Renee grew up in is very different from the one that young activists and providers work in today. Not only did everyone born in or after 1973 grow up with legal abortion, but today's medical students, law students, and activists just entering the reproductive rights field came of age during the heyday of abstinence-only education, and in a time that has seen impressive gains by the anti-choice movement to restrict abortion access. They are in an interesting position, then: while they only know a world with legal abortion, they also only know a world where abortion is heavily politicized and controversial, and where it is all too easy to overlook the very individual and meaningful reasons that women choose abortion.

Women Who Have Abortions

When people know that you work in the pro-choice movement, the stories come out. All of the sudden, you're a safe person; you can be trusted to hear very personal stories about terminating a pregnancy because you won't judge or criticize. And when you go through life hearing such stories, one thing becomes quite clear to you: All kinds of women have abortions. According to the nonpartisan Guttmacher Institute, three in ten American women will have an abortion before the age of forty-five.[7]

Rachel* is one of my mother's oldest friends; I have known her and her husband practically all of my life. But it isn't until I tell them I'm writing a book about reproductive rights that Rachel's own experience with abortion comes up.

Several years into her marriage, in the mid-'70s, Rachel became pregnant. She had already had two healthy pregnancies, but this pregnancy did not progress normally. Rachel was vague on the details when she recounted her story to me, but she made it clear that the abortion was medically necessary. "Had I not been offered that option," she tells me, "I very well could have lost my life, so I will always be thankful for the physician I used. I was able to make a decision that was right for me and for my body and for my family."[8]

Rachel's voice is firm as she says, "I don't fault anyone that does not make a choice to have an abortion. I think abortion is probably one of the hardest decisions a family can make. There'll always be doubts if I did right or I did wrong, but the right thing is

---

* Not her real name.

that people have those choices that they can make. I was fortunate enough that I had what I consider good medical care; I was fortunate that I was able to understand my options, but not everyone has that liberty. To deny a person the same rights that I had as a somewhat educated individual, I think is a terrible travesty. I think it's a terrible situation where one group can and one group can't.

"I'm not the least bit ashamed of what I did," Rachel continues. "In fact, I feel somewhat empowered by the choice I had to make because that was my right." Yet Rachel only agreed to be interviewed if her real name was not used.

The day after I see Rachel, I spend some time with Vicki,* a longtime friend of my father's family. Toward the end of our visit, she mentions that she had had an abortion many years earlier. Months later, Vicki tells me the whole story.

"My ex-husband is the only one who knows," Vicki says. "I wanted to tell my mother, but it happened before I moved back here, and that wasn't something I wanted to break the news about in a long-distance telephone call. That was back when long-distance calls meant something, you know, not like today." Her husband threatened to leave unless she had an abortion; they were living in a city that was hundreds of miles from her parents, siblings, and closest friends, although it was also in one of the few states that had liberalized their abortion laws in the early 1970s. "It was [the state's] law to first see a psychiatrist," Vicki explained, adding that the entire procedure was covered by insurance. "I remember that I told the psychiatrist that if my husband wasn't in the picture I

---

* Not her real name.

would not consider abortion, but I guess approval was routine. I later told the doctor before the surgery that I want[ed] to change my mind, but he said he had the time scheduled—be there." After she had the abortion, Vicki's husband—who had, she says, "badgered" her to get the abortion—called her a murderer.[9]

"If I had known myself as well as I know myself now—I have more confidence to trust my feelings and realized that I was capable of supporting and raising a child on my own—then I would not have had an abortion," Vicki muses. "But," she adds sternly, "the decision should be the woman's. Even before abortions were legal, women still had them generally in seedy, unsanitary places. The United States should not go back to those days."

I couldn't stop thinking about Vicki's story in the following days, about the profound ambivalence that she expressed. When I worked for the National Abortion Federation (NAF), I heard many women express gratitude that they could have an abortion, even as they regretted the particular circumstances—an unstable relationship, economic hardship, age, or a lack of education—that made abortion their best choice.

To appreciate a decision even as you regret the reasons for that decision is a complicated set of emotions, and one that established pro-choice organizations have not always successfully addressed. Groups like Planned Parenthood, NARAL Pro-Choice America, and NAF generally stick to messages about how common and safe abortion is, but they don't offer a great deal of in-depth discussion about the range of emotions women may experience. Instead, they offer first-person stories, which overwhelmingly talk about abortion in positive terms. While studies have shown that this is how most women do indeed feel after their abortions, those women that have more ambivalent feelings following their abortions may not find much comfort or support in these messages.

These are important distinctions. The anti-choice movement has been incredibly persuasive in its insistence that if a woman has mixed feelings following an abortion, then abortion itself must be unethical. Pro-life advocate and therapist Vincent Rue is credited with coining the term "post-abortion syndrome" in testimony before Congress in 1981,[10] to refer to an adverse physical or emotional response to abortion. While neither the American Psychological Association nor the American Psychiatric Association recognize this as an official syndrome or diagnosis,[11] the term quickly gained traction in the anti-choice community, and in 1987 Ronald Reagan asked then–Surgeon General C. Everett Koop to write a report about the effect of abortion on women. The avowedly anti-choice Koop had believed, prior to taking office as surgeon general, that abortion traumatized women; he even coauthored a book, *Whatever Happened to the Human Race*, which discussed post-abortion trauma.

Even so, he was reluctant to do as Reagan asked, suspecting that the request was motivated more by politics—anti-choice advocates and the religious right were significant sources of support for the president—than public health concerns. After conducting his own research and reviewing that of his staff, Koop concluded that there were no rigorous, unbiased scientific studies on the effects of abortion on women's health that could support either a pro- or anti-choice position. As a result, Koop explained in a January 1989 letter to the then-outgoing president, he could not conclude one way or another that abortion was harmful to women.

This conclusion shocked and incensed conservatives and anti-choice advocates, who had assumed that Koop would take an anti-choice position. Yet Koop was careful to draw a strong distinction between his personal beliefs and scientific evidence, and he refused to let ideology pressure him into a stance he was not comfortable with. While many in the pro-choice movement applauded his ability to place public health above personal opinion, Koop did suffer for his decision. After President George H. W. Bush declined to appoint Koop as the Secretary of Health and Human Services, Koop left office one month before the end of his second term as surgeon general.[12]

In 1988, the American Psychological Association commissioned a study to review the then-current research around post-abortion psychological effects.[13] After a survey of over two hundred studies, the panel of six experts found that only a handful—nineteen or twenty—met what they considered reliable scientific standards. From those studies, researchers were able to draw a clear conclusion that most women do not experience lasting distress as a result of having an abortion: "The weight of the evidence from scientific studies indicates that legal abortion of an unwanted pregnancy in the first trimester does not pose a psychological hazard for most women."[14] While some women did experience more serious distress, they were definitely in the minority; one study found that for women that had first-trimester abortions, "76 percent of women reported feeling relief two weeks after an abortion, and only 17 percent reported feeling guilt."[15]

It is important to note that women seeking later abortions did report more distress around their abortion, as did women that had difficulty making their decisions. But it would be intellectually lazy to assume that it was the abortion itself that caused this distress, as opposed to the events that led to the necessity of having the abortion.

According to a survey of over 1,200 women who obtained abortions, nearly three-quarters cited the concern that having a child would interfere with the woman's education, work, or ability to care for dependents as the reason that they had an abortion. Economic concerns came in a close second, followed by the woman's desire not to be a single mother or concern over relationship problems.[16]

These are not only compelling reasons to seek abortions, they are valid reasons why a woman might regret that abortion is her best choice. Few women would choose to experience economic hardship or to have a job that could be so disrupted by pregnancy and motherhood; likewise, few women would choose to be in a relationship that could be negatively impacted by a pregnancy. Any of these reasons alone could cause a great deal of emotional distress to a woman that has less to do with the abortion itself and everything to do with the rest of her life. The abortion is not the cause of her problems—it is a symptom of much larger and unwieldy concerns that affect every aspect of her life, including when to have a child.

There are other, albeit less common, concerns that must also be considered. While 88 percent of abortions are performed within the first twelve weeks of pregnancy,[17] women who have abortions later in their pregnancies overwhelmingly cite a delay in making the necessary arrangements, including raising money and getting an appointment, as the reason for having second- or third-trimester procedures.[18] For later-term abortions, the issue of fetal abnormality must also be considered; many birth defects that are incompatible with life are not discovered until the fourth or fifth month of pregnancy, or even later.

It is not surprising that the anti-choice movement would rather blame the abortion for how a woman feels than look at the other facets of her life. The social conservatives that dominate the anti-choice movement are generally not supporters of the kinds of social programs that would actually increase services to low-income women, make workplaces more family-friendly, and expand access to reliable contraceptive methods in underserved communities. If Rue and his cohort really wanted to help women emotionally, they would address the reasons why women choose abortion in the first place. But since that would mean examining the often-complicated reality of women's lives and taking meaningful steps to improve those lives, anti-choice activists have instead chosen to cast abortion as the beginning and end of a woman's problems, and they point to any evidence of mixed feelings or regret as a reason to ban abortion for all women.

Naturally, the anti-choice movement also refuses to recognize its own role in causing stress for women who choose abortion. Yet that is undeniable. From the picketers who stand outside abortion clinics and call women "murderers" to the overall cultural atmosphere of secrecy and stigma surrounding abortion, women are bombarded with the idea that abortion is not a valid choice. These messages are powerful enough that even women who are fully comfortable with their choices have confessed feeling guilty that they weren't conflicted; imagine how much worse those feelings could be for someone who had more difficulty making her decision, or is unable to share her choice with friends and family for fear of negative reactions. That the anti-choice movement can demonize women for choosing abortion, and at the same time portray women as innocent victims of the evil abortion cartel, points to the power and success that the movement enjoys in this country.

The Complexities of Choice

"It's difficult for the pro-choice movement to talk about abortion with nuance," Steph Herold, a reproductive justice activist, says. "I wish we could talk about it with nuance more, but it's hard when abortion is so constantly under attack. It's hard to say, from a messaging point of view, there should be no waiting periods, there should be no obstacles whatsoever, even though some women may regret their abortions. It's difficult to balance that reality with the fact that although most women feel relieved, some women may feel sad, overjoyed, or a mix of those after an abortion. And so the anti-abortion folks have opened their arms up to conflicted women and diagnos[ed] them with this supposed post-abortion syndrome without any evidence that this disease exists, just because women don't feel 100 percent empowered and relieved after their abortions. I think the anti-choice folks have been successful in co-opting a scientific-sounding syndrome for something that's really much more complex."[19]

Steph also brings up the concern that the pro-choice movement may be inadvertently alienating women who have mixed feelings about their own choices. "If we don't offer any kind of support or messaging, or even if we don't even acknowledge that for some people abortion can be a tragedy or something they need to process emotionally, then we lose them. Especially if we keep calling for people to speak out about their abortions, to contact their legislators about abortion, about reproductive health issues in general, we may have to talk with a little more nuance and more personal experience instead of just war-on-women language. While a war on women may indeed be happening, I don't think it's an effective framing that reaches people who don't have as strong opinions on reproductive rights as we do."

"If I felt ambivalent, and I didn't see anything out there that acknowledged my feelings of ambivalence, if I was looking to normalize my own experience, and the only things I could find that were validating my feelings were anti-stuff?" Bess,* another activist, muses. "I can see that it could push me in a direction that I wasn't initially going to go in. I think that the establishment narrative is, women are all sad that they have to have abortions. These are difficult decisions, and every woman struggles with and thinks seriously through her decision. Then she has her abortion, and although she's sad that she had to make the decision, she is entirely relieved and her life goes on without a hitch. And they try to acknowledge that it's a lot more complicated than that, but it's a really hard balance to walk between 'I am woman, hear me roar,' and 'these are normal sad feelings.'"[20]

"The emotionally honest approach is to acknowledge the ambivalence, to acknowledge all of the complex bouquet of feel-

---

* Not her real name.

ings and emotions that comes out of this decision," Norman,* a clinic escort and activist, offers. "That's the emotionally honest approach. But I completely understand the flipside, which is the knee-jerk reaction, where we're under attack by all these anti-choicers, we have to present the cheeriest side, just for PR sake, we have to present women who are relieved. They've made a tough decision, they made the best of a bad situation, but now they're relieved and everything is fine and happy and roses and sunshine and unicorns because that's how to present it public relations-wise.[21]

"It's a tough choice," Norman admits. "Do you be emotionally honest to try and make it easier for the women who are making these choices? Or do you go with the rosy PR image because you want to minimize the chance of attack and you want to maximize the availability overall of abortion care?"

The approach of some high-profile pro-choice politicians and mainstream organizations has been to focus more on the abortions themselves and less on why women have them. In a speech in 2005, then-Senator Hillary Clinton said, "[A]bortion in many ways represents a sad, even tragic choice to many, many women"; Senator John Kerry has opined, "[a]bortion should be the rarest thing in the world."[22] Barack Obama made it clear from the outset of the health care reform debates that he would not seek changes to the ban on Medicaid-funded abortions; that pro-choice leaders in Congress and elsewhere publicly agreed with the administration's approach, even if it conflicted with their own stated beliefs, is cited

---

* Not his real name.

by many in the pro-choice movement as a missed opportunity to take decisive steps towards safeguarding every aspect of women's health care.[23]

The donation sections of both Planned Parenthood and NARAL's websites talk about protecting health care and fighting anti-choice legislation; the National Abortion Federation's brief request is focused on protecting the right to choose. These are important goals, of course, but they don't exactly give the impression that these are three of the leading representatives of pro-choice activism in the country.

Broadening this message to include women's experiences would not be impossible, but as it stands now, the most thoughtful and highly-praised work is coming from independent groups like Exhale and Backline. Both organizations work in the field of post-abortion support and counseling, offering women a nonjudgmental place to explore their positive and negative feelings following abortion. A loose collective of clinic directors and counselors, dubbed "the November Gang,"[24] has also been a vocal advocate for a more nuanced discussion of abortion, one that accepts that there is space for a whole range of abortion experiences, and just because abortion is hard for some women doesn't mean it's wrong for all women. Websites and organizations like the 1 in 3 Campaign and I'm Not Sorry have demonstrated a much greater ability and willingness to share stories that challenge all sorts of cultural assumptions around abortion, as this sample from I'm Not Sorry's website shows:

"I have never regretted the abortions, although I certainly regretted the circumstances under which they came about. I am forever grateful that I had the choice of abortion available to me, or else there would be three more damaged human beings in the world."[25]

"I do not mourn for an unborn child. I do feel sorrow for having so little self-esteem that I wasted my precious time and energy on an emotionally abusive relationship. I did not want to have a child from that relationship (and he certainly was not interested in being a father). I did not then, nor do I now, feel it was my responsibility to carry that pregnancy to term."[26]

"Even though I have not admitted it to myself (or my boyfriend) until just now writing these words before me, I would not have gone ahead with the pregnancy even if there were no adverse medical side effects to use as an excuse. I am starting a new job at a large company later this month. I have no savings. My boyfriend is several years younger than me and does not have a regular source of income. We are not married, and while I don't feel the need to be married prior to having children, our families may very well feel differently. Furthermore, I am just not mentally prepared."[27]

These stories—or, more accurately, these excerpts of stories—only hint at the very wide range of reasons why women seek abortions. But they are all united in their recognition of abortion as a good and right choice and nothing that women need to justify or feel ashamed about.

The pro-choice movement cannot expect to survive if it does not allow every kind of story to be told, even the ones that cause others to examine their own values and biases. Simply framing abortion as a sad or otherwise regrettable choice is capitulating to the anti-choice messaging, which holds that every abortion is a mistake and every women suffers. Without a counter-voice, it's easy for the general public to believe this narrative, despite how common abortion really is.

And while it would be great for that counter-voice to be just as loud and obnoxious as the anti-choice movement's narrative, it can be just as beneficial to talk about these issues in more private settings, among friends or romantic partners. My college years were shaped to a certain degree by the experiences of several close friends who chose abortion following unplanned pregnancies. Their situations did more than make me very aware that you could get pregnant even when using birth control; they also showed me that no matter how deeply pro-choice someone might be, it was still normal to have mixed feelings about having an abortion.

Shannon Connolly, a medical student at the University of Southern California, touches on the value that conversation can have: "Until abortion is normalized, until people are able to say it's just another part of health care, it's just another tremendously difficult but common decision that women make, we won't be able to talk about it in a meaningful way. I certainly would never in a million years fault a woman who had an abortion for not wanting to share that with other people because it's too difficult, but if it were possible for an individual person, I would hope that they would be able to. And I would hope that if you're pro-choice, you're able to say that to people who are close to you, so maybe if they've had an abortion, they'd be able to talk to you about it."[28]

CHAPTER TWO

HANDS-OFF TRAINING

"You have an OB/GYN? Do they do abortions?" New Hampshire abortion provider Wayne Goldner asks me, and to my embarrassment, I realize that I have no idea. "You don't know," he replies, his indignation clear even over the phone. "Walk in there. 'Do you do abortions?' 'No I don't.' 'Great, give me my chart. I'm going to go find somebody who does...' Why aren't we doing that?" he asks. "Why aren't we saying it is unacceptable? How would men react if they found out that their primary care doctors didn't do prostate exams from now on? And from now on you have to travel a significant distance and have a total stranger do your prostate exam? You think men would go along with it? Okay. So then, why are women tolerating it?"[1]

After his hospital merged with a Catholic facility, Wayne found himself unable to admit a patient whose water broke when she was only fourteen weeks pregnant. The pregnancy would have to be terminated, but since an exam showed a fetal heartbeat and the patient had not yet developed an infection or any other indication of immediate harm, the abortion would technically be elective and therefore wasn't allowed at his hospital. The woman did not have her own transportation and couldn't afford the travel expense, so Wayne paid for a taxi to drive her eighty miles to the closest hospital that would perform an abortion.

When Wayne Goldner gives his opinion on abortion care, I listen. A few months after our interview, I go to the gynecologist for my annual pap smear. At the end of the exam, I ask if he performs abortions. Of course, there's the little problem of insurance—my husband works for the federal government, so if I needed abortion care, we would have to pay the entire cost out of pocket. Still, I'm reassured and relieved when the doctor says that yes, if I need an abortion, I can have one at his office.

If I do have an abortion one day, I will be in good company. Abortion is one of the most common surgical procedures in the US; at the current rate, 35 percent of all women in this country will have had an abortion by the time they are forty-five.[2] Over the past three decades, the number of women who have died or suffered permanent injury from abortions performed in the United States has decreased to the point that childbirth carries a higher risk of death.[3]

The history of abortion in America is unlike that of any other country. Up until the mid-1800s, common law held that abortion was legal until the time of "quickening," or when a woman first feels the fetus move, which generally occurs during the fourth month of pregnancy. The legality of abortion up to this point was commonplace. Even the Catholic Church supported it until 1869.[4] Women used drugs or herbal methods to terminate their pregnancies; recipes were often shared between female family members and friends. If medical assistance was needed, a midwife generally provided it.[5] Indeed, midwives performed a wide range of reproductive health care services, not just abortion. They were the ones who delivered babies and tended to the health of both women and their children. Being able to provide all of these roles gave midwives an insight into the various aspects of their patients' lives that many doctors today do not have, due to the increasing specialization of medical care. This allowed midwives to look at abortion and birth on a continuum of choices, not as two opposite decisions. The decision not to have a child came out of a specific set of circumstances, and in many cases was seen as the best option for the woman and her family.

As Barbara Ehrenreich and Deirdre English discuss in their influential book *Witches, Midwives, and Nurses: A History of Women Healers*, the role of midwives began to change during the nineteenth century. During the early years of that century, formal medical schools didn't exist in the US, and few European doctors, who had received more rigorous training, had immigrated to this country. In many communities, the men and women who served as healers did so because they had a genuine interest in health and a desire to help people, and they were able to learn by apprenticeship.[6]

But as the nineteenth century progressed, both medical education and training did become more common, at least among white, male, upper-class members of society. These "formal" physicians seem to have taken a page from the concurrent drive toward industrialization that was also occurring in the 1800s, as they sought to distinguish their method of practicing medicine as the "proper" one and the more traditional methods as outdated and dangerous. Certain segments of society responded well to this campaign—having a "trained physician" was seen as a sign of status and prestige.[7]

As the medical field underwent these shifts in training and public opinion, so did laws regulating various aspects of health care, including abortion. The purpose of these first laws was to protect women's health. Infection was common, and there was concern that women were putting themselves in danger by using certain medications. The regulations prohibited the commercial sale of these medications but allowed women to purchase them via the mail or in person from a doctor or pharmacist.

There were also more paternalistic reasons for regulating abortion care: physicians wanted more control over their midwife competitors. Even as they bolstered themselves with newly-created organizations like the American Medical Association (created in 1848) and the establishment of rigorous medical schools, trained physicians were very aware that they were competing for patients who were more comfortable with midwives and other "lay" physicians. One way that this new class of doctors could attract patients and establish their practices was by casting aspersion on the old methods, which they blasphemed as old-fashioned and scientifically suspect.

The establishment of medical schools themselves was another way in which the medical field was regulated. As both trained and lay practitioners struggled to assert their field's right to practice medicine, the training required for formal physicians began to look more like what is common today. By the end of the 1800s, medical education required students to first complete four years of college, officially setting the medical degree beyond the reach of many working class people.

Many medical schools were initially reluctant to admit women, but female students were eventually accepted into medical programs; in 1849 Elizabeth Blackwell became the first woman to receive a medical degree from a US medical school,[8] and in 1850 the country's first medical school for women, the Women's Medical College of Pennsylvania, opened.[9] And when women became formal physicians, they sought to achieve the same respectability their male colleagues had begun to enjoy. Female lay practitioners were removed from the faculties of women's medical colleges, and female physicians joined their male peers' already well-established campaign against midwives.[10]

The push to regulate abortion also had strong backing from so-called nativist politicians, concerned that, as the birth rate among middle-class, white, Protestant women declined, the children of immigrants would soon outnumber "natural-born" babies. Other fears focused on how the traditional balance of the home could be affected as more women sought paid employment; if they were able to control their reproduction, it would be easier and more accepted to work outside of the home. All of these concerns resonated with lawmakers across the country, and anti-abortion laws became more widespread.[11]

There is a certain irony in the fact that anti-abortion laws were initially enacted to protect women from illness and death because the increasing regulation of abortion in the nineteenth and twentieth centuries, and the related changes to the medical field, had the opposite effect. Even though midwifery was still practiced into the twentieth century, the medical field never let up on attacking it as old-fashioned and unhygienic. This purposeful campaign counted on sexist, racist, xenophobic, and classist assumptions[12]—namely, that white males were best equipped, intellectually and physically, to practice medicine.

Fodder for the attacks was further driven by the recognition on the part of physicians that medical students were graduating without adequate experience in actually assisting a labor and delivery. Getting rid of midwives meant more opportunities for doctors to get the practice and knowledge that the medical schools did not provide.[13]

The campaign to eradicate midwifery also included a media outreach component, with anti-midwifery articles appearing in prominent women's publications like *Harper's Magazine*. This material omitted the fact that many midwives had received training, not to mention far more hands-on experience than any physician, and that their maternal death rates were lower than those found in hospitals at the time. There was also the legislative component: the legal rights of midwives to practice were compromised as more states decided that only physicians could be licensed.[14]

As midwives were increasingly forced out of practice, women were left without many options. Trained physicians were expensive, so low-income women often sought out untrained practitioners or addressed their health concerns themselves. In the case of abortion care, this meant they had two choices: seek out physicians who lacked the training and skills of experienced midwives; or attempt to self-abort. If complications arose and women sought help in public hospitals, they were treated, but they also faced intense judgment and scrutiny, and it was not uncommon for care to be withheld until the woman told the authorities who had performed her abortion. In some cities, the police would punish men whose lovers died following an abortion, but for the most part it was women who bore the brunt of having an unwanted pregnancy.

"Our generation assumes that abortion is a choice that we all have," OB/GYN resident Justin Diedrich observes. "Few of us have ever seen women take matters into their own hands. The 'septic abortion wards' do not exist anymore," he points out, referring to the wards, commonly found in hospitals until the 1970s, where women suffering complications from illegal or unsafe abortions were treated. "OB/GYNs of that era saw firsthand the detrimental effects of restrictive abortion law. They saw women die. They saw families torn apart. And we don't even hear about this anymore."[15]

This history is not the only crucial piece of information that medical students are not hearing about anymore. Today, abortion care itself has become elusive within medical programs, and just as midwives did not lose their footing as care providers without a bit of help, the loss of adequate abortion training amongst family care practitioners and OB/GYNs is no accident.

The Abortion Hour

In March of 1993, Dr. David Gunn was shot and killed by Michael Griffin at the Pensacola Women's Medical Services clinic in Pensacola, Florida,[16] making him the first physician killed in the US because he performed abortions. Around the same time, Jody Steinauer and thousands of other medical students received an anti-choice pamphlet at their homes. By its tone and content, it was clear the mailing was intended to intimidate students. The brochure included a "joke" that read, "Q: What would you do if you were in a room with Hitler, Mussolini, and an abortionist and you had a gun with only two bullets? A: Shoot the abortionist twice."[17] At the time, Steinauer was a first-year student at the University of California, San Francisco School of Medicine. As she and her fellow med students became aware of the potential threats they faced as physicians, they realized just how little formal abortion training was in their curriculum. Motivated to make a difference, Steinauer and a group of other students founded Medical Students for Choice (MSFC) in response to these issues. Twenty years later, more than 75 percent of medical schools in North America, as well as schools in nine other countries, have their own chapters dedicated to the dual causes of increasing the number of abortion providers and including more abortion education and training in medical schools.[18] But while about half of the country's 243 OB/GYN residency programs incorporate abortion into their residents' rotations, it often remains a struggle for medical students to receive any education on the subject during their initial years of schooling.[19, 20]

"We only get an hour of abortion training in our whole four years," says Megan Evans, a student at The George Washington University's School of Medicine and Health Science who, at the time of our interview, was the president-elect of MSFC's board of directors. "What can you talk about in an hour? And then we get an hour of contraception. We have these case-based studies that we do every week in a small group the first two years of medical school," she continues. "They had taken out the abortion case our second year. Not because it was controversial, [but] because they felt the second year students needed more time [for other cases].

But out of all the cases they picked that one, even though the other cases were about diabetes and heart disease—which are important, but we'd already seen them over and over again. So, we fought to get the abortion case put back in, and then fought to edit it because it was so terrible. They let us do both, which was really fantastic.[21]

"I think that the administration is fairly apathetic about the whole idea of teaching abortion," Megan adds. "They're not going to do anything different unless we demand it. They're not going to be like, oh, here's information about abortion. We have to request it and fight for it."

Louisa Pyle, a dual-degree student pursuing both an MD and a PhD at the University of Alabama, Birmingham (UAB), and her classmates had a similar experience. "My class was taught that EC [emergency contraception] was illegal. This was 2004, 2005," Louisa recalls. "We were able to go into the class notes and say okay, this is wrong. We added a little blurb into the transcript that, all respect to the lecturer, who is not a specialist in reproductive health care, we were able to verify with references."[22]

But even this victory highlights the larger problem. Louisa continues, "How many people out there are teaching that IUDs are unavailable, or that IUDs are inappropriate if you've never had a kid?" she asks. "They don't know any better; it's not malicious. How many people are going to pay a price for that lack of knowledge?"

"Honestly, I find it extremely frustrating that my own medical school and others across the country are still so behind in educating the future generation of doctors on abortion and contraception," Melissa Weston, a member of MSFC and student at the

University of Chicago–Pritzker School of Medicine, says. "I think that it is safe to say that my institution is more of a welcoming environment when it comes to these issues, as our OB/GYN department has a very active family planning section."[23]

When Melissa was in college, she volunteered at her university's sexual assault center. After graduation, she spent a year working in direct services at a domestic violence center. "I talked to 200-plus women that year," Melissa recalls, "in the hospital after a partner kicked their pregnant bellies; in jail cells when the scratch marks on their partner's face showed up before the bruises on their necks; in their homes; sometimes in a dorm, or in the middle of a cornfield as they explained to me that their neighbors [wouldn't] believe them. I still see their faces and hear their voices. Sometimes when I feel like I am losing touch as I get through [my] day in the classroom or hospital, all I have to do is remember."

At the time of our interview, Melissa was MSFC's regional coordinator for several midwestern states. Her school's chapter is very active, but she still feels that "we could be doing so much more than what we do now. We basically have some mention of hormonal birth control methods during the first year's reproductive endocrine lecture, a spring elective exclusively on these issues (after MSFC organized it and brought faculty in to teach it), and part of a lecture during the second year, when we talked about pregnancy complications. We know that the D&C [Dilation and Curettage][24] is one of the most commonly performed surgical procedures, but my classmates and I have not learned about it yet by third year and will most likely not be trained on it until residency *if* we seek it out."

"When I was in medical school [from 2003–2007], we were not taught about abortion," physician Justin Diedrich recalls about his education at Case Western Reserve University. "I believe in our course syllabi and lecture notes there was a single paragraph that stated that women have abortions and that there were a couple different techniques. Period. Nothing was really even said about birth control, except for contraceptive pills."[25]

In his third year of medical school, Justin was able to arrange a rotation at a local abortion clinic; through the assistance of the Barnett Slepian Memorial Fund and Medical Students for Choice, he also trained at the University of California, San Francisco, and San Francisco General Hospital. There, "I realized what open discussion could be," Justin says. "I saw how medical students could be taught and *should* be taught about contraception and abortion. I realized the dearth of information and teaching, and, honestly, discussion, of the most common surgical procedure in the country at my own medical school."

When Bhavik Kumar began medical school at Texas Tech Health Sciences Center School of Medicine in 2006, he wasn't sure what field he wanted to go into. "I came to med school and I was completely lost," he recalls during our phone conversation.[26] "The first year of med school was kind of just floating; I went from plastics to cardiology to I-don't-know-why-I'm-in-medicine." Shortly before he began his second year of school, Bhavik went to a MSFC leadership training program, "and that's when I had my moment," he tells me. "That's when I kind of had my first, 'Wow, this is really something I'm passionate about, something that I love,' the first time that I felt like I had purpose and that medicine was interesting and there's an area that I really could enjoy."

Texas Tech is located in Lubbock, a city in West Texas that Bhavik calls the buckle of the Bible Belt. Nationally, in 2010 (the most recent year for which figures are available), 367,752 children were born to women ages 15–19—47,751 of them in Texas.[27] "Sex education in Lubbock is nonexistent," Bhavik points out. After he attended the MSFC training program, "I figured, we're med students, maybe we should be talking to the students and getting something through."

What Bhavik and his fellow students wanted to get through was a more balanced sexual education curriculum than the abstinence-only classes taught in Lubbock's public schools. They didn't start with the schools, however, but decided instead to lead discussions at the local Boys and Girls Club. For the teaching materials, Bhavik worked off of an abstinence-based curriculum that had been approved by the Texas legislature that presented facts about contraception. "We stayed with sources that were certified. That way, we weren't using information that was third party or could be controversial. It was factual information. It was abstinence-based. It stuck with their guidelines, but very loosely.

"We talked about healthy relationships, abstinence, [and] we also talked about where they can get contraception. Of course they had to get permission from their parents, but all the kids enjoyed it."

Following the positive response to the Boys and Girls Club presentations, the medical students asked the school district to allow them to present their curriculum in the local schools. The district agreed, though with a few restrictions. "There were three things that the school department told us not to mention or talk about, and that was abortion, homosexuality, and masturbation," Bhavik recalls. "They said that we don't want those three topics mentioned because they're controversial and it would lead to big discussions [that were] not appropriate. I told [the med students], if somebody comes up to you [and] privately asks you a question, feel free to give them the information privately."

What Bhavik and his fellow MSFC members were able to accomplish is impressive. But it is also ironic that, even with such limits, these medical students were able to speak with adolescents more openly than many med students can speak with their professors. We hear a great deal about how politicized sex education at the middle and high school level has become over the past decade, but what gets far less attention is just how controversial it can be to teach abortion in a medical school.

An Incomplete Education

A 2005 study published in the *American Journal of Obstetrics and Gynecology* examined abortion education in US medical schools and confirmed the concerns about just what students are learning. Of 126 surveys sent to the clerkship directors of OB/GYN rotations at medical schools, seventy-eight were returned. Twenty-three percent of the directors said they didn't know if any abortion education was included in the preclinical years of medical school; 44 percent said no formal education was given during this time; 19 percent said there was a lecture specifically about abortion; and 11 percent had "a small group discussion of abortion and/or a clinical experience in abortion care."[28] When asked about education in the third year of medical school, 25 percent reported no formal abortion education, and 45 percent reported offering a clinical abortion experience.[29] Among those schools, 74 percent of the clerkships were integrated into the curriculum to some degree, so that students were notified of the opportunity in advance either verbally or in writing. At schools that offered the experience in a less-integrated manner, students had to take the initiative to arrange their own training.[30] Not surprisingly, schools that offered abortion education in the first two preclinical years of medical school were more likely to offer education in the third year.[31]

Seventeen percent of schools said there was no formal education in either the preclinical or third year of their programs.[32] Just over half, 52 percent, of the schools said that they offered a reproductive health elective in the fourth year of medical school, but of those who offered this elective, 92 percent said that participation was low, with 10 percent or fewer students enrolling.[33] While the paper did not discuss reasons for the low participation rate, it's hard not to wonder why expertise in reproductive health and family planning is an elective, not a required element of medical training.

Shannon Connolly, a medical student at the University of Southern California who, at the time of our interview, was on the board of directors of Medical Students for Choice, gives some insight into the myriad difficulties that prevent most from learning about the abortion procedure. If a student wants to have hands-on training, for example, "you have to contact the administration and ask for away time to go to a Planned Parenthood, because very few abortions are provided in academic medical centers, and all medical students train in academic medical centers," Shannon explains. "When you're a medical student, you have a tremendously busy schedule and you're always tired and sleep-deprived. It's not like you can just take your free Saturday and go to Planned Parenthood, because you're supposed to be working every Saturday at the hospital. A lot of med students have to squeeze in what little abortion training they can get on top of their already fully extended schedules."[34]

Shannon brings up an even greater barrier: What if a student wants to learn how to perform abortions, but lives in a state where there are no clinics at which to train? MSFC does offer a reproductive health externship program, which provides funds so a student can go to another state for several weeks to learn abortion provision. Since its establishment in 1995, the externship program has funded over one thousand students and residents; in 2011, seventy-seven students and residents received stipends from the program.[35] While the program relieves the financial burden of receiving this education, the student still must be able to take time off from their regular course load. This is no easy task, as the third and fourth years of medical school, when a student would be advanced enough to receive the training, are already packed with required rotations at the student's "home" hospital. And since it is at the discretion of the student's school to accept the credits, unfriendly administrations may decline to count the externship as part of the student's education.

The barriers to receiving abortion training extend further to residencies, which are potentially more troubling, given that this is the phase of a doctor's training where they learn how to diagnose and treat actual patients in their specialty. Following a period of decline for abortion training in residency programs—in 1985, 23 percent of OB/GYN programs included training in first-trimester procedures, and 21 percent included training in second-trimester abortion provision, but by 1991, these numbers had declined to 12 and 7 percent, respectively—in 1995, the Accreditation Council for Graduate Medical Education (ACGME) required that abortion training be a part of OB/GYN residency programs.[36] While residents had the right to opt out of training for personal or religious reasons, everyone was required to learn how to manage abortion complications. Despite safeguarding residents' rights to opt out of the training, the mandate was not safe from political meddling. The following year, Congress adopted anti-choice legislation known as the Coats Amendment, which maintains the federal funding for and the legal status of programs that refuse to comply with the ACGME requirements.[37]

From the standpoint of patient care, there are myriad benefits for residents to receive training in abortion care. Resulting competency in treating miscarriage alone is significant, since miscarriage affects an estimated 10–25 percent of all pregnancies[38]; while the majority of these occur during the first thirteen weeks, an estimated 1–5 percent of pregnancies are lost between thirteen and nineteen weeks gestation, and stillbirth occurs in 0.3 percent of pregnancies between the twentieth and twenty-seventh week of gestation.[39] Students also gain a deeper understanding of how to examine a patient, and they are better able to ensure that a patient receives the most accurate information.

Even residents who opt out of the actual procedure training but still learn about managing complications have reported that this education has value: in addition to learning technical skills such as sizing the uterus, they also improve their skills in talking with and counseling patients.[40]

A committee opinion released by the American College of Obstetricians and Gynecologists (ACOG) in 2009, fourteen years after the ACGME mandate, remained pessimistic about the state of abortion training. In 1998, two years after the ACGME mandate was in effect, 81 percent of all programs surveyed reported offering first-trimester training, but only 46 percent of those offered it "routinely," and 34 percent offered it as an elective.[41] A follow-up study from 2005 was not much more encouraging: 51 percent of the OB/GYN program directors reported routine training, 10 percent offered no training, and 39 percent said they offered elective training.[42] Despite these dismal numbers, anti-choice activists are not satisfied with the state of abortion training either.

Anti-Choice Tactics Move Behind the Scenes

In 2011, Representative Virginia Foxx (R-NC) introduced an amendment to H.R. 1216, a bill concerning a federal grant program for graduate medical education. Foxx's amendment would bar the program from either paying for abortions or paying for training physicians in abortion care, under the rationale that since the program is federally funded, taxpayer money could be used for abortion services.[43] The House approved the Foxx amendment by a vote of 234–182 (thirteen Democrats voted for it, and ten Republicans against), as well as H.R. 1216 itself.[44] Whether the Senate will consider the bill remains unclear.[45]

In withholding funding from a medical education program, Foxx—and her 233 colleagues who voted in favor of the amendment—demonstrate a breathtaking disregard for women's health. As previously discussed, there are many ways in which learning basic abortion care enhances the physician's knowledge of her specialty and treatment of patients, even if she never actually performs an abortion. Whatever the circumstances, quality medical care means treatment by doctors who are familiar with all the medical procedures that their specialty encompasses. The Foxx amendment sanctions the common anti-choice tactic of exoticizing abortion, portraying it as so repugnant that not even doctors should be allowed to learn about the procedure.

Republicans are fond of using the idea of taxpayer-funded abortions to justify political maneuvers. In the spring of 2011, as Congress negotiated a spending plan intended to avoid a government shutdown, Republicans insisted that certain policies be included that would severely affect women's ability to access and pay for abortion care. Among other demands, the party wanted the government to stop providing federal funds to Planned Parenthood and instead distribute the funds to state health departments to use as they saw fit.[46] This measure was particularly contentious because the federal funding that Planned Parenthood received went to preventative services like cancer screenings and breast exams; however, conservatives justified the proposed cuts by arguing that the federal funding allowed Planned Parenthood to direct private donations towards abortion care.[47] While the move to defund Planned Parenthood gained a great deal of traction, particularly in the House, the organization's funding did remain intact.

Federal funding for abortion has been outlawed since the passage of the Hyde Amendment in 1976, and doesn't show any sign of changing any time soon. Hyde prohibits the use of Medicaid for the procedure except in cases of rape, incest, or if a woman's life is in danger from a "physical disorder, physical injury, or physical illness, including a life-endangering physical condition caused by or arising from the pregnancy itself."[48] But any clinic employee or woman on Medicaid can vouch for just how difficult it is to get Medicaid to pay for the procedure even under those conditions.

"It's hard to think of something more backwards than the Hyde Amendment," reproductive rights attorney Mark Egerman says. "This is an ongoing, annual process, whereby we prevent women who have the fewest resources from getting the assistance that they need to control their lives, to exercise the choices that all people have. We are allowed to shame poor women who are disproportionately women of color, and in a way that you would never allow shaming people who are not poor."[49]

While Virginia Foxx and her colleagues are busy on the federal level, individual state legislatures are also embracing such myopic thinking. In June 2011, the Republican-controlled Wisconsin legislature amended an existing law to classify the University of Wisconsin Hospital and Clinics as a "state agency."[50] Under this new classification, anti-choice advocates argued, the hospital could not use public funds to pay or train medical residents in abortion provision.

This anti-choice attack is particularly galling because abortions aren't even performed at UW Hospital and Clinics. Residents who want to train in abortion care do so at Planned Parenthood clinics, and that portion of their training is paid for by another hospital.[51] Yet Pro-Life Wisconsin, a local anti-choice group created by "dedicated and experienced pro-lifers who realized that the pro-life movement needed to refocus on principle to achieve total protection for all preborn children,"[52] is convinced that the UW facilities are in danger of becoming "ground zero for training abortionists."[53] The group, along with the conservative Alliance Defense Fund, has asked the state's attorney general to prevent residents from receiving any abortion training at all.

This request makes it clear that the real concern isn't where the training takes place or who is paying the residents' training salary. It's that abortion training is occurring at all. Pro-Life Wisconsin, and its sister organizations across the country, want to eradicate legal abortion entirely. Since court challenges have thus far been unsuccessful, the anti-choice movement has methodically shifted its focus to other targets and has correctly realized that if there are no qualified doctors to perform abortions, the procedure itself might as well be illegal.

Wisconsin is not the only state whose elected representatives seem more willing to jeopardize the health of their constituents than to allow doctors to perform abortions. In early 2012, the Kansas legislature began deliberating a massive anti-abortion bill that would, among other provisions, prohibit medical residents at the University of Kansas Medical Center from performing abortions. This prohibition would mean that the university's residency program would be in violation of its accreditation requirements.[54]

In mid-March, a legislative committee approved an amendment to the proposed bill that would protect the program's accreditation. The following day, however, the state house adopted an amendment that would prohibit state funds from being used for abortion care and bar state workers—which the medical residents are classified as—from performing abortions "during the workday."[55] (There's no word yet on what legal health services would be banned after the workday.) Much like in Wisconsin, no abortions are actually performed at the University of Kansas Medical Center.

This strategy also reveals the dangerous disregard the anti-choice movement has for all women. While the Coats Amendment undoubtedly complicates the issue of accreditation, if the Wisconsin attorney general decides that UW must remove abortion care from its program, the program would be violating ACGME and ostensibly could lose accreditation. That would put a whole range of OB/GYN services in jeopardy, not just abortion care.

As of this writing, the Kansas Senate has indicated that they won't consider the anti-abortion bill in the 2012 legislative session; so the KU Medical Center still has its accreditation, as does the UW Hospital and Clinics—for now. Wisconsin's OB/GYN residents are still able to seek abortion training at Planned Parenthood if they want to.

And that might be the thorniest issue of all. Because just as it doesn't matter how legal abortion is if doctors don't know how to do the procedure, it also doesn't matter if there aren't doctors willing to do the procedure.

Between 1982 and 2000, the number of abortion providers in the US declined by 38 percent, from 2,900 to 1,800.[56] While there were undoubtedly many factors that contributed to this decline, including a shift from provision in hospitals to provision in free-standing clinics, one result was that women's access to these services was affected. In 1978, 77 percent of all counties in the US lacked an abortion provider; by 2000, that number had risen to 87 percent, while during the same time period the proportion of women of childbearing age who lived in these counties increased from 27 percent to 34 percent.[57] As of 2008, the number of all US counties that didn't have a provider remained at 87 percent, and the number of reproductive-aged women residing in those counties had risen slightly, to 35 percent.[58]

Between 2005 and 2008, the number of abortion providers remained stable: 1,787 in 2005, and 1,793 three years later. Not all of these providers perform abortions up to the same point in pregnancy, however. Sixty-four percent offer some services for patients who need second-trimester procedures; 23 percent offer abortions up to twenty-three weeks; and 11 percent offer services at twenty-four weeks.[59] Nearly every practicing OB/GYN—97 percent—has had, or will have, a patient who wants an abortion, but only 14 percent perform them.[60]

A large number of providers are nearing retirement age. According to one survey, 64 percent of providers are at least fifty years old.[61] While a greater percentage of younger physicians have expressed a willingness to provide abortion care—a survey of OB/GYNs found that 22 percent of doctors aged thirty-five and younger are likely to perform abortions, whereas only 12 percent of those aged 36–45 are[62]—that still means that barely over one-fifth of OB/GYNs are willing to provide this service. Given the millions of women who will seek abortion care in their lifetimes, this low number of potential providers is cause for concern.

Thanks to her pursuit of both an MD and PhD, MSFC member Louisa Pyle has been a student at University of Alabama, Birmingham's medical school longer than most of her peers. "I'm so lucky," Louisa tells me, smiling. "I'm like a seventh-year med student, so I've gotten to see all these people personally who have come in maybe feeling like, 'of course abortion should be available, of course contraception should be available, but what's the big deal?'" Louisa's tone changes, becomes more urgent to reflect the student's transformation: "'Oh, wait, I see now there's an issue. Okay, well, I'll make sure my fellow med students know about contraception; okay well, maybe they need to know about abortion too.'" Now her tone is more insistent and determined, "'You know what, doggone it, I'm going to be a provider, come hell or high water, I'm going to make sure that happens.'" In her normal voice, Louisa continues, "You see them progress through those different steps as they learn more and more about it and come back to more meetings. So I think the potential is there for it to get a lot better."[63]

CHAPTER THREE

ISOLATED, STIGMATIZED, AND ROMANTICIZED

Several years ago, I watched the *Frontline* documentary "The Last Abortion Clinic," which is about the only abortion clinic still open in Mississippi after a successful anti-choice campaign to regulate and limit the procedure. The documentary was so moving that by the time the credits rolled I was ready to enroll in medical school so I could become a provider, despite the fact that I actually have no interest in being a doctor.

I doubt it was the filmmakers' goal to present the clinic's physicians and staff in this kind of inspiring, almost superhuman light. Likewise, the 1996 HBO movie *If These Walls Could Talk*, in which Cher (Cher!) plays an abortion provider who is extremely matter-of-fact about her work right up to the minute that she is shot by an anti-choice protestor, does not have to work hard to highlight the strength and bravery of those who risk their lives to provide women with this essential choice. Even though both fictional and actual abortion providers downplay the huge risks their work involves, it is almost impossible not to feel a measure of awe at their career choice. It is one thing to support abortion; it is another to head directly into the ring of fire and make personal sacrifices to make sure that the right to abortion is protected, and the service is available.

"When I started medical school I thought 100 percent, absolutely, I want to be an OB/GYN, I want to be a provider," says Maura Porto, a medical student at the University of New England College of Osteopathic Medicine and a member of MSFC. Yet, as she learned more about the realities of the field, Maura began to reconsider. "There are so few providers out there that if you are a provider, that may be all you do, and it may change your patient base. I'm slowly learning about the ramifications of being a provider, and I guess I'm a little bit disenchanted about how that works. I think idealistically there should be more providers, but when it comes to my practice and what I ultimately want to do, my ideals are strong, but maybe my backbone is weaker. I'm definitely questioning [my plan]."[1]

It's interesting that Maura cites the actual logistics of being an abortion provider as her concern because that would seem to pale next to the very real threats to providers' physical safety. But her concern is echoed by a number of other medical students, all of whom are keenly aware that the limited number of providers in this country means that if they choose to go into the field, abortion provision may well be all that they do. A physician who provides abortion care as part of a larger practice may be able to establish longer-term and more varied relationships with her patients, but those who work at Planned Parenthood or independent reproductive care clinics often don't have as much patient interaction and may not have the opportunity to see patients beyond one appointment for the procedure itself and one for the follow-up visit.

An obvious corrective to this concern would be a better integration of abortion care into the work of traditional medical clinics. But anecdotal evidence shows that while individual family medicine and OB/GYN practitioners are willing to perform abortions on a case-by-case basis to patients with whom they have existing relationships, they are not openly advertising abortion care. Marciana Wilkerson, a retired OB/GYN, recalls how her clinic approached this issue when she practiced during the 1980s and '90s. "What we did to protect me in private practice was, if someone called and asked for an abortion on the phone and she wasn't one of our patients, the staff politely told her that I didn't perform that service," Marciana tells me.[2] "But if they knew who she was, they'd bring her in and I'd speak to her face-to-face. There was a big need for it; women would usually come and say 'could you refer me to someone?' and they were thrilled when they found out I could offer that service and not send them out."

Abortion provision in hospitals can be even more complicated. Elective abortion in a hospital setting is a contentious issue, bumping up against federal funding restrictions, the policies of Catholic facilities, and the objections of nurses and doctors who do not want to assist with the procedure. The first so-called "conscience clause," the Church Amendment, was passed in 1973 and stated that neither individuals nor facilities that received public funds could be required to perform abortions or sterilizations, or make either personnel or facilities available to perform those services, if doing so was contrary to either the individual or facility's "religious beliefs or moral convictions."[3] Within five years, nearly every state in the country had passed its own form of conscience laws. In 1996, Congress passed the Coats Amendment, which stated that the federal, state, and local governments are not allowed to discriminate against "health care entities" that do not undergo abortion training, provide this training, perform abortions, or refer individuals for such training or treatment.[4] The following year, Congress amended Medicaid and Medicare programs such that while a plan couldn't prevent doctors from providing abortion referral or counseling, it could refuse to pay them for doing so.[5]

Toward the end of George W. Bush's second term in office, his administration passed a regulation that allowed health workers, hospitals, and insurance companies to refuse to provide abortions or other services that violated "a religious belief or moral conviction."[6] The regulation also required facilities that received federal money to certify their compliance with those protections.[7] In February 2011, President Obama repealed the regulation but also issued a new rule that retains federal conscience protection for abortions and sterilizations.[8]

Nine months later, in December 2011, a federal judge ruled that twelve nurses employed by a New Jersey hospital who opposed providing abortion services on moral and religious grounds did not have to assist in any part of elective abortion care—including caring for a patient before and after her procedure. The nurses would have to provide care in a life-threatening situation, but only if no other nurse was available, and only until another nurse could take over.[9]

When I first read about this case, I thought about a training exercise used by a pro-choice organization. Its purpose is to explore personal biases. Participants grapple with issues such as who "deserves" an abortion more, a thirteen-year-old raped by her father or a married, unemployed thirty-year-old with two children?

There are other difficult but equally realistic scenarios, such as women who have had multiple abortions and women who picket an abortion clinic one day and sit in the same waiting room as a patient the next. The purpose of the exercise is not to answer these complex questions but rather to illustrate that while it is normal to have biases, it is important to ensure that personal opinions do not prevent a woman from getting the care she needs.

"When I first thought about choice I thought, well, it's okay for a woman to have an abortion, but after her third abortion it's not okay," medical student Megan Evans tells me. "I would set up all these, 'It's okay, but . . .' Then I got to a point where I just felt like, to me, abortion is not a gray issue, it's very black and white. I know very few people feel that way. But I don't feel like there's any point where I should determine what's best for that other woman. I think there will probably be times where it may be difficult to perform the abortion, but once I start putting 'I won't do this because I don't feel it's right,' or 'I wouldn't do this,' then I feel like I've lost touch with what choice means. Like Dr. Tiller [said], you have to trust women. If she believes getting the abortion is the best thing for her in her life, I will perform the procedure and support her decision."[10]

Megan refers to George Tiller, an abortion provider who performed abortions beyond the twenty-first week of pregnancy and was shot and killed in May 2009. Activist Kate Palmer recalls when, in 2001, she was offered the chance to do an internship at Dr. Tiller's clinic in Wichita. "Besides being ideologically pro-choice, I had never really confronted my own feelings about abortion and what it meant to have a later-term abortion," she shares. "I almost backed out of the internship because I wasn't sure how comfortable I would be representing Dr. Tiller and his clinic in the community. After spending time with Dr. Tiller and understanding the broader issues surrounding abortion, I soon realized how important it was for women to have abortion as [an] option, even later in their pregnancies."[11] As can be seen in these personal struggles, the principle of leaving one's own biases at the door, in order to provide the best care and truly allow for patient consent and individual decision-making, is a fixture of medical and nursing ethics.

The nurses in New Jersey, however, are not the only group of healthcare employees who have made national news for refusing to provide care. In February 2012, a federal judge ruled that the state of Washington couldn't force pharmacies to sell emergency contraception, such as Plan B, if they had religious objections to doing so.[12] The state has appealed the decision, arguing that protections are already in place for pharmacists who refuse to fill prescriptions for personal reasons,[13] and that existing regulations stipulate that pharmacists must fill prescriptions in a timely manner.[14]

It is difficult to imagine another line of work that routinely lets its workers refuse to do some aspect of their job and still keep their position. There's the classic example of military service: if someone joins the military and decides, after several years of service, that he is now a pacifist and doesn't believe in military intervention, he would be discharged. There is also the broader example of retail discrimination; that is, a store that is open to the public may not discriminate against people of a certain race or religion. In both cases, individual beliefs are not allowed to interfere with the purpose of the individual's job.

Conscience clauses are especially odd because nurses and doctors already have well-developed codes of ethics designed to cover all aspects of their career. The Nursing Code of Ethics does not explicitly address abortion services, but it does have some interesting things to say about nurses' responsibilities: "The need for health care is universal, transcending all individual differences. The nurse establishes relationships and delivers nursing services with respect for human needs and values, and without prejudice. An individual's lifestyle, value system and religious beliefs should be considered in planning health care with and for each patient. Such consideration does not suggest that the nurse necessarily agrees with or condones certain individual choices, but that the nurse respects the patient as a person."[15]

On the subject of a nurse's personal responsibility to her or himself, the code recognizes that, "Nurses have both personal and professional identities that are neither entirely separate, nor entirely merged, but are integrated. . . . In situations where nurses' responsibilities include care for those whose personal attributes, condition, lifestyle or situation is stigmatized by the community and are personally unacceptable, the nurse still renders respectful and skilled care." The code does state that, "Where a particular treatment, intervention, activity, or practice is morally objectionable to the nurse, whether intrinsically so or because it is inappropriate for the specific patient, or where it may jeopardize both patients and nursing practice, the nurse is justified in refusing to participate on moral grounds. Such grounds exclude personal preference, prejudice, convenience, or arbitrariness. Conscientious objection may not insulate the nurse against formal or informal penalty."[16]

And herein lies one of the difficulties of conscience clauses: while no one should be forced to do something she disagrees with morally, it is equally unacceptable to withhold treatment from a patient whose decision you find objectionable. After all, it could be argued that opposition to abortion is as much a personal preference as moral argument—and aren't one's morals determined by their personal beliefs, and vice versa? While that question may be better answered by philosophers, what the Code of Ethics indicates is that a nurse's primary responsibility is to the patient.

It is also instructive to consider the ripple effect that a health care professional who refuses to provide abortion care or contraception care can create. Women in need of such services don't exactly have a lot of time to search for a physician, nurse, or pharmacist who will perform the procedure or fill the prescription. If they can't receive the service that they need from the facility closest to them, they might not have the time, transportation, or financial resources to seek out another option that requires more travel.

Perhaps hospitals like the one in New Jersey should consider conducting bias workshops for their employees, along with medical schools and residencies. Reproductive health choices are hardly the only controversial issues in medicine: What about the use of fertility drugs, or a pregnancy that involves multiple embryos? What is the most ethical course of treatment for someone in a persistent vegetative state, or for an extremely premature infant? How might a doctor feel having to help a patient who sustained his injuries while committing a heinous crime? And what about if a patient insists on undergoing medically unnecessary and potentially risky cosmetic surgery?

Medical care is full of situations that could easily put a physician or nurse in the position of providing care that goes against his or her own moral beliefs. If hospitals are willing to allow employees to opt out of providing abortion care, they should be cognizant of the precedent that they are setting. And health care professionals would be doing themselves and their patients a disservice to not think deeply about how they can best perform their jobs, even when their own senses of morality are challenged.

Given that one state has now said that it's okay for personal beliefs to trump patient care, it's tempting to think that abortion service should just be the province of independent clinics whose primary goal is to care for girls and women who need abortions, with a fully supportive and skilled staff. These are the very reasons that independent clinics have long been seen as a vital component of the pro-choice movement. Abortion clinics originated as a response to the hospital-based model of abortion care that dominated provision up until the early 1970s, which was not always particularly focused on counseling, support, or women's rights. By opening their own clinics, activists and providers were taking the opportunity to create the environment they felt women deserved, one centered around affirmation, empowerment, and understanding. Yet shifting the bulk of abortion care to freestanding clinics has helped create the very environment that medical student Maura Porto and other prospective providers fear, one where their work becomes isolated and repetitive almost by definition. Moving these services out of hospitals and more traditional clinics also means that women, particularly those in rural communities, are often forced to travel great distances to receive abortions.

Even in the years before *Roe*, it was possible for some women to obtain safe abortions in a caring setting, outside of the hospital. Many cities had informal yet effective networks of sympathetic clergy and providers who helped women receive care; perhaps the best known of these services, the Jane Collective in Chicago, was run by female activists who were trained in abortion provision and helped thousands of women receive safe care between 1969 and 1973.[17]

Renee Chelian, the director of the Northland Family Planning Centers, was introduced to abortion provision in the early 1970s when she worked in a doctor's office while attending nursing school. While abortion was not yet legal in her home state of Michigan, it was legal in New York, and her employer would travel to Buffalo on the weekends to provide abortions. Renee began making the trip with him, and after *Roe*, the doctor decided to open a clinic in the Detroit area. "[After we] opened it up, I started being very, very unhappy with the way women were treated," Renee remembers. "There was no recovery room, and I wasn't allowed to really answer questions. I was getting women who were calling the office and asking questions about abortion and my boss suddenly was telling me all the time, 'I don't think you should sit on the phone and answer questions for patients.' So I was at odds with him every day."[18] When Renee was given the chance to open her own clinic, she overcame her initial reluctance: "I was twenty-two, the idea of being the boss and running something was frightening." With the support of her husband and family, she said yes.

Renee took a decidedly low-budget approach toward advertising the clinic. "We made up these [cards and stickers] that said 'legal abortion for women,' with a phone number on them. We put them in public bathrooms, in bars, restaurants, malls. Women started calling, and we could give them information about everything. You couldn't call the health department and get this kind of information."

Today, Renee's three Detroit-area clinics are a model for patient-centered abortion care. The procedure rooms are clean and well stocked; the recovery room features comfortable chairs and hot tea that the staff has selected for its calming and soothing properties. The literature they have on hand for patients includes detailed workbooks that help women who are unsure about their decision to sort through their feelings.

The clinic that I visited is tucked away in an anonymous office building in a Detroit suburb, but neither the clinics nor Renee have always enjoyed such a low profile. "I really was shocked when antis started showing up [at the clinic, in the 1980s], and then the media would show up for a bomb threat and shove a microphone in my face," Renee says. "I was put much more in the public eye, and we did become a target. I'm from the inner city; I'm somebody who can fight," she adds with more than a hint of pride. "They were in the vestibule; they were everywhere. That was when I learned how to start fighting. When they targeted my house, that's a whole different story. My kids were scared," Renee recalls of her daughters, who at the time were barely school-aged. Her youngest daughter cried every night during the picketing. Even though Renee successfully lobbied the city council to pass a ban against residential picketing, she has tears in her eyes when she says, "It was one of the worst times. But it never made me feel like I should give up."

Just as Renee remains fiercely committed to keeping her clinics open, established providers are just as committed to staffing such clinics. Willie Parker, a former director of Planned Parenthood Metropolitan Washington [DC], has no doubts about why he provides abortion. "I'm clear about the decision I made to do this work," Willie tells me over coffee. "I think about that there are people who feel strongly enough that they might try and act out and harm me. Am I concerned about my well being, do I want to live a long time? Of course I do. But in weighing my concern about what happens to women against my concern about what happens to me, my concern about what happens to women [is greater]."[19]

Wayne Goldner also takes the threats to his safety seriously. "You never take it lightly," he tells me during a telephone conversation in July 2009, "but I always say, look, you're more likely to get shot as a divorce lawyer than as an abortion provider. I knew George Tiller, and I think it's a horrible thing. But that's terrorism, and if I allow them to stop me from doing what I believe in, that would be wrong. I think it would insult the memory of George Tiller for me to quit doing this because he got shot. It would be to let him die in vain. I'm going to keep doing what I want to do. I'm going to do more."

As perhaps the best-known abortion provider in the country, Dr. LeRoy (Lee) Carhart has spent a lot of time thinking about security—and with good reason. On September 6, 1991, fires were set on Lee's property. He and his family were unharmed, but the blaze claimed the lives of seventeen horses and two other pets. No one was arrested in connection with the fire, but as Lee notes, the blaze was set on the day that the state passed a parental notification law. (Nebraska now has a parental consent law.[20]) "We felt that it was a celebratory type [of] thing. [We received] a letter telling us that killing the horses was justified [because I kill] children. And the obvious message was, you need to stop; that's what they were trying to say."[21] The following day, a nurse who worked at the clinic where Lee worked part time performing abortions had her garage set on fire, and anti-abortion literature was found on her property.

In response to the arson, Lee, a former Air Force officer, decided to start performing abortions on a full-time basis. "In the military you're taught you never negotiate with terrorists," he says now by way of explanation. But at the time, "I just thought, well, if they're willing to spend that much energy to try to make it unavailable, then I would spend time trying to train people to do abortions. That very next Monday [after the fire], I went to the director of the hospital [at my other job] where I was on the surgical staff and said, I'm going to resign."

Lee still lives in Nebraska, but since late 2010 he has spent part of most weeks working in an abortion clinic in suburban Maryland. Just thinking about traveling across the country every week, to say nothing of the personal risks, sounds incredibly daunting to me. But Lee offers a different perspective on his work. As a medical student in Philadelphia, he trained in abortion care, but he also saw what he calls the "devastation side of abortion," particularly women who tried to self-abort. When an acquaintance approached him about working at her clinic after he retired from the military, Lee went to the clinic to observe.

"I went one Saturday and it was like going back twenty years. The women were equally desperate, and the stories were the same, but they were taken care of, and home in an hour or two. Being able to see somebody that's desperate one day and have them happy … and healthy [the next] is the best feeling I think you can have. I just really feel that I am helping people. I think my home is now an airplane, and that's where I sleep," Lee laughs. "I'm getting to do what I love here."

When it comes to the future, Lee says that his "hope and dream" is that abortion care "does, at least for the early procedures, get back into the doctor's private practice. I think that they can be safely done in the private practice environment. For the later abortions, the fact that there are [multiple] clinics in the United States that are doing it right now is probably the ultimate safety and the best situation there is for women.

"I think when it was just George, it wasn't enough," Lee continues. "And that left him to be the big target that he was. Now, the average person could take out George and figure well, they ended late-term abortions. But I think now that there's as many of us as are doing it, the average person's not going to be able to get to all of us. Plus I think it's good for the patients because you shouldn't have to travel to Wichita from New York. Wichita really was a great location for the clinic—it's in the middle of the country—but it meant everybody had to travel."

While the accessibility of abortion services is indeed a concern to providers and patients alike, perhaps a more pressing concern is the ability of clinics to even remain open. In early 2011, Virginia's General Assembly voted to regulate abortion clinics as hospitals, not doctor's offices. Supporters of these regulations claimed that they were acting in the best interests of women and said that the new regulations would make the clinics safer for patients.

The state already prohibits clinics from performing second- or third-trimester abortions; ironically, those must be performed in a hospital. First-trimester abortions are considered to be the safest form of an already incredibly safe medical procedure: fewer than 0.3 percent of all women having abortions experience complications that require hospitalization.[22] In Virginia, approximately 28,520 abortions were performed in 2008.[23] In the ten-year period between 1999 and 2009, one woman died as a result of abortion-related complications.[24] Details of how this death occurred have not been released. However, while even one death is lamentable, it is important to consider in comparison that eleven women died in that state in 2009 alone from pregnancy-related complications.[25] Yet state politicians decided that it was of the utmost importance to mandate the ceiling height of clinic rooms and require that all existing clinics have covered entryways, along with a host of other structure-related requirements that had nothing to do with patient safety and everything to do with imposing onerous and expensive regulations on abortion clinics—and only abortion clinics. Other freestanding medical offices that perform equally if not more invasive services, like cosmetic surgery (which, unlike first-trimester abortion, routinely requires administering general anesthesia and is therefore statistically more risky) and eye surgery, are not held to the same standards. It's interesting that patient safety only becomes an issue when women are the patients, even when the procedure already has an excellent safety record.[26]

Virginia currently has twenty-one abortion clinics that will be affected by the new regulations. Early estimates from pro-choice advocates predicted that up to seventeen of those clinics would not be able to afford to implement all of the new requirements after the regulations went into effect, and would either have to stop performing abortions or close entirely.

The emergency regulations went into effect on January 1, 2012, but the state's Board of Health did not release its proposed regulations until June 2012.[27] And that's when things got complicated, not to mention political. Though the board voted in favor of the regulations, it also approved an amendment that would have "grandfathered" in existing clinics—so while new clinics would have to meet the requirements laid out in the regulations, existing clinics would not have to retrofit or renovate their facilities to do so.[28] Virginia attorney general Ken Cuccinelli felt that the amendment was beyond the board's "scope of power" and refused to certify the exemptions.[29]

Before the board voted on the issue again in September, Virginia governor Bob McDonnell appointed a new member: Dr. John Seeds, an anti-choice physician and vice-chairman of OB/GYNS for Life.[30] For his part, Cuccinelli let members know that if they "did not heed his advice" regarding the exemption, "his office would not defend them in any resulting litigation, and . . . they could be personally on the hook for legal bills."[31] Perhaps not surprisingly, the outcome of the second vote was to adopt the regulations without providing any exemptions for existing clinics, a decision that Cuccinelli certified. Within a matter of weeks, Virginia Health Commissioner Karen Hemley resigned, citing the clinic regulations as a reason for her departure.[32] As of this writing, McDonnell has not yet signed the regulations, although he is expected to do so.

While these regulations would be the first of their kind in Virginia, the model that they follow has been around since the mid-1990s. Targeted Regulation of Abortion Provider (TRAP) laws seek to nitpick clinics out of business by insisting that abortion clinics adhere to arcane and arbitrary building requirements that have little to do with patient safety or quality of care. For example, TRAP laws in Mississippi decree that an abortion clinic "be located in an attractive setting," and the grounds must be free from grass that could harbor insects.[33] In Louisiana, politicians tried to mandate the angle of water fountains in clinics.[34] More troublingly, many TRAP laws authorize state health inspectors to search both the offices and medical records of abortion providers, as this South Carolina law shows: "[Health] Department inspectors shall have access to all properties and areas, objects, records and reports [of the abortion facility], and shall have the authority to make photocopies of those documents required in the course of inspections or investigations."[35] While similar provisions have been overturned in other states, the fact that any state gives inspectors this kind of access to medical records is troubling and points to just how much power the anti-choice movement can wield over individual abortion clinics.

Yet for all the concern expressed about building specifications and landscaping, a high-profile case in Philadelphia has raised questions about why state regulators fail to investigate actual dangers in clinics that do threaten women's safety. Dr. Kermit Gosnell performed abortions in the city for decades, despite the fact that, according to authorities, he wasn't trained in abortion care and employed no trained medical staff.[36] While Gosnell didn't advertise his services, word spread about the doctor who would provide abortions up to thirty weeks for a lot less money than any other clinic.[37]

For years, state regulators ignored both complaints about Gosnell and the forty-six lawsuits that were brought against him; since his clinic opened in 1979, it was inspected only five times, and never after 1993.[38] In 2010, Gosnell's clinic was raided on suspicion of drug violations, and the authorities finally took his unhygienic, horrific clinic seriously. An investigation resulted in eight murder charges being brought against Gosnell: one involving a woman who fatally overdosed on painkillers before her procedure, but the other seven involving fetuses that were allegedly born alive after Gosnell "induced labor, forced the live birth of viable babies in the sixth, seventh, eighth month of pregnancy and then killed those babies by cutting into the back of the neck with scissors and severing their spinal cord," according to District Attorney Seth Williams.[39] This unprofessional and unsafe "method" is so greatly at odds with the procedures that are practiced by trained, caring providers that what Gosnell did can hardly be called abortion provision. Rather, his actions are those of an unscrupulous individual who took advantage of low-income, young, and immigrant women who wanted—and deserved—safe abortions but could not afford to go anywhere else.

Nine other clinic employees were also charged with crimes.[40] As of this writing, Gosnell is being held without bail and is awaiting trial.[41]

Pennsylvania officials did not react to the Gosnell scandal by holding state agencies accountable for their failure to act. They haven't addressed the fact that so many low-income and immigrant women sought help from Gosnell because they could not afford safe, reputable care. Instead, the official response was to pass Senate Bill 732 in 2011, a restrictive anti-choice bill that will require clinics to comply with new, expensive state regulations, such as widening hallways and elevators.[42] How these requirements will make women safer is unclear; indeed, if existing clinics must close their doors because they can't afford to implement the changes, many more women will be forced to seek care from less-reputable but also less-expensive providers . . . like Kermit Gosnell.

Happy Hour Conversations

Politicians treat abortion provision like an exotic form of medical care, one that requires unique rules and restrictions, in part because that is how society still views abortion itself. Being able to talk about abortion with nuance and honesty is one way to achieve a more balanced perspective, but getting to that place even in private conversations, much less public discourse, can be difficult, as several of the people interviewed for this book know firsthand. Their experiences illustrate just how complicated this issue can be, even for those who spend their professional lives working with issues of choice.

"I always identified as pro-choice and certainly always supported the cause and directed my vote many times, having grown up in Florida," activist Alexis Zepeda says during our interview in Washington, DC. "My mother's side of the family is Boston Irish-Catholic, and sort of cool in that New England way, and didn't talk about things like this, although we talked about politics a lot as a family. It wasn't until I started working in it that the women in my family talked about it without any restrictions," Alexis recalls. "Given how liberal and how open my family is on all other political issues, the fact that they never really talked about it speaks more than anything else I've heard about in support of the argument that the shame that surrounds abortion is so palpable and so real in this country."[43]

"Being an Abortioneer is like being gay, or having HIV (not to trivialize the struggle of those groups of people)," activist and blogger Anti-Anti* says in our e-mail interview. "It's something that is very difficult to disclose to others, even to the ones you love, for fear of isolation or stigmatization. And even if they are accepting, they can still make you feel awkward or different. So I'm playing it safe and protecting the confidentiality of myself and others."[44]

Anti-Anti uses the same pseudonym for our interview that she does in her writing for the group blog The Abortioneers; her cowriters also use pseudonyms. The blog, which chronicles "the ins and outs and ups and downs of direct service in the field of abortion care,"[45] touches on issues that are both broadly political and startlingly personal, and Anti-Anti is equally open in our interview.

"My relationship with my significant other was a bit strained at times," she says about how her work has affected other parts of her life. "He comes from a super anti [choice] family and I've had to bite my tongue more than my fair share of times. It's a big deal for me; being a woman and a minority to boot, I've been encouraged all my life to be as loud as possible. I've never been ashamed of myself. But here I am, telling his mom and dad that I still haven't found a job but I'd keep them updated on my search. Pathetic! In

---

* Not her real name.

fact, after I told him about the call [about a job in the field], he pulled me onto his lap, stroked my hair, and said 'Baby, you can't take that job. What would I tell my mother?' Good grief! That probably even solidified my commitment to work there. It was the first time I felt real feminist pangs. Like, even this man, who fell for me because I speak my mind and don't take anybody's shit and am just as witty and clever as he is and can give him tastes of his own medicine . . . wouldn't 'let' me do this work because his mother— his mother!—wouldn't stand for it? I feel bad for him. It's taken him some time to adjust, but his mom still doesn't know."

"My parents don't really know what I do," Amanda, a reproductive justice attorney, says candidly. "My dad's a minister and I was raised in a very, very anti-choice home, decorating the 'abortion stops a beating heart' signs in the basement of our house as a little kid and going to rallies. When I decided to develop a superstrong feminist and pro-choice and progressive identity in college, I think they [initially thought] this might be a phase. But then I went to law school, and I realized that these two things that I care so much about, the law and reproductive rights, I can actually do them at the same time." If her extended family asks about her work, Amanda explains, she says she works in public interest law. "For the most part, I think [my parents] have a willful blindness thing going on. They're very proud of me but not like they tell their buddies, oh my daughter's working in this movement, isn't it great."[46]

"I can't really talk with my family about what I do," Erin, a prochoice activist, admits. "I have to be vague, and I think my extended relatives don't know what I do, can't know what I do because it might cause a fight. It's intense because my family is Catholic and

I think that many of them are probably not pro-choice. I don't really know; I've never asked. I just try not to have the discussion so it that doesn't turn into [an] argument." Among her peers, however, Erin is more open, to the point that, as she says with a laugh, "When I'm out some friends are like, 'Can you not talk about abortion?' If someone asks me what I do and they have questions, my friends are, like, 'Oh god, talking about abortion again.'"[47]

"I will bring up abortion at the bar, like every weekend," Erin's friend and fellow activist Raina Aronowitz tells me enthusiastically. "I'm totally for de-stigmatizing the word abortion or feminist, all of it. Erin actually sent me this link [for an] 'I Love Abortion' T-shirt I would absolutely love to have. I bring it into my everyday life. Even within the reproductive health movement, people shy away from it, and I feel like that's what drew me to it. People will do domestic violence, people will do sexual health, and contraception, and emergency contraception, and birth control, but so few people will actually do abortion, even within the movement. It's stigmatizing and it's polarizing and it's hard. People want to shy away, they're not going to do things that are really hard and really stigmatizing. There's a huge stigma to it. I want to do the things that no one else will, especially because I see it as one of the most important things."[48]

"To live in this state as an abortion provider, I never know what I'm going to say," says June Ayers, the owner and director of an abortion clinic in Montgomery, Alabama. "Somebody says what do you do and usually I [say] I'm a nurse and they say where do you work, and I'll say Reproductive Health Services. Some people go, oh, and then some people will [say], good for you, I got my pregnancy test done there. I'll never forget about eight years ago I went in to get a sign remade," June recalls, referring to a metal sign that hangs in the parking lot outside. "I told [the business's owner that] I needed it for Reproductive Health Services, [and] he said we're not doing business with you. That's like being hit in the gut. And you know, well, I respect your opinion although you don't respect mine, I respect your opinion, I'll take my business elsewhere. You just don't know; it's not something where people let you know whether they're pro-choice or they're not and so you just don't know until you put yourself out there."[49]

"The work stays with me after I leave the office, but I can't really imagine it being any other way," says Roula, an activist who formerly worked in direct service. "It's not just an accidental job for me. I feel like it's really important to me and I wouldn't feel the same way about doing some other things I could also do. It's not like I take it home with me because I'm traumatized, but because I'm really into it. I don't know how to explain—I mean, you go to happy hour and you're talking about abortions the whole time, it's not necessarily like a terrible or neurotic thing."[50]

"I've lost a couple of friends who I never would have guessed were anti-choice," pro-choice activist and former clinic employee Sara Skinner says. "That was painful but now I do have a litmus test when I meet people," she points out. "Something that was really great for me was I told my cousin what I did and I really thought that she was going to be really upset, and she said, 'I think that's great.' I think sometimes pro-choice activists assume the worst in people, with reason, but at the same time I don't think we should quiet ourselves and assume that people will react with problems. It's taught me that I need to be a little less judgmental about how I think people will react to the work that I do."[51]

And others have found that their work in the field has resulted in surprisingly positive feedback from relatives and community members. "Growing up, I was very involved in my Methodist church," activist Kate Palmer tells me. "When I got my first job at Northland Family Planning clinic [in Detroit], I was nervous about how my church community would react. I didn't really care if they supported me, but I didn't want it to become an issue or to make people feel uncomfortable. I was really surprised by most people's reactions. Once people found out where I had started working, older women kept approaching me to tell me that they were proud of me and the work that I was doing. They would whisper their own abortion stories to me during the coffee hour at church on Sunday mornings. It made me realize how supportive most people are of abortion, even though it's not often discussed."[52]

"I've had two abortions, one a few days after I turned eighteen," medical student Shaundell Hall tells me at the beginning of our conversation. "I became pregnant with someone who was abusive. When I initially found out, I thought I would choose adoption because I considered abortion to be sort of a last resort for people who were in really bad situations. I didn't realize that mine was that bad.[53]

"It was actually my mother who suggested that I consider abortion," Shaundell continues. "I knew my family was pro-choice, but it was never something that we really talked about. I ended up talking to the minister at my church, and he and his wife were both very supportive and he even offered to go with us to the clinic. We went to a clinic that was about three hours away; it was in St. Louis. I never regretted it." Shaundell plans to specialize in family practice; as part of her work, she says, she will provide abortions.

However, even when support for abortion is found, Dr. Willie Parker points out that there is a kind of cultural sentiment in favor of continuing a pregnancy. "If you're now pregnant with a pregnancy that you never desired in the first place, the decision about whether or not to continue that pregnancy to me is not a choice, it is a resolution of a dilemma," he explains.[54]

"I think when we call it a choice, this is the notion of a kind of lightness-of-heart decision that isn't really there. And I think that it's that rhetoric that has made it problematic for people outside of that decision who are trying to understand," Willie continues. "It's easy for them to say, 'Oh, why would you not choose to have a baby?' Because the social context around having a baby is a celebrated event, it's desirable, and kind of a biological imperative that you're supposed to do no matter what the context. In the context of that rhetoric, it's problematic for gaining a public understanding and awareness, and . . . compassion for people who might have made that decision."

As Rozalyn Love found out, even that amount of compassion often does not exist for people who choose to perform abortions or help women acquire abortions. When she was a medical student at the University of Alabama, Birmingham, Roz wrote an essay for the *Washington Post* about her evolution from a teenager who didn't believe in abortion to a medical student and activist committed to education and choice.[55] Published shortly after George Tiller's murder, the reaction to Roz's article was swift and overwhelming.

Roz received eight hundred e-mails. She recalls, "The positive mail far outweighed the negative mail, which surprised me. I think so many people were afraid, or knew I would get hate mail and be called awful things, that they felt almost obliged to send me a piece of positive mail.

"Then there was your usual round of the awful stuff," she continues. "People took it very personally. It was beyond over-whelming. Most of the negative nasty stuff came on blogs, a lot of it not true. People were saying that this was all concocted by the *Washington Post* and that I didn't exist; [that] I used a pseud-onym, because how ironic would it be that my last name was Love and I planned to murder babies; that I grew up Catholic. I don't know where that came from. I'm not Catholic at all. To sit back and watch people actively blog about you is really scary."[56]

Beyond the disorienting experience of seeing her very existence questioned, it was the reaction of Roz's family that seemed to touch her most deeply. "[My family's] immediate reaction was kind of shock. And heartbroken, that this is what I would choose to spend my life's work doing," she explains. "I think [my family] never really heard a legitimate argument for the other side. Whether you make that decision or not, it should be a personal decision, and it is certainly a decision between you and whatever spiritual being you ascribe to. It was a good conversation," Roz says. "My family understands now that the article wasn't a personal attack on them; it was just talking about the culture of the South and particu-larly my hometown. We talked a lot about how we do a lot of pre-tending, especially with difficult topics like sex. That can promote unhealthy behavior, unhealthy relationships."

Willie Parker has also seen a personal benefit to being open about his work. "My immediate siblings know what I do, and all of my family, they respect what I do," the physician says. "If they're conflicted at all, they're conflicted in a good way in terms of, they know me for who I am and they know the principle of why I do this work. So the world became less black-and-white to them and more gray."

The Personal and the Political

Every provider and activist has a different reason that he or she became involved in pro-choice work. When asked, most have many, and don't mention one specific instance or experience. But Dana Weinstein's pro-choice activism came about in an intensely personal way.

"I was twenty-eight weeks pregnant, and during a routine examination they saw something a little off with the baby's brain," Dana explains over coffee. "I went for an MRI two weeks later and they found significant problems with the baby's brain, that the brain had never even really developed at all. I made the heartbreaking choice to terminate.[57]

"They couldn't give me any indication of how long the child would survive after it was born, but they did say that I would need a resuscitation order in place prior to delivering her, and she would need significant medical intervention to exist," Dana continues. "They gave me the option of adoption, there are apparently families and places that will adopt children like this, that will die. They didn't give me the option of abortion and I had to ask the question.

I was not at all prepared for the diagnosis ... so to have to turn around in front of my husband and ask about ending the child's life was horrible. I said to my husband over and over again, 'Don't think I'm a bad person. Please don't think I'm a bad person for asking about termination so quickly after learning our diagnosis.'

"As soon as he saw me, [the doctor] was compassionate," Dana adds. "I think he has to be tough for what he does, but he was compassionate and just apologetic for the situation I was in.

"When my first child was born, I remember having a conversation with a friend of mine about how having [him] changed my perspective on abortion, in that I found it harder to understand why someone could end a pregnancy," Dana tells me. "You see a heartbeat, you see the beautiful face, you see ten fingers and ten toes. Now I think back to the sonograms, the beautiful sonograms I had of my sick baby. She had a beautiful heartbeat, beautiful face, ten beautiful fingers and ten toes, but the whole insides were wired completely wrong. I feel a little guilty that I was so judgmental after having my son. Anti-choicers use that image and that's very emotional and provocative, but it does not tell the [whole] story, certainly not for someone like me. I doubt anyone walks into it, whether at six weeks or at thirty-two weeks ... I don't think anyone makes the choice lightly."

The café where we sit is not very crowded, and though Dana's voice is soft, her words are clear. At some point during our conversation I realize that a part of me is tensed, wondering if any other customers are listening, and what they might think.

"I never in a million years thought that I would need a late-term abortion," Dana says. "I honestly thought people who had late term—I didn't think they were naïve and all of a sudden decided they didn't want to have a baby, but I did think well, maybe they didn't go to checkups and finally they learned something went wrong. [I] never thought you could go to every single appointment, you could have every test—amniocentesis wouldn't have caught this. Nothing, no surgery, no drugs, nothing that would have changed the outcome for my child. To have it be debated, and so difficult to be able to terminate is just so wrong. I would challenge any politician to walk in my shoes."

Dana has done just that by sharing her story, despite how painful it is for her to talk about the end of a much-wanted pregnancy. "I think part of [deciding to speak out] was a need to have some legacy for my child," she says thoughtfully. "I was thirty-two weeks when I ended my baby's life, and I just had a hard time saying good-bye. And if I can do anything to help anyone else, then I feel like my baby had a purpose. I feel like if my voice can make any difference in this, then I want to be out there loud and vocal and not ashamed of it by using my name, by using my story.

"I have the utmost respect for people who make a different decision," she continues, "but the fact of the matter is, it's a choice. We have a right to make the choice that's best for our baby."

Dana says that when she first told her family that she was going to speak out about her experience, "my mother-in-law, a very strong, independent woman, said I don't think you should use your name. I remember saying to her, 'You know what? If an antichoicer or someone who comes from a different opinion threatens me or calls me a baby killer or puts that imagery in front of me, it won't be nearly as awful as the image I have of the MRI of my baby's brain completely malformed. So, bring it because I just cannot possibly fear anything.'"

"Until I went off to college it never really occurred to me that people would be anti-choice. It just didn't make any sense to me," physician Justin Diedrich tells me in an e-mail. "So in college I first started really thinking critically about what I believed and why. And the more work I did in women's health, the more certain I became of what I believed—what I *knew*. Abortions happen whether they are legal or illegal, and whether they are safe or unsafe. Criminalizing one of the most common surgical procedures in the world does not make it disappear. It only makes it less safe.[58]

"Abortion stirs up more commotion than any other word in the medical dictionary," Justin continues. "There will always be fanatics. Sometimes we can have a dialogue, but usually we cannot even agree to disagree. And they are entitled to their beliefs. They are a just as much a part of this landscape as I am."

"Do I think about safety?" he asks during our second interview. "Of course. Naïveté is irresponsibility. 'Safety' is an ongoing conversation. I think of my wife, and I think of my future. But I also think of my future patients. I am an abortion provider. And I will continue to provide full reproductive health care to every one of my patients."

Physicians who came of age pre-*Roe* had no reason to expect that their work would ever draw the kind of anti-choice harassment and violence that became common in the years after abortion was legalized, when anti-choice groups shifted their focus from the courtroom to the places where abortions were being performed. In contrast, today's medical students and residents have seen all too clearly the physical dangers of providing care. Each murdered provider and clinic worker has brought a fresh round of media attention, and high-profile clinic attacks have become national news. Yet not a single medical student or resident interviewed for this book cited a fear for their physical safety as a reason to not go into the field.

Even so, seasoned providers remain doubtful that their younger colleagues will follow in their footsteps. "I worked with med students who were interested in performing abortions, but I found that over the years I heard from [fewer and fewer] young physicians who were interested in learning the skill," retired physician Marciana Wilkerson tells me. "It's a very specific skill. And I don't think that there are too many young physicians who have that skill anymore, and a lot of them don't want to learn. There's so much noise now about *Roe v. Wade*, about the pro-life people, that I think a lot of the younger people choose not to do it."[59]

"Doctors are not going to come out en masse and go into abortion practice, just because when you're coming out of medical school and you're $200,000–$300,000 in debt, you're not going to start a solo practice," contends abortion provider Lee Carhart. "And there's not going to be very many group practices except on the coasts where you can say I want to do abortions and they're going to say it's fine. But I do think the positive effect from Medical Students for Choice is phenomenal in that it can expose a lot of future doctors to [the] thoughts of women about abortion, how important it is to them.

"I also truly believe that, at least in the present medical environment, when these doctors have worked for fifteen to twenty years, the same as I did, there's going to be a significant portion of them that will say, 'You know, I wouldn't mind doing abortions for Planned Parenthood one day a week,'" Lee continues. "But . . . as long as this harassment goes on, it's going to be a field of medicine that's predominantly middle-aged providers looking for a second career that are burned out with what they're doing. And that's whom I started training back in the '90s, people from all walks, radiologists, internists, family practice people."

Lee also raises a provocative point about doctors who provide abortions in a more clandestine manner and the effect that that has on how abortion can be viewed. "When the docs are hiding, then it's hard to say that your patients should want to be identified [as having had an abortion]," he observes.[60]

Louisa Pyle and Rozalyn Love have both spent a lot of time thinking about what course they want their careers to take. And despite their passionate commitment to MSFC and their deep belief that there need to be more abortion providers, neither is sure that she will go into the field. "I'm completely committed to the idea of getting trained. I'm absolutely committed to the idea of providing. I've thought a lot about what my best role might be, though," Louisa says. "I think my strongest role might be in some sort of leadership in an individual medical school, or on a larger administrative scale, trying to make sure that appropriate information is in the curricula across one or multiple medical schools, for abortion or contraception."[61]

"I don't see myself opening my own abortion clinic here in Birmingham," Roz says. "Making sure that I can provide them as part of comprehensive health care [is] more what I would do. Sometimes I wonder, 'Am I taking the easy way out, am I choosing that because I think that's where my gift lies or where my talents are, or is it because I'm too scared to be Dr. Tiller?' And sometimes I don't know. Being a full-time abortion provider is not what I got into medicine to do."[62]

"Unlike many of my peers, I went to medical school for the sole purpose of becoming an abortion provider," medical student Shannon Connolly says. "After I graduated from college, I didn't know what I wanted to do with my life. I ended up taking a job at Planned Parenthood in Boston, [and] I worked with women who were either seeking family planning or just gynecological health care. For the first time, I understood on a far more sophisticated level what the consequences of poverty and poor access to health care were, and what the circumstances are of many women who are seeking abortions. I realized how difficult it was to get accurate information, to find the clinic or a doctor that would provide the service, and to actually get there and pay for it. I decided that I wanted to be an abortion provider because I felt passionately that I wanted to help these women and I felt that I could do it, and I was willing to take it on as my life's mission."[63]

Shannon has also found that Dr. Tiller's death has only strengthened her commitment to providing abortions. "He was such an amazing, kind-hearted soul," Shannon says. "His loss is acutely felt by many, many people, but it makes it that much more important that people from my generation step up and agree to be abortion providers. If not us, then who, right?"

Life on the Front Lines

So, what is it like for the activists and providers actually working in this often-demonized field? Challenging, frustrating, intense—and rewarding.

"I get paid to cause trouble—but in a good way," is how Melissa Bird explains her job as the executive director of Planned Parenthood Action Council and the vice-president of public policy for Planned Parenthood of Utah. "One of the most important things that I do is build relationships with elected officials regardless of party or 'choice' affiliation in order to educate elected officials about who we are as an organization, and what we really do for the community." In addition to that work, Melissa has also helped pass legislation that secured funding for STD education and ensured that sexual assault victims had access to emergency contraception in the ER, among other reproductive health issues.

"Being pro-choice to me isn't just about abortion," Melissa says. "It is about making sure that girls and women are equipped to take control over their health care and their bodies and that they always have access to all forms of reproductive health care and that abortion is safe, rare, and legal."[64]

"I oversee all of the field work in Colorado, Wyoming, and northern New Mexico," Katie Groke Ellis, the field manager for Planned Parenthood of the Rocky Mountains [PPRM], says. "I am in charge of our on-the-ground outreach [and] work with our field organizers to reach out to our activists who are doing grassroots activities in support of our political issues. We run phone banks, canvasses, fun events like movie nights [and] rallies."[65]

Katie's colleague Adrienne Kimmell, the executive director of the Florida Association of Planned Parenthood Affiliates, stresses the importance of outside activists. "We have activists or volunteers who engage more on the policy or political side of things, by doing things like phone banking; we run phone banks all the time. Submitting letters to the editor really makes a huge impact and is so important with getting our message across, advancing our pro-active policies. We usually have a lobby day where people can come up to our state capitol in Tallahassee and meet with their elected officials and educate them about who Planned Parenthood is, what we do, why we think that young people need to have access to comprehensive sex education and women ought to have increased access to birth control to prevent unplanned pregnancies. So there are certainly a lot of ways people can get involved that [are] outside of the more clinical aspects of things."[66]

At the time of our first interview in 2009, activist Steph Herold was working in an urban clinic as a counselor, and she discussed the differences between that job and her earlier work at an abortion fund. At the fund, "it was much easier for me to disconnect from the work at the fund when I came home every day. I was talking to women on the phone, not in person. I was providing people with one part of the abortion experience, helping them raise the money, and that's easier than looking them in the eye and talking about their complex feelings about abortion.

"Being a clinic counselor is more intimate than a phone conversation, but there's also more at stake. Sometimes I have to tell people you know what, you have this medical condition, we need you to get medical clearance and you'll have to come back in a week. And people want to punch me in the face—they want the abortion immediately. That can be very frustrating for the patient and for me. Of course I want her to have the abortion as soon as she wants to, but we're talking about a medical procedure. It's my job to make sure she has a safe abortion, not a quick abortion."[67]

"I come very much from a privileged background, [as] a white middle-class woman," activist Sara Skinner says. "I saw how women of color were being treated and the lack of choice and just a lack of education about their own bodies, including myself," she recalls about her direct-service work at an urban clinic. "I can honestly say before I started working there I didn't even know about the different types of birth control. I didn't even how an abortion worked; I knew on some sort of level, but it was very much a learning experience for me. I think the job really opened up a lot of what it means to be a woman in America, what is really an option, what is really choice and how having abortion be legal on the books doesn't really mean anything at all.

"It's a privilege, you know, it's such a privilege to be invited into someone's life," Sara says thoughtfully, "but at the same time I don't find it to be very empowering for the other person sometimes. We just want to feel comfortable solving the problem, so we're not asking everything that needs to be asked: What do you have? What can you do? I'm not talking about abortion but what do you want to do, how are you planning on getting the money together.

"Sometimes people who work [for access funds] say that they have dreams about phones that never stop ringing," Sara adds. "I hope that when I have children, if I have children, that the phones will have stopped ringing, and that at that point women will be able to choose what they want when they want it and not have to worry about what's in their wallets."[68]

"I can see it in my mind's eye, the woman calling has a piece of paper with all these phone numbers, people's names, clinic names, arrows drawn everywhere, things scribbled on back, they're doing their math, things like that," Alexis Zepeda says of her time as a case manager for the DC Abortion Fund. "They're in total crisis and because of that can't think about putting one foot in front of the other. That's one of my stock phrases that I say every time, let's just think about putting one foot in front of the other, we'll get there, I'm with you, we'll get there.

"You hear the worst stories of people's lives of chaos and how everything is out of their control, including their reproductive lives," Alexis continues. "Many women who call us, they're not good at controlling their lives, that's why they are where they are. That's not a judgment on them or any ability they have; it's that they're supported or not supported by what I like to call inter-locking systems of oppression that put them in these lives of chaos that it's incredibly hard to dig yourself out from. All we are is a hand with this one particular problem, and we can't fool ourselves into thinking that once we help them with this pregnancy that their lives are going to be changed and everything's going to be perfect. It just won't, but we're there for this one thing."[69]

"We have people from all over the state call, from the big met-ropolitan areas to the tiniest little towns," law student Kyle Marie Stock says about the Lilith Fund, an access fund where she volun-teers in Austin, Texas. "A lot of people are already parents; that's definitely one of the things that comes up often. People already have children and they can't necessarily provide adequately for another kid, and they're really trying to make sure that they're able to raise their family in a healthy manner.

"It's interesting to me because Texas is so large and there aren't a lot of abortion providers," she says. "Certainly they're out there, but often they're in the metropolitan areas, so if you're in a rural area you may have to travel four, five hours. Especially if you're in West Texas; there, you may have go to New Mexico. It's frustrating, and also because Texas is religiously and ideologically conservative, the conversation itself is even hostile. I mean, when you're sitting in the Austin bubble, sure, people are more conversant about it. But I remember speaking to someone on the hotline where she was like, you are literally the first person I've told that I'm pregnant and I'm getting an abortion. She would be horribly ostracized and probably coerced, in terms of the way people present the argument, into not getting the abortion at all."[70]

While the stress and frustration experienced by women seeking abortion care is significant, those working in direct service have their own share of frustrations, too, that go beyond the rather academic annoyance at laws and regulations that make it so difficult for women to access services. Cursing Henry Hyde is one thing; being cursed out by a woman who's been trying for three weeks straight to raise money and is now being told that she still doesn't have enough is completely different. Even when you know that she's yelling at you because she can't yell at her partner or boss or Medicaid case manager; and even when you don't blame her because you'd be yelling too if you were in her shoes, being face-to-face with such anger and desperation can be harrowing.

Burnout is not uncommon; a number of activists who worked in direct service when I first interviewed them have since left their jobs to pursue graduate degrees or other employment. And even volunteering for a fund can take a toll on people. "One of the biggest challenges for small abortion funds is that our resources are so limited that often we can not adequately train people to deal with some of the hard cases," the Lilith Fund's Kyle Marie Stock says. "If there was something that I [didn't] know how to handle, I would often call one of my colleagues and talk it out with them and debrief and take care of myself first, to make sure that I was available to my client, to make sure that I wasn't doing them more harm than good. I think that if we could do a better job training, people would burn out less. I definitely got to a point where I was like, I can't do this anymore. The best thing to do is know your limits and use other resources when you've reached that point. We certainly have people who answer the hotline who have MSWs [Masters in Social Work], people who do abortion counseling at clinics, people who are extremely well trained, and then there [are] other people that are new. But it's really important to have as much new blood in the organization, to be drawing people into the community and really having people participate as much as they can, so it's kind of a balancing act."[71]

"Sometimes I question myself, have I become desensitized?" social worker Kira Baughman Jabri says as she reflects on her work in abortion care. "Because it's nothing for me to say, okay, you're fourteen and your father raped you, and I'm here to help you. I know incest exists, I know that women get raped, I know all these horrible, horrible things that not just women, but children and their families, go through.[72]

"I remember having a long conversation about an eleven-year-old with [a clinic employee] and I don't know what happened, but we just both stopped and said, you know we've been talking about pediatric abortion and that [term] should not exist," Kira says. "We just jumped right into helping mode; we're happy that we can provide this service, but I don't like saying pediatric abortion—it's very difficult. So I think those are the cases that get to me. But then on the flip side, I know that for the rest of their lives we're actually giving them a fighting chance that they didn't have."

"Talking to women in crisis means meeting them in the middle of what might be the worst time of their life, but also the time when they were forced to find out what they are really made of," documentary filmmaker Angie Young says about her direct-service experience. "I loved being at the front lines of the abortion issue helping real women dealing with this issue; it gave me a very powerful education about what the real issues are surrounding abortion, and overwhelmingly reaffirmed my position that abortion should be safe, legal, and accessible for all women. More than anything, I think this job really taught me how to listen and have empathy on a deep level. Sometimes conversations would last for hours and afterwards the person would thank me and say it was the first time she felt like someone really heard her. Those were the best days."[73]

Angie channeled her passion and talent into the 2008 film *The Coat Hanger Project*, which examines the importance of legal abortion. This was Angie's first film, and the result is a moving and thoughtful exploration of the pro-choice movement. Likewise, Steph Herold drew on her experiences to create the website I Am Dr. Tiller.

"[The] website came out of a staff meeting at my clinic," Steph tells me. "We met right after Dr. Tiller's death; it happened on a Sunday, and we were all back in the clinic on Tuesday. We were all talking about what we thought we could do and how we were feeling, and it came up that we never really talked about why we do this work, and how maybe we could prevent these acts in the future. I got to thinking about what it would be like to humanize abortion providers, and I had the idea for this website. I immediately text messaged Yahel and told him, buy the domain I Am Dr. Tiller and I'll explain to you later. We set it up really quickly that night."[74]

"She had this idea," Yahel Carmon, who helped build the site, adds. "It started out with the idea of women holding up signs saying 'I am Dr. Tiller,' and telling their stories. Dr. Tiller works in Alabama; Dr. Tiller volunteers in Philadelphia, et cetera, et cetera."[75]

Shortly after the site was launched, Bill O'Reilly mentioned it on his show, *The O'Reilly Factor*. "We don't have cable in our apartment," Yahel explains, "so I got a text message from my little brother saying oh my god, Steph's and your site was mentioned on Bill O'Reilly. My first reaction was, why are you watching Bill O'Reilly?

"My first reaction," he continues, "when I heard that he had mentioned Steph by name on the show, was to lock down her server, close her Linked-In account, make sure that her Facebook and Twitter were restricted."

"We got a lot of e-mails after that," Steph says. "A big influx, really frightening—'You're going to hell,' that sort of thing. At the same time a few blogs picked it up and said obviously Bill O'Reilly has no idea what [that site] is really about. Then on the other side, a lot of pro-life websites picked it up saying oh my god, this website is like a den of terror."

"When I started, I had my difficulties with dealing with the reality of abortion," Michelle Fortier, the director of North Florida Women's Health and Counseling Services, tells me when I visit her clinic. "What really brought it home with me is listening to the women and their stories about how important this choice is and about how necessary it is. For a lot of the women that we see, this is the option that they feel that they need to have, that they need to obtain an abortion.[76]

"You had that saying, I believe in abortion but I could never choose abortion," she continues. "Working here, I think all of us in the facility are like, it's a reality, I'd probably choose it. Finally being able to say that and give legitimacy to our choices instead of being the good person—for some reason it's considered the right thing to say that you support abortion but not for you. We even have patients that come in here and they're like oh, I always supported abortion rights but I never thought I'd be in this situation."

The very fact that abortion is something unpredictable—that it results from an unexpected occurrence, such as a fetal anomaly or failed birth control—speaks to how important it is to safeguard the availability and accessibility of the procedure. Any woman could find herself in need of abortion care at any point in her reproductive life, and any man could find himself in a situation where abortion is the best choice for his partner and family. And it is this universality that makes it imperative that reproductive rights remain protected and robust.

"This is your vote, your choice, and your voice," activist Melissa Bird says. "My body is not your political platform, and my voice is bigger than yours. Don't freak out, do something, be powerful."[77]

CHAPTER FOUR

(MIS)REPRESENTATIONS OF REALITY

Popular culture is both a reflection of and a leader for society. Thirty years ago, *The Cosby Show* was considered groundbreaking because it focused on a highly educated black family. Now black surgeons, attorneys, and executives are common all over television and film—and the country itself has a black president. *The Cosby Show* is not responsible for Barack Obama's 2008 or 2012 victories, but it did play a role in changing the way that a lot of the country viewed black families.

Similar parallels can be drawn between the gay-rights movement of the 1970s and the plethora of ways gays and lesbians are depicted in pop culture forty years later. *Longtime Companion* and *Cruising* are no more responsible for sexual diversity in entertainment than *thirtysomething* and *L.A. Law*, but these four very different presentations of homosexuality have certainly increased the visibility and acceptance of the LGBTQ (lesbian, gay, bisexual, transgender, and queer/questioning) community.

When it comes to the subject of abortion, however, mainstream films and television shows have demonstrated a marked reluctance to approach the issue. An unplanned pregnancy has long been a convenient way to add dramatic tension or comic possibility, or take an established character in a new direction. Yet the outcome of this common plotline rarely deviates from one of two resolutions: the woman continues her pregnancy or the woman chooses to have an abortion but suffers a conveniently timed miscarriage instead. It is exceedingly rare to see a female character decide to have an abortion and actually go through with the procedure. And even with the persistent popularity of TV medical dramas, it's even more uncommon for a character to provide abortions.

As of spring 2012, it has been nearly impossible to find published research that specifically tracks and examines the references to, and representations of, abortion in film and television. However, academic papers and dissertations have included the issue in research exploring concerns as varied as how women's rights are portrayed in the media, how framing a controversial issue influences viewer reaction, and how early films about abortion reflected popular attitudes of the times. Andrea L. Press and Elizabeth Cole's book, *Speaking of Abortion: Television and Authority in the Lives of Women*, looks at how viewers spoke about and responded to depictions of abortion on television. Press and Cole's work is valuable in looking at the range of opinions women hold on abortion, but its focus was not to offer a thorough review of television portrayals.

Outside of academics, entertainment and culture journalists have discussed the issue in relation to films or individual episodes of television shows that address abortion, or the overall media approach to the topic. Yet in my own research, I've found that the most comprehensive resource was a nonexhaustive timeline of abortion stories found on the website The Abortion Diaries.[1] As a result, the majority of the films and television shows discussed in this chapter are examples I came across through personal interest or my own research.

Flirting with Choice

In 2007, three very different movies about pregnancy opened within seven months of each other and received tremendous attention. They were *Knocked Up*, a highly successful, raunchy comedy about a one-night stand; *Juno*, a comedy about teen pregnancy, which won its screenwriter an Oscar; and *Waitress*, an independent film about a woman in an abusive marriage that garnered both critical acclaim and a surprisingly strong box office showing. At first glance, endearing depictions of independent single moms, and nonshaming treatments of teen and casual sex, may seem like a step forward. However, especially when seen together, a theme emerges. Each movie features a woman who did not plan to become pregnant and would have extremely valid reasons for choosing abortion. Yet, in every instance, she continues her pregnancy.

Knocked Up asks viewers to believe that a brand new couple wouldn't so much as raise the question as to whether to continue the pregnancy. More implausibly, *Waitress* contends that a desperately unhappy woman, whose close friends are ready to help her however they can, would automatically decide to have her hated husband's child (only to spend the bulk of the movie talking about how she detests her unborn child up until the very end). When Jenna takes a pregnancy test, her friends are in the bathroom with her waiting for the results. "Negative, negative, come on negative," her friend Becky murmurs. "Come on. Dear Lord, protect our Jenna from the hell of unwanted pregnancy."[2]

Jenna, a talented baker, says that she doesn't want a baby; she just wants to make pies. And her other friend, Dawn, expresses surprise that Jenna was even having sex with her husband, Earl. After Becky explains, "He got her drunk one night," Jenna adds, "I should never drink. I do stupid things when I drink, like sleep with my husband." When they see that the test is positive, Jenna's friends ask if she's all right. Jenna replies by talking about a new pie that she wants to make called "I Don't Want Earl's Baby Pie." When Dawn says she doesn't think they can use that name, Jenna responds, "Then I'll just call it Bad Baby Pie." After another minute she says, quietly and with resignation, "I ain't never gonna get away from Earl now."[3]

In contrast, after the title character of *Juno* becomes pregnant by her friend Paul, her initial decision is to have an abortion. Juno makes the appointment and goes to the clinic. However, as she later tells her best friend Leah, that's where she changes her mind.

"Couldn't do it, Leah. It smelled like a dentist's office in there. And there were these horrible magazines with water stains. And then the friggin' receptionist is trying to get me to take these condoms that look like grape suckers. . . ."[4]

And, Juno adds, she saw an anti-choice classmate outside the clinic. "And she was like 'Oh, hi, babies have fingernails.' Fingernails! . . . I'm staying pregnant, Leah."[5] And so she does, in short order deciding to place her baby for adoption, finding adoptive parents, and sorting out her own feelings about Paul and relationships in time for a happy ending.

Television shows have presented similarly narrow responses to unplanned pregnancy. In general, the woman either continues the pregnancy, decides to have an abortion but miscarries instead, or decides to continue the pregnancy after she considers having an abortion and then carries to term and has the child. This third storyline shows no sign of losing popularity, as shows as disparate as *Beverly Hills, 90210*, *Felicity*, *Roseanne*, *Dawson's Creek*, *The O.C.*, *E.R.*, *Melrose Place*, and *Sex in the City* all presented their own takes on this situation in the 1990s and 2000s. In every case, valid concerns were raised about having a child: economic worries, the lack of a supportive partner or family, the woman's educational goals, her age (which tended to be either late teens or mid-thirties to early forties, but nothing in between), and her own mixed feelings about becoming a mother for the first time, or adding to the family that she already had. Yet in every case the woman decides to continue her pregnancy.

More recently, one of the lead characters on *Desperate Housewives*, a mother of four in her forties, grappled with whether to continue her own unexpected pregnancy. In a befitting fashion for this primetime soap, the woman, Lynette, decides to continue the pregnancy only after talking about it with her friend Susan, whose daughter is in the hospital after being strangled. After Susan congratulates her on the pregnancy and Lynette says that she's been upset about it, Susan asks why. Lynette answers, "I'm in my forties, my husband is back in school, I don't know how I'm going to do this whole baby thing again, and also because . . . because I can't quiet that one voice in my mind that keeps saying . . . maybe I shouldn't." Susan reacts sympathetically and tells Lynette that she can do "whatever you think it is you need to do." "Yeah, I know. Lucky me," Lynette responds. Susan points out some of the downsides of pregnancy, but then she talks about how all that day she thought she was going to lose her daughter. "I realize that I would have traded everything I own, I would give everything I ever would have, for just one more day as Julie's mom. But I'm not telling you what to do," Susan adds. "Actually, you are," Lynette says. "And I'm glad you did."[6]

There is nothing wrong with depicting adoption or unplanned parenthood as valid choices; in fact, both *Knocked Up* and *Waitress*, not to mention several of the shows mentioned above, could have benefited from even a cursory exploration into the woman's reasons for choosing to continue her pregnancy. But by consistently making abortion the option that dare not speak its name, no matter how rational a choice it might be, its validity and acceptability is diminished. The choice becomes so foreign that it cannot even be addressed, at least not by characters who have to remain sympathetic and relatable to viewers. The popular media's lack of diversity when it comes to pregnancy options is a reflection of, and more fodder for, the secrecy and shame surrounding abortion. It stands in stark contrast to real life, where 49 percent of all pregnancies in the United States (about 3.2 million) are unintended and 43 percent of those pregnancies end in abortion.[7] If these plotlines were more realistic and featured discussions of the circumstances, feelings, and beliefs that a woman actually experiences when making such decisions, media could help normalize and destigmatize this common choice.

Abortion Goes Primetime

Nowhere is this lack of discussion more evident than on the hugely popular MTV reality show *16 & Pregnant* and its spin-offs, *Teen Mom* and *Teen Mom 2*. Each episode of *16 & Pregnant* follows a teenage girl in the months leading up to and immediately following her child's birth. Family dramas, relationship stress, and worries about school and finances are all explored with clockwork regularity. Few of the girls' relationships survive the birth of their children. While a small number of girls profiled choose to have their children adopted, the vast majority decide to parent. *Teen Mom* and *Teen Mom 2* take a more in-depth look at the challenges and successes eight girls featured on *16 & Pregnant* encounter as they adjust to being mothers—or, in the case of one young woman, to having placed her child for adoption.

The *16 & Pregnant* franchise does not shy away from presenting teen pregnancy in all its complicated, relationship-destroying, education-derailing glory, but one aspect of pregnancy is rarely mentioned. You guessed it: abortion. During the first three seasons, a parent or friend might very briefly raise the subject, asking the teen if she'd ever considered not having the baby. The question tended to receive vague, mumbled responses like "Not really," or "I thought about it." Substantial conversation about why the teens didn't feel that abortion was the right choice, or—given the prevalence of parental involvement laws and the difficulty many young women have accessing a clinic—didn't feel it was even a realistic option, was never included in a single episode.

However, as the series has progressed, MTV has become more

forthright about the topic. In late 2010, the network aired an excellent stand-alone special called *No Easy Decision*.[8] The commercial-free, half-hour show featured Markai, a former *16 & Pregnant* participant, who found out that she was pregnant for a second time and decided to have an abortion. Filmed footage of Markai discussing her options with her partner, mother, and best friend made it clear that she struggled with her decision. She and her partner wanted to give their child a better life than they had had. However, Markai also made it clear that she wouldn't choose abortion as a first option for anybody.

No Easy Decision also shared the stories of two other young women. One discussed how she needed a judicial bypass in order to get an abortion and noted how costly an abortion could be. The other woman said she had thought about adoption but concluded that it wasn't the right choice for her. All three women were clear that there was no one "right" way to feel about abortion, that it was okay to feel both sadness and relief, regret and pride.

This message came up again in an episode during the fourth season of *16 & Pregnant*, which featured a young woman who became pregnant at the same time as her older sister. The pregnant girl, Briana, explains that her sister Brittany chose abortion because her then-boyfriend was not supportive of the pregnancy. Briana decided to continue with her own pregnancy because her boyfriend had said he would help her parent. In the ensuing months, however, Briana's boyfriend becomes more distant and unwilling to participate in either Briana's life or the life of his unborn child.

Throughout the episode, both Briana and Brittany talk about

their different decisions. Their mother tells both of them that she wanted Brittany to "live her life . . . be successful and accomplish everything that you know you can," and adds that she wants Briana to do the same, though it now feels like Brittany would be able to "do it all" while Briana could not.[9] "That's the choices that we made," Briana points out. "I can still live my life; I just have to live it a different way."[10] Later in the conversation, Brittany admits that sometimes she wishes she could take it back, and she confesses that it was hard to see her sister and mother prepare for the arrival of a baby.

Briana also admits ambivalence about her decision. After her daughter is born and it is clear that her child's father is out of the picture, Briana tells Brittany, "If I could go back and make the decision you made, I would do it. I'm not saying I regret her or anything, but you made a very, very smart decision."[11] While MTV has never repeated *No Easy Decision* (though the show is available on the network's website), it is likely to repeat Briana's episode just as relentlessly as it replays every other episode of *16 & Pregnant*.

Is this same ambivalence expressed in scripted shows where characters not only decide to have abortions but actually go through with them? For the most part, yes. Abortion is rarely presented as an unequivocally positive choice; instead, characters express doubts and confusion. While this is representative of how many women feel about having an abortion in real life, it also omits that a lot of women consider having an abortion to be an empowering and appropriate choice.

The very first abortion depicted on television occurred on the soap opera *Another World*, with its 1964 storyline about Pat Matthews' illegal abortion.[12] Very little has been written about this particular storyline, in which the word "abortion" was never used.[13] The lack of attention given to either the storyline or the response it generated makes me wonder if, first of all, there was not much in the way of either advertiser or viewer response, and, second, if the reason for *Another World*'s dismissal stems from its genre. Almost from their inception, soap operas have been considered little more than "women's entertainment" and not worthy of serious consideration from those who study the entertainment industry. While it is true that soaps in general, and *Another World* in particular, have had more than their share of outlandish plotlines and groan-worthy acting, the very fact that it was a soap opera that first tackled such a controversial topic speaks to the ability of this genre to address social issues years before more mainstream entertainment felt comfortable doing so.

When a primetime show finally did discuss abortion, however, it really made waves. In 1972 the sitcom *Maude* aired the iconic two-part episode, "Maude's Dilemma," which movingly depicts the surprise and anguish that Maude, a middle-aged grandmother, and her husband, Walter, feel over her unexpected pregnancy. The show is set in New York, a state that had legalized abortion two years earlier. Two CBS affiliates initially refused to air the episodes, and a number of others were pressured not to rerun them the following summer. Sponsors, including Pepsi, pulled their ads from the rerun following pressure from anti-choice groups.[14] Yet despite—or, perhaps because of—the controversy, sixty-five million people watched those episodes when they ran for a second time.[15]

The most unapologetically pro-choice abortion storyline ever featured on television is, not surprisingly, one of the most recent, appearing nearly forty years after the *Maude* episode. Dr. Cristina Yang, a primary character on the medical drama *Grey's Anatomy*, has twice experienced unplanned pregnancies and twice decided to have an abortion. The storyline involving her first pregnancy aired in 2005; that pregnancy was ectopic and she required emergency surgery. The storyline about her second pregnancy began in 2011, and this time she did go through with the abortion even though her husband strongly objected to her choice.

All of the dramatic tension surrounding this storyline was about what Cristina's choice meant for both her and her husband. There were painful conversations and one blistering fight after Cristina tells him that she is going to have the procedure, but when her husband shows up for the appointment and holds her hand, viewers are left with the sense that all has been resolved. As far as portraying the procedure itself, the show chose a very low-key approach: Cristina on a table, waiting for the doctor to start, and the camera cutting away soon after her husband comes to her side.

That's the classic manner in which films or TV shows depict the abortion procedure, regardless of whether they're showing an illegal abortion or one in a clinic: the woman on a table (either kitchen, hotel, or examining room), the doctor at her feet, a sheet covering her body. For all the anti-choice talk about how gruesome the abortion procedure is, the birth scene in *Knocked Up* is far more graphic than any filmed abortion scene could ever dare to be.

What is especially unique about Cristina's storyline is that it doesn't disappear after one episode. During the next season of

Grey's Anatomy, it becomes clear that her husband still resents her for having an abortion. His feelings erupt during a young child's birthday party, leading the couple to seek counseling—where their different perspectives are made strikingly clear. After summarizing some of their past issues, Cristina says, "But now we're fine." "Except for the part where you aborted the child that I wanted," her husband says. "Except for the part where you held my hand while I exercised my right to choose, and then four months later you screamed I killed your baby in front of all our friends," Cristina replies, just as calmly.[16] This scene, and the ensuing plotlines involving the abortion, fulfill what show creator (and Planned Parenthood, Los Angeles board member) Shonda Rhimes said the show was hoping to achieve. "I think for me the point is, it's a painful choice that a lot of women have made in their lives and we just wanted to portray it honestly and with a really good conversation . . . [a]nd see what happens after."[17]

In that same interview, Rhimes said that while she had some "strong conversations with Broadcast Standard and Practices"[18] during the first Cristina-abortion storyline in 2005, the 2011 episode incited no similar discussions; and as far as she was aware, the overall reaction to that episode was pretty quiet.

Rhimes's impression was accurate: while plenty of entertainment news outlets carried stories about the episode, there was no mention of anti-choice groups boycotting the show or advertisers pulling their ads.

It is interesting that neither Maude in "Maude's Dilemma" nor Cristina on *Grey's Anatomy* use the conventional "right" reasons for choosing an abortion. Both women were financially stable and in committed relationships with supportive partners. Neither was pregnant as a result of rape, and no mention was made of potential harm to the woman's health or problems with fetal viability. Rather, both women chose to have an abortion because it was the best decision for her, full stop.

In the years between Maude and Cristina, other television shows have depicted primary characters choosing abortion. Erica Kane, a popular lead character on the soap opera *All My Children*, had a legal abortion in 1973; this milestone, however, was negated in 2006, when the show revealed that the doctor who performed the abortion had actually implanted the aborted embryo into another woman's uterus. While such a twist is standard fare for soaps, fans were outraged and saw the revision as a disgrace to what had been a socially significant storyline.[19]

The Canadian teen series *Degrassi High*, which was broadcast in the US through the CBC, kept things more realistic in 1989. After a summer romance, high school student Erica Farrell realizes she is pregnant. She decides to have an abortion. The Canadian version of the show aired a scene in which Erica and her twin sister, Heather, fight their way through a crowd of anti-choice protestors in front of the abortion clinic. The US version deleted this scene, and in fact did not explicitly state what Erica's decision was.[20] However, subsequent episodes aired in the US made it clear that Erica chose abortion, and that her choice causes conflict between herself and her sister, as well as problems with an anti-choice classmate. Those later episodes also showed that while Erica regretted the tension with her sister, she did not regret her choice.

Fifteen years later, with a new but similar storyline in 2004, the

Degrassi franchise encountered censorship again. This time, it was from the cable channel TeenNick, which aired *Degrassi: The Next Generation*. When fourteen-year-old Manny finds out that she is pregnant, both her boyfriend and her best friend want her to continue the pregnancy. Manny eventually decides that an abortion is the best decision for her, has the procedure, and has no regrets. TeenNick initially refused to air this two-part episode. After petitions and protests from fans, it finally aired the episodes in 2006, two years after they aired in Canada.[21]

In late January 2010, two very different dramas also addressed unplanned teenage pregnancy. On the sports drama series *Friday Night Lights*, Becky, a high school sophomore, becomes pregnant by a classmate she likes but hardly knows. The daughter of a single mother who had been a teen herself when she gave birth, Becky was well aware of both her mother's struggles and how limited her educational and career prospects would be if she has a child. Becky has a number of conversations with her mother, the boy involved, a close friend, and her school principal, before deciding that having an abortion is the best decision.[22]

Equally realistic is the way in which *Friday Night Lights* depicts the fallout for Becky's principal, Tami Taylor. The teenage boy's religious parents file a complaint with the school board after finding out about the abortion, convinced that Becky would have continued the pregnancy if Tami had not given her the information she requested about abortion. The ensuing controversy over, and discussion about, appropriate adult guidance, parental involvement, and the rights of teenagers to make their own decisions accurately reflects the ongoing national conversation over these issues and provides ample room for Tami and other characters to voice their compassion for Becky and support for her choice. Most refreshingly of all, Becky herself moves forward with her life, relieved and healthy. The entire storyline is progressive and direct and reflects a more nuanced depiction of abortion than many mainstream television shows may have attempted even ten years ago.

The same week that the *Friday Night Lights* episode aired, the glossy medical soap opera *Private Practice* (which, like *Grey's Anatomy*, was created by Shonda Rhimes) also featured a pregnant teenager. Here, it is the fifteen-year-old daughter of two of the lead characters, both physicians, who is pregnant. Her father is adamant that he will support whatever choice his daughter makes, but her mother is equally resolute that her daughter will ruin her life if she has a child so young and, despite being anti-choice, insists on an abortion. The girl eventually talks with another doctor, who had had an abortion herself several years earlier; their even-handed discussion serves to underscore the confusion that the girl is feeling about what to do (driven in part, it seems, by the fact that her mother always told her abortion was wrong yet is now demanding that she have one). In the end, for reasons that are not explicitly explained but seem to stem both from the girl's confusion and her awe at seeing a baby being born, she decides that she wants to continue with the pregnancy, and raise her child herself.[23]

(Like *Grey's Anatomy*, *Private Practice* has addressed abortion and reproductive rights issues in multiple episodes. A 2011 episode of *Private Practice* involved a patient who discovered that her first-trimester abortion did not work, and had to decide if she wanted to have the procedure or continue with the pregnancy, which by then was at 19 weeks.[24] In this episode, the show's main character describes herself as an abortion provider.[25])

While all of the above shows have received varying amounts of controversy, praise, and attention, one thing they do have in common is that they made it to air. That's more than the animated show *Family Guy* can say about its abortion-centered episode, which was scheduled to run during the show's eighth season, which aired from 2009–2010. *Family Guy* has a well-deserved reputation for off-color, provocative humor, so the real surprise might be that it took the show so long to get around to the subject of abortion.

The executives at Fox, which broadcasts the show, felt that an episode in which lead character Lois Griffin agrees to be a surrogate mother, then chooses to have an abortion after the biological parents suddenly die, was too controversial for the network. "I think the network is making a decision that is, unfortunately, probably correctly based on people's current ability to handle and dissect controversial narratives, which is far less than it was in the '70s,"[26] *Family Guy* creator Seth MacFarlane said in an interview about the episode, adding that Fox was aware that the show planned to address the topic but made it clear that the episode might not be aired on TV (the episode was later released on DVD). For Fox's part, the network's entertainment president said that not airing the episode "was a business decision" in response to a "fragile subject matter at a sensitive time."[27]

That explanation, honestly, should come as no surprise. Like pretty much any television studio—or any company, really—Fox wants to make money, and though controversy can help attract viewers and ratings, it can alienate advertisers.

Few show creators or writers will talk on the record about all the ideas that never make it to the screen and the reasons why those storylines fail. So it's difficult to speculate with any confidence why certain television shows may have chosen to have a character continue with an unplanned pregnancy rather than choose an abortion, particularly if the abortion option makes more sense in the context of the show. But let's take another look at the handful of shows discussed in this chapter: *Maude*, *All My Children*, *Degrassi High*, *Degrassi: The Next Generation*, *Private Practice*, *Friday Night Lights*, and *Grey's Anatomy*. One of those was a soap opera, which aired to a primarily female audience in the middle of the day, and expectations in terms of both ratings and advertiser revenues were much lower than for primetime shows. Two were Canadian shows that were written for audiences in that country. *Maude* was helmed by Norman Lear, who had a very well-established reputation for being controversial but also a track record that demonstrated just how well courting controversy had worked for both his shows and the network that aired them. Likewise, both *Private Practice* and *Grey's Anatomy* are run by Shonda Rhimes, who has created several financially successful and popular shows for the ABC network. On the opposite side of the spectrum, *Friday Night Lights* garnered great critical acclaim but perpetually low ratings. It is not too difficult to imagine that while the network's executives knew the storyline was potentially risky, there was also little to lose in terms of viewers and advertisers—and much to be gained in terms of publicity and critical attention. Regardless of a show's specific circumstances, abortion remains a gamble.

These storylines are also taking a chance from an entertainment perspective. While abortion plotlines can be dramatic and thought provoking, they aren't always the most entertaining way to pass thirty minutes or an hour. Too often, abortion stories get the same sort of "very special episode" treatment that so many other social issues receive, where characters spend a lot of time talking about an issue they've never mentioned before and never will bring up again—and their way of talking about it seems more like a public service announcement than actual conversation. As much as I love *Degrassi High*, I'll be the first to admit that the dialogue in that show's abortion episodes often makes me cringe because it sounds so clunky and awkward.

Aside from the business angle, there is also the challenge of writing about abortion in a way that neither lectures the audience nor trivializes the subject but merely tells a story. This is a tricky balance to achieve, but when it works—when abortion is represented as the common choice that it actually is for so many women—society is better off for it.

A Different Kind of Hollywood Ending

Despite all of the challenges, all of the abortion storylines discussed above work. They successfully show that abortion is a complex yet common decision that will affect, but not ruin, a woman's life. This is a much more considered and thoughtful approach than the more common resolution to unplanned pregnancy plotlines in which a woman knows all the reasons having a child is not the right option for her, yet she decides with a distinct lack of further discussion to continue the pregnancy regardless.

This treatment has found traction in a wide range of movies, such as *Knocked Up*, *Juno*, and *Waitress*, but these are far from the only popular films that rely on this narrative. However, just as the storylines presented on *Degrassi* and *Grey's Anatomy* have taken pains to present storylines detailing different options, some notable films have succeeded in portraying abortion as a logical and common choice for female characters.

Two examples can be found in well-regarded 1980s movies. The teenage Stacey in *Fast Times at Ridgemont High* doesn't agonize over her decision to have an abortion; rather, she calmly schedules her appointment and gets the money together. In *The Big Chill*, the adult Meg sums up her college abortion in a simple sentence: "It probably—no, it was the right thing to do at the time."[28]

Neither movie made abortion the focus of its plot, choosing instead to present the unplanned pregnancy as a part of an individual character's story. Likewise, the 1987 film *Dirty Dancing* revolves around a summer romance, and the illegal abortion that sets the plot in motion is just a background element (albeit an important one).

"If you do a documentary on coat hanger abortions, the only people who see it will be those who agree with you anyway," Eleanor Bergstein, the film's writer, said in a 2010 interview. "If you put one in a wide-based musical with pretty clothes, and lots of romance, it may surprise people and make them think of things they didn't think of before."[29] In the same interview, Bergstein mentioned that the illegal abortion plotline caused the film to lose a national sponsor, but the movie was massively successful. *Dirty Dancing* was the eleventh-highest-grossing film of 1987,[30] won an Academy Award,[31] and remains enduringly popular to this day.

As with their television counterparts, films that depict abortion as an acceptable and realistic choice are still the exceptions that prove the rule. While the financial and creative barriers to changing this narrative have already been discussed, there is another element that allows these barriers to remain: the audience. It may be a cliché that viewers get the entertainment they deserve, but if viewers just passively complain about what they see and make no effort to demand change—either through their consuming habits or through creating the entertainment they want—then they can't expect change to just happen.

Not every member of a movie audience is pro-choice, and not every person who's watched a TV show that features a conveniently-timed miscarriage or waiting-room change of heart has rolled her eyes and said out loud, "Are you kidding me?" But a whole lot of people who consume media also believe in reproductive rights, even if they're not all that vocal about their beliefs.

Changing the way media represents abortion means becoming more vocal. If pro-choice individuals can't even talk about their views in their own lives, even with people who disagree, they will never be able to successfully demand that others talk about abortion to a larger audience—and they can never expect that the idea of abortion as a valid choice will ever receive the representation it deserves in the mass media.

This larger representation does matter. Television and movies and books and songs matter. Perhaps they matter more than they should; perhaps an MTV show shouldn't be a primary way for teenagers to learn about birth control. But to deny that power is naïve, and it would behoove the pro-choice movement to use that significant platform to their advantage. After all, at their best, film and television have the power to facilitate necessary discussions about issues as diverse as sexuality, race, and class, and to help attitudes evolve in more inclusive directions. By repeatedly ignoring abortion, movies and TV shows are paying lip service to the anti-choice idea that abortion is somehow a wrong and undesirable choice for a woman to make.

It's easy to rant and rave about how abortion is represented—or worse, simply ignored—in pop culture. It's a lot harder, but also a lot more worthwhile, to direct all that energy and intelligence into an honest conversation about why choice is important and continue to work for a world in which abortion is just one more choice that a woman can make: an everyday, legal, unremarkable choice.

CHAPTER FIVE

THE AMAZING TALKING
FETUS OF OHIO

In March 2011, Ohio lawmakers heard testimony regarding a so-called "heartbeat bill." The measure would outlaw abortions once a fetal heartbeat could be detected via ultrasound, which can be as early as the sixth or seventh week of pregnancy—or before many women even know that they are pregnant.[1]

For the hearing before the House Health Committee, the anti-choice group Faith2Action announced that two fetuses would "testify." Two pregnant women would be given ultrasounds in the hearing room so the assembled politicians would both see the ultrasound images of the fifteen-week and nine-week fetuses and listen to their heartbeats. Faith2Action's president, Janet Porter, crowed that this would result in "testimony from the youngest to ever come before the committee—a nine-week-old unborn baby."[2]

The stunt's impact was diminished, however, when the heartbeat from the nine-week fetus turned out to be faint and difficult to hear. Yet H. B. 125, which read in part that ". . . no person shall knowingly perform an abortion on a pregnant woman with the specific intent of causing or abetting the termination of the life of the unborn human individual that the pregnant woman is carrying and whose fetal heartbeat has been detected according to the requirements of division (C) of this section," still passed the House by a vote of 54–43 in June, before going to the Senate for debate in December 2011.[3] That same nine-week fetus, now a nine-week infant, was brought into the hearing room, presumably as evidence that because politicians had "heard her heart" months earlier, she was given the chance to live.[4]

This veneration of the infant was strikingly at odds with political decisions made by the House Republicans not twelve months earlier. In June 2011, the Republican-majority House voted along party lines to approve Republican governor John Kasich's proposed 2011–2013 budget,[5] which included drastic cuts to the state's education funding and to "just about every state service and program,"[6] even as a proposed pay cut to lawmakers was removed from the final version and an estate tax that mainly affected wealthy taxpayers was ended.[7] Anti-choice politicians proclaim that they want to protect the unborn, which is very literally correct, since their consideration for children stops at about time that the infant emerges from its mother's womb. As far as Ohio Republicans, like so many others in the anti-choice movement, are concerned, once the child is born, both it and its mother are on their own.

Further evidence of the lawmakers' desire to ignore the realities of actually raising children can be found in their refusal to allow a young mother to testify at the March 2011 hearing. The state chapter of NARAL had asked that this woman be allowed to testify via video because one of her children had severe disabilities and required constant care. The bill's sponsor, Lynn Watchmann, denied the request, citing the technical difficulties of allowing video testimony (Sen. Watchmann apparently didn't consider these difficulties to extend to projecting real-time ultrasound images).

It seems more likely that the request was denied because the woman's testimony flew in the face of the anti-choice party line. The woman, who was not publicly identified, later told a reporter that she had spent her whole life "making 'pro-life' choices,"[8] but when she was pregnant with a wanted third child, she found out that the fetus had a fatal anomaly. Although neither her hospital nor her insurance was willing to help her end her pregnancy, the woman did decide to have an abortion. "[Y]ou can't tell anyone else what to do," she said in an interview with *The Nation*. "Everyone's situation is so different."[9]

Altogether, in 2011, 135 state provisions related to reproductive health and rights were enacted in thirty-six states, representing an astounding increase from the eighty-nine that were enacted the previous year and the seventy-seven enacted in 2009.[10] Out of those 135 provisions, ninety-two restrict access to abortion services.[11]

Restricting access to abortion care can take many forms. For instance, in 2011, Alabama, Oklahoma, Kansas, Indiana, and Idaho joined Nebraska in banning abortions after twenty weeks of pregnancy.[12] Not to be outdone, in April 2012, Arizona's Republican governor Jan Brewer approved the country's first ban on abortions done after twenty weeks of gestation.[13] This is notable because gestational age is generally defined as the number of weeks from the first day of a woman's last normal menstrual period, but in a typical pregnancy, conception generally occurs anywhere from eleven to twenty-one days after this date.[14] So the Arizona law actually outlaws abortion at a much earlier point than any other law in the country.

The primary rationale for these laws rests on the controversial concept of fetal pain. Despite its "scientific" appeal to anti-choice politicians, there has been scant evidence to support that a fetus feels pain at that point in pregnancy. A 2005 study published in the *Journal of the American Medical Association* found, after reviewing reports and studies on the topic, that fetuses are unable to feel pain until approximately the seventh month of pregnancy.[15] And a more recent review done by the UK's Royal College of Obstetricians and Gynaecologists found that the area of the brain that processes responses to pain is not fully formed until the twenty-fourth week of gestation.[16]

Another popular method of curtailing abortion access is through mandatory waiting periods, which require women to make multiple trips to the clinic. The first visit isn't for any real medical purpose; rather, it is to receive counseling, often including inaccurate information, about abortion. Women who work often must take time off for their appointments, and women who have very young children have to arrange child care. Now imagine having to go through the same hassles again within the next twenty-four or forty-eight hours, only this time you'll be at the office even longer because now you can actually have the procedure you need. On the surface, there is nothing wrong with receiving counseling before an abortion. On the contrary, many clinics have excellent counseling programs where women are able to ask as many questions as they need about the procedure and to talk through any concerns or feelings that they have about getting an abortion. In addition, it isn't uncommon for clinics to suggest to a woman who is unsure take some time, be it hours or days, to make the decision that is right for her.

Counseling sessions become problematic, however, when the state requires that 1) a set amount of time must elapse between the counseling and the procedure; 2) the counseling must be provided in person; and 3) clinic employees are required to give women information that is medically inaccurate or otherwise biased. Out of the thirty-five states that require counseling as of April 2012, twenty-six detail what information a woman must be given.[17] Eleven states require that a woman be given unproven information about fetal pain; five states include inaccurate information about abortion and future fertility; of the six states that include information about breast cancer, five inaccurately claim that there is a link between abortion and an increased risk of this cancer; and eight states only describe negative emotional responses to abortion.[18]

"I think that there's nothing more—well, there's a lot of things that are degrading," pro-choice activist Kira Baughman Jabri says with a rueful laugh. "It's extremely degrading that we say, 'Oh, so you weren't smart enough to come to a decision when you first came to the clinic. Go home and think about it some more.' I think that's absolutely insulting. We don't do that for any other procedure."[19]

Occasionally, such mandatory counseling has been checked by the law. In mid-2011, North Carolina Governor Beverly Purdue vetoed a bill that would have required a twenty-four-hour waiting period and mandated that women would have to view an ultrasound image of the fetus and hear a detailed description of the image. The North Carolina General Assembly managed to pass the bill even after Purdue's veto, but in fall 2011 a federal judge granted a prelimi-nary injunction against the law's "intrusive measures."[20]

Another federal judge issued an injunction against an even more intrusive waiting period law, this time in South Dakota. The bill, which was signed into law by Governor Dennis Daugaard in March 2011, would have required not only a three-day waiting period but also that a woman must seek counseling at a crisis pregnancy center.[21] Crisis pregnancy centers are largely run by Christian charities, and they were established to counsel pregnant women against having an abortion. The federal judge very logically found that, among other problems, the requirements for a doctor to provide, and a woman to receive, certain information violated their First Amendment rights; and that both the waiting period and the requirement to go to a crisis pregnancy clinic placed an undue burden on the woman.[22]

Texas Governor Rick Perry had better luck with his combined waiting period/mandatory ultrasound bill, which stated that a patient must receive a sonogram at least twenty-four hours before her abortion, that she see the image, and that she hear both a description of the image and the fetal heartbeat. While the woman may decline to see the image and hear the heartbeat, she cannot decline to hear the description. The law also stated that physicians and facilities that didn't comply with the law would be subject to penalties of up to $1,000 per violation, per day.[23]

As in South Dakota and North Carolina, the Texas law came before a federal court, this time in the summer of 2011. Judge Sam Sparks found that the law violated the First Amendment and blocked enforcement of several measures, saying that "the Act compels physicians to advance an ideological agenda with which they may not agree, regardless of any medical necessity, and irrespective of whether the pregnant women wish to listen."[24]

But several months later, the Fifth US Circuit Court of Appeals overturned the injunction and cleared the way for Texas to begin enforcing the new law, which it did in early 2012.[25] The appeals court decision was based on its belief that the requirements didn't violate free speech and that, in fact, a sonogram should be required because a woman might change her mind. "The provision of sonograms and the fetal heartbeat are routine measures in pregnancy medicine today. They are viewed as 'medically necessary' for the mother and fetus. Only if one assumes the conclusion of Appellees' argument, that pregnancy is a condition to be terminated, can one assume that such information about the fetus is medically irrelevant," the court wrote in its opinion.[26]

Given that the argument centers on women who are seeking abortions and therefore do consider their pregnancies conditions to be terminated, it seems that such a conclusion can indeed be assumed. This case is not about whether a woman should be required to hear a fetal heartbeat and a detailed description of how a fetus is developing for a pregnancy that she chose to continue. It's about the rights of women that have chosen to terminate their pregnancies, and about how the state of Texas apparently has such little faith in the decision-making capabilities of these women that it really feels it must insert itself into the examining room at every turn.

Women aren't stupid. They know what having an abortion means, and they know how to make the best decisions for themselves. According to a 2008 Guttmacher Institute report, 61 percent of women who have abortions also have at least one child—so they also know about fetal development and what an ultrasound image looks like.[27] Not to mention that given the financial realities of obtaining abortion care, the procedure is far too expensive and time-consuming to ever be a snap decision. By the time a woman enters the clinic, she has already devoted more time, energy, and resources to this decision than many people devote to other medical procedures—and that's before she discusses anything with a counselor.

In the specific case of Texas, have any of these anti-choice legislators thought about the reality of obtaining an abortion in their state? Texas is a geographically huge state where a third of all women live in a county with no abortion provider, so the travel time alone is likely to be significant.[28] That's not even considering the financial aspects, time commitment, and potential opposition that a woman might have to deal with from her partner, family, or friends. But apparently the state's politicians neither thought nor cared about these very real concerns because their belief that women can't really know what an abortion is unless they're shown an ultrasound or hear a heartbeat makes me think that the bill's supporters actually think a woman just wakes up one morning and thinks, "Hey, you know what'd be fun to do today? Get an abortion!"

A lot of laws on the state level are passed without drawing much national attention, but the Texas sonogram bill did make headlines, thanks to some marked similarities with another controversial bill in Virginia. That state's proposed anti-choice legislation also mandated that an ultrasound be performed at least twenty-four hours before a woman could obtain an abortion, and that the woman be given the option to see the image. In addition, the original version of the bill also specified that if the fetal age could not be determined through a transabdominal ultrasound, then the woman would have to undergo a transvaginal ultrasound.[29]

From a medical standpoint, this makes sense. Most pregnancies are simply not advanced enough before twelve weeks for an embryo or fetus to be visible on an abdominal ultrasound, so it's not uncommon for a physician to use a transvaginal ultrasound instead. Of course, most doctors are not told by the state that they must perform that ultrasound, and most pregnant women are given the choice of whether to have a transvaginal ultrasound or not.

The Texas bill did not specify if transvaginal ultrasound would be used,[30] but given that 88 percent of abortions are performed in the first twelve weeks of pregnancy, it's likely that a physician would need to use that method to determine gestational age and detect a heartbeat.[31] Perhaps because the method of ultrasound was not explicitly stated, or perhaps because there were so many other problematic aspects, few of the objections to the Texas bill focused on the possibility that women could be forced to undergo this invasive procedure.

But the idea of state-mandated transvaginal ultrasounds definitely caused a furor in Virginia.[32] Citizens recoiled at the idea that a woman could be required to undergo such a physically invasive procedure, and the bill attracted national attention—and outrage. Petitions, protests, and mocking on *The Daily Show* and *Saturday Night Live* all caused state legislators and anti-choice governor Bob McDonnell to reconsider their support, albeit only for that one part of the law.[33]

It's hard to see how the bill that McDonnell eventually signed into law is much of an improvement. Women will now be allowed to opt out of having a foreign object inserted into their bodies in favor of submitting to an external ultrasound.[34] But women must still have that exam, regardless of whether it's medically necessary, and the doctor is still required to offer the patient the option of seeing the image and hearing the heartbeat. In addition, the twenty-four-hour waiting period remains and, as Judith Lichtman, senior advisor to the National Partnership for Women & Families, points out, "To add insult to injury, in Virginia [the patient] has to pay for it! The doctor doesn't think it's necessary, she doesn't need it, and she has to pay for it because some political person and body has deemed that she [should]."[35]

While the total cost of an abortion varies from clinic to clinic, the average price of a first-trimester abortion in Virginia is between $260 and $495. The final version of the mandatory ultrasound bill will add a significant cost to the procedure—anywhere between $300 and $1,200—and the ultrasound itself may not even be medically accurate.[36] As Virginia state senator and pediatric neurologist Ralph Northam notes, "[T]hey are telling us to do a costly and unnecessary procedure that won't even work,"[37] since the final version of the bill means that doctors may have to do an abdominal ultrasound at a point so early in pregnancy that the ultrasound won't show anything. Rather than protecting a woman's health or respecting the doctor-patient relationship, the Virginia bill, much like its Texas counterpart, simply gives the government the right to intrude on a private situation.

In Wisconsin, the infamous union-busting governor Scott

Walker ignored the plea of the 12,500-member strong Wisconsin Medical Society to veto another piece of anti-choice legislation that would require doctors to ensure that women are not coerced into having abortions.[38] While this phrasing sounds innocuous, the society is concerned that the language of the Coercive and Web Cam Abortion Prevention Act is ambiguous, intrudes on the doctor-patient relationship, and threatens physicians who fail to precisely follow the bill with the possibility of being charged with a felony.[39] The bill also bans "telemed" abortions, where a woman who has chosen a medication abortion speaks with the physician via webcam rather than in person—even though no abortion clinic in the state offers that option.[40] Governor Walker signed the bill into law in April 2012.[41]

Penumbras, Burdens, and Other Legal Hazards

While the past two years have brought a seemingly endless assault on reproductive rights, using legal channels to restrict abortion access is far from a new anti-choice tactic. When asked which legal cases are most significant, reproductive rights attorney Mark Egerman says, "*Harris v. McRae*[42] really made me want to work full-time on abortion rights. I just remember thinking, this is one of the worst rulings, one of the most appalling in this country."[43]

Shortly after the Hyde Amendment was passed in 1976, attorneys from the ACLU, Planned Parenthood, and the Center for Constitutional Rights brought a class-action lawsuit on behalf of women who needed Medicaid abortions, doctors who wanted to provide Medicaid abortions, and the Women's Division of the

Board of Global Ministries of the United Methodist Church (New York City Health and Hospitals Corporation filed a companion suit).[44] Several years of litigation followed, and in 1980 the Supreme Court heard the case. The Court ruled five to four that the Hyde Amendment did not violate the Fifth Amendment; that states that participated in Medicaid were not required to fund medically necessary abortions; and that a woman's freedom of choice did not include "a constitutional entitlement to the financial resources to avail herself of the full range of protected choices."[45]

"What the court said was, the federal government may not put obstacles in the way of poor women who want to exercise the right to an abortion, but it need not remove obstacles not of its making," Mark says, paraphrasing the decision. "It just shows such an ignorance of poverty. The idea the federal government has nothing to do with poverty, nothing to do with educational opportunities, workplace opportunities, in ensuring all Americans have a chance to succeed in the world and specifically, reproductive poverty is part of poverty. Denying people reproductive choices creates a cycle of poverty, and it ensures that those who have few resources . . . remain that way, especially lacking an otherwise robust social safety net, which we in the US have never really . . . committed to. *Harris* is a pretty clear signal that we're not going to get much more from the Supreme Court."

In a country where abortion is supposed to be a protected right, *Harris* is just one of several landmark cases that helped create the current tenuous state of abortion rights. The modern legal history of reproductive rights began in 1965, when the Supreme Court, led by Chief Justice Earl Warren, heard the case of *Gris-*

wold v. Connecticut, a challenge to an 1893 Connecticut law that prohibited the use of contraception. *Griswold* was the culmination of decades of grassroots attempts to change Connecticut's contraception law by working through the state courts. The defendants, Estelle Griswold, executive director of the Planned Parenthood League of Connecticut, and Dr. C. Lee Buxton, a physician and Yale Medical School professor, had opened a birth control clinic and, as expected, were arrested and found guilty of violating the contraception ban. Two subsequent appeals, first to the Appellate Division of the Circuit Court and then to the Connecticut Supreme Court, failed to overturn their conviction. However, the US Supreme Court ruled in favor of Griswold and Buxton, holding that dispensing medical advice and contraception to married couples was protected by several "penumbras, formed by emanations"[46] that guaranteed an individual's right to privacy from government intrusion. The seven to two decision also held that the Fourteenth Amendment protected "the right of marital privacy,"[47] even though the Constitution did not specifically mention marriage, and that the Ninth Amendment supported this idea.

"*Griswold* is a hard ruling to understand," Mark admits. He notes that the Ninth Amendment, which was considered in the *Griswold* case, "is sort of an amendment that doesn't really get its fair time in the sunshine. There are unenumerated rights that an individual will obtain, and [that] has come up in the past. A classic example is if the state wanted to pass a law redistributing children, it couldn't. It could not come and take your children away despite the fact that there may not be a constitutional guarantee that you have a right to raise your own child. That is the kind of thing that the Ninth and Fourteenth amendments' privacy guarantees essentially protects."

Thanks in no small part to *Griswold*, individuals tend to assume their decisions concerning contraception and family planning are private and protected by the law, and therefore free from government interference. Historically the private affairs the courts had kept safe from government obstruction were economic rather than social, and extending the right to privacy to sexual matters was unprecedented. So, without decades of precedent to lean on, the typically high-flown language of Supreme Court cases, full of "penumbras" and seances with the Founding Fathers, suddenly looked radical.

However, *Griswold* only applied to married women. While single women in search of contraception could simply put a ring on the third finger of their left hand—and many did—this legally enforced discrimination lasted until 1972. In *Eisenstadt v. Baird*, the Court ruled that a Massachusetts law prohibiting distribution of contraceptives to unmarried people violated the Equal Protection Clause of the Constitution.[48]

Meanwhile, activists and providers took to the lower courts to challenge anti-abortion laws under various legal theories. These cases were significant not just for the rulings themselves, but also for what this activism represented on a national scale: individuals were challenging a century's worth of conventional wisdom that criminalized a basic medical procedure. *Roe* can be seen as the culmination of this fight, but there is another significant case that occurred around the same time: *Doe v. Bolton*. *Doe* challenged Georgia's abortion law, which allowed for abortion for state residents in cases of rape, severe fetal deformity, or the possibility that the mother could sustain a severe or fatal injury to her health.

The plaintiff, using the pseudonym "Mary Doe," a married mother of three, was nine weeks pregnant at the time she sued the state's attorney general, Arthur Bolton, for the right to an abortion. In its ruling, the Supreme Court found that the existence of the three conditions allowing abortion violated the Fourteenth Amendment, and that the residency requirement violated the Privileges and Immunities Clause.[49]

In *Doe*, the Court unambiguously favored the woman's right to preserve her health over the government's power to meddle. In the majority opinion, Justice Harry Blackmun wrote that the decision to have an abortion "may be exercised in the light of all factors— physical, emotional, psychological, familial, and the woman's age—relevant to the well-being of the patient."[50] The *Doe* decision was released the same day as *Roe v. Wade*, a case brought by Sarah Weddington and Linda Coffee on behalf of "Jane Roe," a pregnant Texas woman.

"Jane Roe" was the pseudonym used for Norma McCorvey, who had tried to obtain an abortion in Texas in 1969. At the time, Texas law allowed the procedure only if the woman's life was in danger. Weddington and Coffee challenged this law in US District Court; the defendant was Harry Wade, the Dallas County district attorney. The district court ruled in favor of Roe, but after an appeal, the case went to the Supreme Court in 1970. The Court delayed hearing both *Roe* and *Doe* until late 1971 (*Roe* was reargued in 1972), and the decisions in both cases were released on January 22, 1973.[51]

In its lengthy opinion in *Roe*, the Court presents a wonderful overview of how abortion became such a controversial procedure, and it's hard not to wonder if such pains were taken to detail the evolution of a controversy because Harry Blackmun, the lead majority justice, and his colleagues knew how closely their decision would be studied and argued in the coming years.

"*Roe* created a three-trimester framework that essentially created an increasing level of state regulation the further along a pregnancy progressed," attorney and clinic escort Noah Schabacker summarizes. "In the first trimester, almost no state interference was allowed; some state interference was allowed in the second trimester; and in the third trimester we have what becomes the familiar life/health of the mother limitation. These were bright-line rules that specifically limited the amount of governmental interference in choice and tied those limits to temporal guideposts."[52]

This framework was intentional, and it reflects the high regard in which Justice Blackmun, a former general counsel for the Mayo Clinic, held the medical profession. As Jeffery Toobin notes in *The Nine*, his book on the Supreme Court, a great deal of the majority opinion of *Roe* is "expressed in terms of the rights of the physician, rather than those of the woman."[53]

Roe also makes clear that though limiting abortion only to save the woman's life violated the Due Process Clause of the Fourteenth Amendment, individual states also had a compelling interest in regards to health, medical standards, and prenatal life. Therefore, the state "may, if it chooses, regulate the abortion procedure in ways that are reasonably related to maternal health."[54] Further, as the pregnancy progressed closer to fetal viability, the state "may, if it chooses, regulate, and even proscribe, abortion except where it is necessary, in appropriate medical judgment, for the preservation of the life or health of the mother."[55]

So while women were granted the right to make private health decisions, states retained the right to regulate those decisions, especially after the first trimester. This restriction became even more defined in 1992, when the Supreme Court heard *Planned Parenthood of Southeastern Pa v. Casey.*

Casey arose out of an amendment to Pennsylvania's Abortion Control Act.[56] In theory, the purpose of this bill was to provide an escape clause during an immediate medical emergency, but in practice it severely restricted access to abortion with five controversial provisions: (1) A woman must receive specific information at the clinic about the procedure, and then give her consent. (2) A woman must wait at least twenty-four hours after this appointment before returning for her abortion. (3) Minors must have either the informed consent of one parent or have obtained a judicial bypass stating that a judge allowed her to have an abortion. (4) A married woman must acknowledge in writing that she has notified her husband. (5) Certain reporting requirements are imposed upon clinics that provide abortion services.

A consortium of doctors and clinics sued on the grounds that the provisions placed an undue burden on women wishing to have abortions. After a brief bench trial, the US District Court for the Eastern District of Pennsylvania declared the provisions unconstitutional and entered a permanent injunction against the state's enforcement of them.[57] When the case went before the Third Circuit Court of Appeals in 1991, however, a different decision was reached. Two of the three appeals judges ruled to uphold all of the regulations except for spousal notification; the third judge, future Supreme Court justice Samuel Alito, supported all of the requirements, maintaining that the spousal notification law would affect very few women.[58]

According to statistics used in the case, 70–80 percent of women seeking abortions were single; among married women, 95 percent involved their husbands in the decision.[59] Therefore, Alito concluded that the notification law "cannot affect more than about 5 percent of married women seeking abortions or an even smaller percentage of all women desiring abortions.... Of the potentially affected women who could not invoke an exception, it seems safe to assume that some percentage, despite an initial inclination not to tell their husbands, would notify their husbands without suffering... substantial ill effects."[60] Given that, Alito reasoned, the law did not impose an undue burden on women.

If a woman is unable to tell her spouse about a pregnancy, she may have good reasons to maintain her silence. According to the American Pregnancy Association, 240,000 pregnant women in the US are subject to domestic violence each year, and pregnant women are at twice the risk of being battered than nonpregnant women.[61] Samuel Alito did not seem to consider this a valid concern; he also didn't seem to understand that even a small percentage of women experiencing "substantial ill effects" from telling their husbands that they wanted an abortion is a small percentage too many.

After the Court heard *Planned Parenthood v. Casey* in April 1992, the justices were divided on what parts, if any, of the Pennsylvania law to uphold. Justices Stevens and Blackmun wanted to strike down all of the restrictions; Chief Justice Rehnquist and Justices Scalia, White, and Thomas had gone on record as wanting to overrule *Roe*, and Justices O'Connor, Souter, and Kennedy were in the middle. Those three judges joined Stevens and Blackmun on some parts, to issue a part-majority, part-plurality opinion ruling that spousal notification constituted an undue burden; the other regulations were upheld. This mixed ruling was not the only notable outcome of *Casey*; the three middle judges declared Justice Blackmun's famous trimester system outdated and no longer applicable in relation to the law.[62]

"We have seen how time has overtaken some of *Roe*'s factual assumptions: advances in maternal health care allow for abortions safe to the mother later in pregnancy than was true in 1973," the Court explained. "But these facts go only to the scheme of time limits on the realization of competing interests, and the divergences from the factual premises of 1973 have no bearing on the validity of *Roe*'s central holding, that viability marks the earliest point at which the State's interest in fetal life is constitutionally adequate to justify a legislative ban on nontherapeutic abortions."[63]

In discussing the impact of *Casey* on future abortion law, attorney Noah Schabacker returns to his earlier description of the trimester system establishing bright lines, legally speaking. "*Casey* replaced these bright-lines with the 'undue burden' standard," he contends. "[It] became an invitation to anti-choice legislators and activists to throw regulations into the path of women, and then have courts evaluate whether or not they posed 'undue burdens,' which means that obstacles—twenty-four-hour waiting periods, required scripts for health care providers, mandatory ultrasounds, parental notification [or] permission statutes—were suddenly being evaluated by (usually) white, middle-aged male judges who either couldn't, or pretended not to, understand that these regulations are specifically designed to prevent women from getting abortions."[64]

Eight years after *Casey*, the Supreme Court heard *Stenberg v. Carhart*, which also considered where, or if, the interests of an individual woman and the state collided. In this 2000 challenge, which was brought by Nebraska physician LeRoy Carhart against the state's attorney general, the court was asked to consider whether Nebraska's ban of a specific abortion procedure, intact dilation and extraction, was unconstitutional.[65]

Intact dilation and extraction—which is also known as D&X, IDX, or its most common and inaccurate moniker, "partial-birth abortion"—is performed by dilating the woman's cervix with the aid of medications, then removing the fetus through the birth canal.[66] To safely remove the fetus, it is necessary to reduce the size of the head, which is done by the physician making an incision at the base of the skull and inserting a suction catheter to collapse the skull.

Intact dilation and extraction has come under fire from anti-choice activists and politicians because of the necessity of reducing the size of the skull and because delivery via the birth canal means that a portion of the fetus's body is outside of the woman before the procedure is complete. This method is rarely used—one study estimates that only 0.17 percent of all abortions performed in 2000 used intact dilation and extraction[67]—which makes sense, given that the technique is only used for later-term procedures, and 88 percent of all abortions in the US occur in the first trimester of pregnancy.[68] In general, if a physician chooses to use intact dilation and extraction, it is because he has determined that it is the best and safest procedure for his patient; in addition, if the reason for the abortion was because the fetus was diagnosed with fatal abnormalities, this method allows for an autopsy to be performed in certain cases to help determine the cause of those abnormalities. Another benefit to intact dilation and extraction is that the fetus is delivered intact, so the expectant parents are able to see and hold their child, if they choose.

The *Stenberg* case was not the first time that intact dilation and extraction had come under political fire. In 1996 and 1997, President Clinton vetoed attempts by Congress to ban the procedure.[69] Though the Supreme Court ruled in *Stenberg* that Nebraska's ban was unconstitutional, on the grounds that it violated the Due Process Clause, this victory was short lived.

In 2003, President Bush signed the Partial-Birth Abortion Ban Act[70] into law, which stated that intact dilation and extraction was never medically necessary for a woman's health and did not include a health exemption.[71] Citing the lack of this exemption and the vague language of the act, US District Courts in California, New York, and Nebraska all ruled that the act was unconstitutional. The federal government, led by Attorney General Alberto Gonzales, appealed the rulings, bringing the case to the US Court of Appeals for the Eighth Circuit in 2005. That court upheld the ruling of the Nebraska court, finding both that the government had offered no new evidence to set this case apart from *Stenberg* and that the act was unconstitutional because it did not include an exemption for the health of the mother.[72] Gonzales petitioned the Supreme Court to review the Eighth Circuit's ruling.

That same year, the resignation of Sandra Day O'Connor and the death of Chief Justice William Rehnquist gave President Bush the chance to move the Supreme Court in a more conservative direction. Both of the judges appointed to fill the vacated seats—Samuel Alito and John Roberts, respectively—had been reticent during their confirmation hearings about their views on abortion, but their actions concerning *Casey* strongly indicated that they would overturn *Roe* (Roberts, a deputy solicitor general at the time, had signed a brief urging the justices to do just that).[73] It was before this Court that *Gonzales v. Carhart* was argued, and the outcome made clear that when it came to abortion, the Court was heading in a more restrictive direction.[74] The five to four ruling overturned the Eighth Circuit's decision, finding that the act did not impose an undue burden on women based on its lack of a health exemption and, further, the language used was clear enough to not meet the definition of vagueness. Writing for the Court, Justice Kennedy also suggested that banning intact dilation and extraction was actually in the interest of women because, in an effort to protect their patients, physicians may withhold the details of what the procedure entailed. His reasoning drew in part from a brief filed by the anti-choice Justice Foundation, which relies on dubious scientific evidence to promote the anti-choice concept of post-abortion syndrome:[75] "While we find no reliable data to measure the phenomenon," Kennedy wrote in his opinion, "it seems unexceptionable to conclude some women come to regret their choice to abort the infant life they once created and sustained. . . . Severe depression and loss of esteem can follow."[76]

"I took a class in law school where we read these cases," attorney Courtney Lewis recalls about *Gonzales*. "Students were swayed by the gory facts of a dilation and extraction. I spoke to a lot of my classmates individually about why I thought this was bad case law: We are banning a medical procedure that doctors think is the safest procedure for women. Why are we banning it? Because it sounds icky! Dangerous precedent in my opinion."[77]

Other interviewees took a more optimistic view of what *Gonzales* might herald for future abortion cases. "I just read the abortion cases in Con [Constitutional] Law 2," Keely Monroe, a law school student, tells me. "My con law professor noted the *tone* of *Carhart*, which was much different than in *Casey*. What I think and hope is that even though justices may not personally believe in abortion, they do believe in the fundamental right that is associated with abortion. I think that although *Carhart* was a blow because it did not leave a health exception for women, it shows that the Court still believes in a woman's fundamental right to choose an abortion and physical autonomy and that the state's interest in unborn life can never trump those rights."[78]

Both *Casey* and *Gonzales* ultimately upheld a woman's right to have an abortion, but both cases also significantly chipped away at the protections originally granted in *Roe*. In the later months of pregnancy, the Court now permits an increasing level of state interference in health and medical standards. More perniciously, *Casey* introduced the idea of "undue burden," to evaluate not only restrictions related to health but also strong anti-abortion rules like parental notification, waiting periods, and mandatory ultrasounds. With the undue burden test, the Court expressly states that it's okay to place burdens in the way of a pregnant woman seeking an abortion—so long as that burden is not, in the eyes of a judge, undue. *Gonzales* then stretched the phrase to the breaking point, essentially stating that it's permissible to outlaw an entire medical procedure because that somehow won't place an undue burden on the woman who may need it and the physician who feels it is the best option for his patient. These precedents set the stage for the rash of prohibitive state laws and mandates that we are seeing today. While *Roe* is often seen as a sweeping civil right, today's Supreme Court sees something far narrower.

Despite the best attempts of anti-choice activists, however, neither of these decisions managed to overturn *Roe*. This feat remains the golden grail for the anti-choice movement, which continues to develop ballot measures and state initiatives that seek to restrict some aspect of reproductive rights. The hope is not just for the individual measure to succeed but also for the pro-choice movement to challenge its legality, which could lead to a court case with a high likelihood of being heard by the Supreme Court.

None of these attempts have yet resulted in the kind of court case that the anti-choice movement is hoping for, and indeed several of the more high-profile actions have suffered equally high-profile defeats. In 2006 and again in 2008, anti-choice activists and politicians in South Dakota attempted to ban virtually all abortions in the state through a ballot initiative; both times, voters in the state defeated the measure by substantial margins.[79] Another approach is to amend state constitutions to define personhood as beginning the moment a human egg is fertilized (which would not only outlaw abortion and certain forms of birth control but could also negatively impact fertility treatments and scientific research). Despite suffering high-profile defeats in Colorado and Mississippi, personhood supporters have remained determined to put the issue on ballots across the country,[80] and in early 2012 the Oklahoma Senate passed a bill that grants full rights to embryos from the moment of fertilization.[81] Though the bill was expected to pass in the Republican-controlled House as well, the House Republican Caucus unexpectedly voted not to hear the bill during the legislature's current session.[82] House Speaker Kris Steele's comment that the measure "would not have any substantive policy effect"[83] seems to indicate that the reason for tabling the bill was driven less by any ideological change of heart and more by a concern with its wording and impact.

One of the popular criticisms of *Roe* is that it failed to anticipate advances in medical science that could move the point of viability to earlier than the third trimester of pregnancy, or around twenty-four weeks. While such a failing is to be expected—the justices, after all, were not psychics—the wording of the decision did leave the door open for challenges to its validity, based on when, exactly, fetal viability can be assured. While it is by no means ideal to deliver a baby after only twenty-four, or even twenty-eight or thirty weeks of pregnancy, science has advanced to the point where such early deliveries do not automatically mean that the infant will not survive or will face a lifetime of severe and traumatic health problems if he or she does survive.

But medical science has also advanced in other ways since

1973, and one of those is in its ability to provide expectant parents with ever-increasing amounts of information about their fetus's development. Tests can detect abnormalities earlier in pregnancy, and they can alert obstetricians to conditions that aren't visible until after the second trimester of pregnancy. The current trend to outlaw abortion as early as the midpoint of the second trimester, as is now the case in Arizona,[84] means that while it is still possible to diagnose genetic diseases and severe abnormalities, it will be extremely difficult for a woman to choose to terminate the pregnancy, even if she feels that it is the best option for herself and her unborn child.

It seems, then, that banning abortion after either eighteen or twenty weeks of pregnancy would cause an undue burden on a pregnant woman—it also seems that this is exactly the kind of restriction that the pro-choice movement would love to challenge. While no cases have been brought as of this writing, this certainly doesn't mean that activists and attorneys aren't laying the necessary groundwork for such a challenge.

There are many elements to consider in undertaking such a potentially high-stakes court case. Legal challenges require time, money, and energy, and as it is constantly fending off attacks on a variety of fronts, the pro-choice movement may be understandably cautious in deciding where to allocate its finite resources. Given the current composition of the Court, there is no guarantee that a case that seeks to prove that a twenty-week ban places an undue burden on a woman, or any similar argument that could raise the issues of fetal pain and fetal rights, would find support from a majority of justices. There is also a school of thought among pro-choice scholars, attorneys, and activists that addressing these restrictions through legal channels is not the best approach to take—and that, in fact, it hasn't been since *Roe*.

"I think we're seeing right now, lawyers are not the right people to be making all those decisions," attorney Mark Egerman says with his customary candor. "Lawyers ruin social movements very quickly; [they] are trained to see the world in a very limited way [and] tend not to have a long history of radicalism or involve- ment. And I think specifically the canonization of *Roe*, the belief that the Court gave us this right, means that in the reproductive rights movement lawyers get too much of a say; the belief that the Supreme Court at any moment could take [this right] away from us, so we need to put all our resources into attorneys—resources that could be going to access, resources that could be going to edu- cation, to campaign, that could be going to train doctors. I'm not sure that this is the correct way for the movement to be addressing some very serious conflicts."[85]

The Trouble with *Roe*

While *Roe v. Wade* is celebrated as a victory for the pro-choice movement, it is interesting to think about how that decision may have prevented a different type of success from developing around the country. Some speculate that the Court overreached with *Roe*, and the pro-choice movement would be better off today if states had been allowed to come to their own conclusions about the legality of abortion. The tone and composition of the modern anti- choice movement would very likely be different, neither as cohesive nor as aggressive, if its target were individual state laws rather than a national decision.

Before *Roe*, a number of states were well on their way to liberalizing their abortion laws. Between the mid-1800s and early 1960s, almost every state outlawed abortion, although some of these states did allow exceptions if a woman's life was in danger.[86] By the early 1960s, forty-four states only allowed abortion in this circumstance.[87] Among the six remaining states, Pennsylvania prohibited all abortions entirely; Mississippi allowed abortion in cases of rape or life endangerment; and Colorado, New Mexico, Massachusetts, and Alabama, along with the District of Columbia, allowed abortion if the woman's life or physical health were in danger.[88] There were strict penalties for violating the law: in nine states, not only the provider but also anyone who aided, assisted, or counseled a woman could face legal consequences; fourteen states made both performing and obtaining an abortion a crime.[89]

In 1962, the American Law Institute (ALI), an organization composed of scholars, jurists, and attorneys, published the "Model Penal Code on Abortion," which made a case for legal abortion when the pregnancy was a result of rape or incest, when the woman's life or health would be at risk by carrying the pregnancy to term, or when a severe defect was diagnosed in the fetus.[90] The ALI's call to amend abortion laws was influential: between 1967 and 1972, thirteen states adopted laws based on the ALI's recommendation, and laws in Hawaii, New York, Alaska, and Washington allowed a woman to have an abortion whenever she and her doctor decided it was necessary.[91] By the time the Court decided *Roe*, all but five states had either reformed their legislation or were considering abortion reform.[92]

Supreme Court Justice Ruth Bader Ginsburg offered her own perspective on the role of the Court in *Roe* during a 2012 talk at Columbia Law School. Ginsburg supported the decision itself, but said that "it moved too far, too fast. . . . The court made a decision that made every abortion law in the country invalid, even the most liberal."[93] Ginsburg suggested that the Court could have delayed hearing *Roe* or a similar case while individual states considered whether to liberalize their own laws, or just overturned the specific Texas law at the heart of *Roe*, which only permitted abortions if a woman's life was in danger. "We'll never know whether I'm right or wrong," Ginsburg pointed out, adding that "things might have turned out differently if the court had been more restrained."[94]

Currently, Louisiana, Illinois, Kentucky, and South Dakota have so-called "trigger" laws in place that would make abortion illegal if *Roe v. Wade* were ever overturned.[95] Arkansas, Mississippi, and North Dakota all have laws declaring their intention to ban abortion, but experts have expressed doubt that those laws could be enforced.[96] It remains an open question whether or not these laws would automatically take effect if the federal law changed, or if they are subject to approval from lawmakers, the governor, and/or the attorney general.[97]

On the flip side, a number of states have laws in place that would protect the right to legal abortion in the event that *Roe* were overturned. Hawaii, Maryland, Nevada, Maine, Connecticut, Washington, and California all ensure the right to abortion in either their laws or constitutions; in addition, the state constitutions of Alaska, Florida, Massachusetts, Minnesota, Montana, New Jersey, New Mexico, Tennessee, and West Virginia have all been interpreted by the courts as protecting a woman's right to abortion.[98]

Just imagine, then, if *Roe* were no longer the law and individual states had the right to decide when and if abortion would be allowed. Women who lived in states that banned abortion would have to travel to legal states and hope that they could make the trip before their pregnancies advanced to a stage where they either couldn't afford the procedure or couldn't find a doctor to perform it. Those who could not afford to travel, like low-income women or teenagers, would have two options: seek out illegal abortions, or continue with a pregnancy that, for whatever reason, is not right for them at the time.

And if those women did have to continue their pregnancies and give birth, it is unlikely that the reasons that made them want an abortion would vanish. Economic concerns, unstable relationships, educational goals, or fetal abnormalities would still be present. In many cases, this would lead to an increased reliance on social services, such as government assistance, Medicaid, and other programs that anti-choice legislatures do not support.

From a public health standpoint, and for society at large, an environment in which women must either turn to dangerous methods of terminating a pregnancy or have children regardless of their life circumstances is unreasonable, to say the least. Every child deserves to be born to a mother—and into a family—who wants that child and can do the best possible job parenting. The way to achieve that is through better social support systems, education, and ensuring that no one needs to become a parent before she or he is ready—not through outlawing abortion.

Nor is the way to achieve that through passing laws that make abortion so onerous to access for one specific class of women that it might as well be outlawed for them. Yet, this is the reality for many pregnant teenagers in this country.

"I think that parental consent [and] notification laws are very contentious," says attorney Courtney Lewis, who has interned for two organizations dedicated to helping pregnant minors access legal information regarding their options. "I think there is much misinformation about [the] laws. Most teenagers tell their parents regardless. Those who cannot for legitimate reasons are the ones hurt by the law. Almost all of my cases were teenagers who lived with a family member [who] was not the teenager's legal guardian, so [they] could not consent, but the family member knew about the pregnancy. The other large section of my cases [involved] cases of physical abuse. Rarely did a teenager call and worry only that her parents were going to ground her."[99]

Twenty-two states currently require that one or both parents of a minor girl give consent before she has an abortion. Another eleven require that one or both parents be notified of her intention to abort, and four states mandate both notification and consent.[100] Under the parental consent law, the teen must get the consent of one or both of her parents, whereas parental notification means only that she must tell one or both parents, but does not require consent.[101]

Like so many other anti-choice laws, the rationale for parental consent and notification laws is that they protect the pregnant girl and promote healthy communication. But requiring that a teenager tell a parent about her pregnancy is yet another example of the state asserting that it knows the realities of a person's life better than she does, and of the state refusing to trust that women—including pregnant teenagers—can make choices for themselves.

These laws ignore the fact that many of the teenagers who need abortions are those who have an honest and justified fear of telling a parent about a pregnancy. They may have reason to believe that their parents will react violently or throw them out of the house; teenagers whose parents are anti-choice may also fear that they will not be allowed to make their own decisions about the pregnancy. In addition, the wording of these laws often ignores the composition of nontraditional families. For example, teenagers who live with their grandparents may still be required to locate a biological parent to provide consent, even if the parent is not involved in their lives. If this is not feasible, the teen may have the option to seek a judicial bypass.

Judicial bypasses are available for minors who feel that they are unable to notify their parents or ask for their consent. The procedure for obtaining a bypass, however, can vary greatly depending on the state—or, indeed, the specific judge. Even in a best-case scenario, where the teenager is able to take the necessary time off of school to meet with a lawyer, go to court, state her reasons for seeking the bypass, and obtain the order, that process often takes at least several days and usually longer. This delay is significant when every week that an abortion must be put off could raise the cost of the procedure.

Texas law student Kyle Marie Stock has seen firsthand the challenges of working around parental consent laws through her volunteer work at a local fund. "[Texas] is a parental consent state.... If [teens] do become pregnant they have a huge barrier to access. That's very problematic because not only do we have a lack of access to information, but a lot of people in Texas are poor.

Waiting to get a judicial bypass often increases the cost of the abortion, so for someone who was twelve weeks along and it was going to cost them $425, now they're seventeen, eighteen weeks along and it's $2,000. If you're sixteen years old and you're afraid to tell your parents, where are you going to get this money?"[102]

Saving FACE but Losing Ground

It is clear that there are legal limitations when it comes to safeguarding reproductive rights. However, legislation has also played an important role in protecting clinic employees, providers, and clinics themselves from anti-choice harassment and violence.

In 2011, the most recent year for which statistics are available, there were twenty-seven reported cases of vandalism and sixty-nine reported cases of harassment against abortion providers in the US and Canada.[103] Three hundred and sixty-five incidents of hate mail and harassing calls were reported, as were 4,780 incidents of picketing and five clinic blockades (a tactic by which groups of protestors physically obstruct the entrances of clinics, usually by standing or sitting on sidewalks, driveways, or near doors to prevent anyone from entering or leaving).[104]

How do these numbers compare with previous years? The prevalence of severe violence, such as murder and attempted murder, has greatly decreased since the mid-1990s,[105] but reports of vandalism increased in 2011 after declining the previous year, as did the number of clinic blockades.[106]

A 2010 report from the Feminist Majority Foundation found that women's health clinics began seeing an increase in threats and activities following the 2008 presidential election.[107] This is not surprising, as historically, incidents of serious violence against providers and clinics have risen during pro-choice presidencies. During Bill Clinton's two terms in office, three providers, one clinic escort, two receptionists, and one security guard were all murdered by anti-choice extremists. During the first year that Barack Obama was in office, Dr. George Tiller was murdered.

A 2010 survey, which was compiled from information provided by 357 providers (out of 595 providers contacted), found that 23.5 percent of the clinics reported incidents of severe violence, up from 20 percent in 2008 and 18.4 percent in 2005.[108] Stalking, death threats, and clinic invasion were the most common types of severe violence reported, and while incidents of death threats and invasion had decreased from their 2008 levels, the incidence of stalking rose from 4 percent in 2008 to 6.4 percent in 2010.[109]

While more clinics reported no incidents of violence in 2010 than did in 2008, the number of clinics that did experience three or more types of violence and harassment rose in 2010: 11.2 percent as compared with 9 percent two years earlier.[110] Nearly 63 percent of all clinics reported experiencing intimidation tactics in 2010. The survey also found a correlation between intimidation and violence: clinics that experienced intimidation were almost four times more likely to also experience violence.[111]

Additionally, the survey found that in 2010, the percentage of clinics reporting potential FACE, or Federal Access to Clinic Entrances, violations to federal law enforcement increased for the first time since 1999.[112] Among the 4.7 percent of clinics reporting potential violations in 2010, however, only 35.3 percent resulted in an investigation being opened, a decrease from 56 percent in 2008.[113]

Passed by President Clinton in 1994, the FACE Act is an example of a law that protects both patients and providers by making it a federal offense to use force, threaten to use force, or physically obstruct people from either providing or receiving reproductive health services. The act also makes it possible for providers, state attorney generals, and the federal government to bring civil lawsuits to recoup monetary damages or get injunctions against certain activities.[114]

Both anecdotal evidence and statistics indicate that in the years immediately following the FACE Act's passage, harassment and violence against clinics and patients did decrease. For example, while there were six reported bombings in 1997, that number dropped to between one and zero per year from 1998 to 2011.[115] Likewise, the number of reported arson incidents declined from fourteen in 1995, to eight in 1997, to three in 2003, and one in 2011.[116]

However, as the report from the Feminist Majority Foundation makes clear, FACE has not put an end to anti-choice violence and harassment. While part of the prevalence of violence and intimidation is related to the current political climate, FACE is a federal law and is enforced through the Department of Justice. Therefore, it will be enforced more or less vigorously depending on how pro-choice the sitting president and his attorney general are.

Between 1994 and 1998, forty-six criminal and civil cases were brought to court under FACE; seventeen of those were criminal cases, and in fifteen of those cases, defendants either pled guilty or were found guilty of FACE violations.[117] Although reports of violence and harassment continued during the eight years of the Bush presidency—and some forms, such as hate mail, harassing calls, and online harassment rose during that time[118]—the Bush administration only brought an average of two criminal prosecutions per year under FACE and never used the law's civil component.[119]

Sixteen states and the District of Columbia have also passed separate laws that protect clinics, providers, and/or patients from a variety of interference by anti-choice protestors, including blockades and harassment.[120] Three of these states—Colorado, Massachusetts, and Montana—also have laws that designate a buffer area around clinics, which protects clinic employees and patients from harassment within that area.[121] How stringently these laws are enforced depends on many factors, from the community's politics to the training the police department receives in anti-choice violence. And as the experiences of June Ayers and Emily Lyons show, having laws in place does not mean that clinics, staff, or patients are always protected.

"The first four or five years were relatively quiet and we operated without a lot of problems," June Ayers, the director of Reproductive Health Services in Montgomery, Alabama, recalls about the years right after the clinic opened in 1978. "Then we started seeing our violence escalate, and we did have a couple of rescues from Operation Rescue. Most of the [problems] were gluing locks, just vandalizing the front, scare tactics. Following people, coming up and parking at the clinic at night when we were inside getting ready to leave—just intimidation tactics.[122]

"Now when the FACE bill came out," June continues, "when it became a point where we could civilly sue them . . . then we did see a lot of the vandalism slow down. We're so mechanized now; most clinics went to automatic locks and cameras. When the violence started to rise and so forth, so did the measures to counteract that, and perhaps that's why we're a little safer today, but obviously we still do not feel safe, even in our own churches."

As much as Dr. Tiller's 2009 murder shook the staff of June's clinic, June points out that for her community, the greater shock came even earlier. "The biggest blow for us was Dr. Gunn.[123] He was a good friend. His death, being the first one, pulled the rug out from under us. That changed our perspective. It was at that point when physicians started wearing bulletproof vests. You know, it's a shame to have to provide medical care in a war zone.

"We don't operate the same like most people do," June continues, as I think about the security camera I passed on my way to the front door. "You are just more aware of your surroundings and hopefully you don't become a victim. We live in the South and a lot of people in the South don't lock their doors and so forth, and no, I don't ever not lock my doors. Part of that comes from just common sense; you don't make yourself a victim if you can help it. But it's translated into why I pound it into my eighteen-year-old, you don't leave the door unlocked no matter what. It's a little bit of an edge there that just makes you a little bit more cautious than somebody, say, going into the hospital, because they've just never had to look at those issues."

These fears are fueled by a history of violence we are all familiar with from a safe distance via headlines and news alerts. However, Emily Lyons, who I interviewed in 2009, did not have this luxury. In early 1998, the New Woman, All Women healthcare center in Birmingham, Alabama, where Emily worked as a nurse, was bombed.

Security guard Robert Sanderson was killed at the scene; Emily was severely injured: one eye was destroyed and the other damaged, a hole was torn in her abdomen, one leg was shattered, and flesh was blown off her body, among other injuries. Over a decade later, her health remains poor. "I've got less than half of my vision. I really didn't see for almost a year, didn't drive for way over a year," she says as we sit in her dining room, her husband, Jeffrey, occasionally poking his head in to make sure she's doing okay. "My hearing's [not good]. I used to have to be in front of you to understand what you're saying. Not any of the social life we used to have, definitely not a whole lot of the friends we used to have.

"I can't even begin to explain the difference," she says in a matter-of-fact tone. "Still a lot of things I can't do by myself; I don't like to go out in public by myself because I don't have somebody to hold on. Without the depth perception, and the awkwardness of walking anyway, if you miss a step or you're off just by a fraction, it throws you. [The] fear is tremendous for that when you're out. It used to be if I was out by myself I didn't know who was around, good or bad. People have written, *you're going to hell, you're going to burn*. People would write that and I'd go, don't they know I've already been there? Look at these burns. I'm not going back," she says with a small smile.[124]

The bomber Eric Rudolph lived as a fugitive in the Appalachian region for five years, wanted by the FBI not just for the Birmingham bombing but also for three bombings in the Atlanta area, one at Centennial Olympic Park in 1996 and two the following year at a gay club and an abortion clinic.[125] "Jeffrey always thought that Rudolph left the country," Emily remembers, shaking her head. "No, he knew this territory, he was comfortable there. Why would he want to leave, [he had people] feeding him, housing him. This is what you do with a hero," she says softly.

After his capture, Emily had two encounters with Rudolph. "I saw him when they brought him to Birmingham, for the judge to read the charges. . . . That was the first time. I was back here, he was up there," she says, gesturing to indicate the short distance she sat from her assailant, "and I couldn't do anything but cry, couldn't stop crying. *What have you done to me? How dare you? You didn't know me, I wasn't a threat to you, I didn't ask you to come down here.* What would life be like now? I can't think that way, but where would life have gone?

"The next time was in Huntsville [Alabama], where he was having his pre-trial," Emily continues. "He was escorted down the hall in front of everyone right there. No expression, just blank, just black. I got up, he was not as far away as the clock," she adds, inclining her head toward a grandfather clock a few feet behind her. "His lawyer was closer to me, but it was intended for him. I didn't care about anybody else in that courtroom. I didn't care about the judge, the lawyers. I flipped him off at the end. His lawyer was, like, *tsk, tsk*. Girl, don't even," Emily says with a laugh. "In your little suit, don't even think about trying to do that; that's not working. The judge wasn't really thrilled about it either, but after all those years, I wanted him to see that."

The future of clinic protection, much like the future of abortion access, is unclear. There are reasons for optimism on both counts as the pro-choice movement refines its arguments in the legal arena and as the public as a whole becomes more aware that reproductive choice cannot be taken for granted.

"This is awful to say and it's really upsetting that it had to come to this," pro-choice activist Abbey Marr says, "but at least I've seen in the people my age around me, that when they saw what happened to Dr. Tiller, they realized that this isn't an issue that was fifteen, twenty years ago, this is an issue happening today, and people on the front lines are being killed. I think that made them angry . . . [s]o maybe some sort of awful silver lining from something about it, people will realize that it's still a really big issue right now."[126]

Likewise, contraception and abortion access continued to make headlines into 2012, as the GOP presidential candidate Rick Santorum continually spoke out about the "dangers of contraception"[127] and Rush Limbaugh excoriated a young woman for speaking out about the importance of affordable birth control.[128] In both instances, women and men from all across the political spectrum responded with disbelief and outrage that contraception was still considered such a controversial issue. "For most women of any demographic, those issues were resolved in the '60s," Judith Lichtman, senior advisor at the National Partnership for Women & Families, points out. "The notion that we should be talking about them now is a total anathema to women, and it gives credibility to the notion that there is indeed a war on women.

"The excesses of the anti-choice people putting issues like legal contraception on the table is a vivid example of women saying, *what?*" she continues. "You know, how in the twenty-first century am I talking about that, and being motivated therefore to take action where they might not have been five years ago when they didn't think any of this was either on the table for discussion or at risk. Today people believe it is at risk.[129]"

Whether this renewed attention on reproductive rights will lead to an increased interest in safeguarding these rights, however, remains to be seen. The Supreme Court remains too close to call, and it is more than likely that the next Republican president will have the opportunity to install at least one anti-choice justice, which would tip the balance definitively toward the anti-choice side. While the Supreme Court—not to mention all the lower courts—has perhaps an outsize role in determining the future of choice in this country, individual attorneys, activists, and providers can play a powerful role themselves, by continuing to work within their communities to show why the right to safe reproductive care is so essential not just for women, but for men and families as well.

"I think that if things are taken away people get up," June told me as she reflected on the future of legal abortion. "But I don't want to see that happen because then we'll lose a lot of really good providers. I'm fifty-five now; I plan to live another twenty years, but if something takes away my livelihood and I have to go into a different direction I don't know if I'll ever come back. We have fought for every piece of ground we have managed to hold onto. I don't think there's any wins; I don't think we've had any wins in twenty years, perhaps even longer than that, but we're still fighting to hold onto the ground that we're sitting on."

CHAPTER SIX

DEFENDING CHOICE, ONE GENERATION AT A TIME

"I was born in 1962, and I was a child in the early '70s, immediately post the Civil Rights era, and saw some of the compensatory benefit," Dr. Willie Parker tells me near the end of our interview. "A bit of opportunity was created in the black middle class in the way that young people of color take for granted. They don't know a world where there are whites and blacks only; they don't know a world where race is segregated. They take for granted the privileges. There's a lack of a sense of history amongst people that [were politicized] after 1973 who take abortion rights for granted," Willie continues, "and then because of that, there has not been [enough] activism opposing [policies] that erode access to abortion services. I think increasingly there are young people, because their lives are so much different and so much better, who don't have a sense that an unplanned pregnancy could happen to them, they would need those services."[1]

"This is the thing that makes me *absolutely crazy*!" Melissa Bird, vice-president of Public Policy for Planned Parenthood of Utah, exclaims. "What is the deal with this complacency and this attitude that they are too busy or too this or that to be involved in this movement. I am so sick and tired of hearing from young men and women that they don't vote because it doesn't make a difference. In local elections, one vote makes all the difference in whether or not we have another pro-family planning, pro-choice person holding office. When will young men and women realize that this is not something they can take for granted? When I tell young women that it is only in the last forty years that they were able to take the pill without their husbands' permission, they simply can't believe that this has happened all so recently."[2]

"The problem that I have is with people who are younger than me, the things that would come out of their mouths were completely ridiculous," says Florida clinic director Michelle Fortier. "I think that they do take it for granted. I think that there might have been a backlash against it for some reason from people who are younger than me. I went to high school in the 1990s and I think there's a different mentality—it was the Clinton years, there [was] a lot more realism, like being realistic that not every pregnancy is a wanted pregnancy. Now I think there's that backlash to the Clinton years with the Bush years. I think a lot of people who are younger than me tend to be more conservative, which is really bizarre," she says, and then adds, "but that might also be because I grew up in New York, so I know a lot more progressive, liberal people."[3]

"I think with some people, [legal abortion] can be seen as a 'given,'" Adrienne Kimmell, the executive director of the Florida Association of Planned Parenthood Affiliates, says. "That said, many women my age are aware that we have to continue to fight for the right to control our own bodies. Having worked with young women for most of my career, it is clear to me that many young women are aware of the continuing threats around abortion and choice. Also, many post-*Roe* women see choice as part of a larger social justice framework and are aware of the threats but view them differently or articulate their feelings in a way that might be different than second-wave feminists."[4]

"I think my generation gets a bad rap in the sense that the post-*Roe* generation doesn't care and assumes that it will always be legal," argues Katie Groke Ellis of Planned Parenthood, "but the post-*Roe* generation [also] feels neglected because the pre-*Roe* generation is always bashing them."[5]

"I think the whole idea of the apathetic younger generation is really overblown," says law student Kelsey Collier-Wise. "I see energized young people all over this movement. There's this perception that back in the 1970s, everyone was a feminist and everyone was pro-choice. Obviously, that was not the case. The women's movement was a counter-culture movement and it's only grown since. I think ageism definitely contributes to this misconception. It's difficult for young people to be taken seriously by the big organizations. You see younger people either working in low-level positions or at the grassroots level, in organizations and on campaigns. I'm not sure what the naysayers need to see to be convinced that young people care. It seems like unless people see an exact rehash of the 1970s, they don't believe actual feminist work is happening. Which doesn't make any sense—different times call for different tactics, and movements evolve."[6]

Movements do evolve, but the means by which that evolution occurs brings its share of controversy as well. In February 2010, a twenty-seven-year-old mother from Florida took to her blog and Twitter feed to offer a real-time account of her medical abortion.

Angie Jackson repeatedly said that her goal was to let other women know what to expect from a medical abortion, but her posts did more than that. In addition to the hundreds of comments she received, both positive and negative, her method of discussing abortion sparked an intense debate about the use of social media. While not every younger activist agreed with Jackson's approach, and not every older activist disagreed, the generational divide did generally fall along such lines. Long-time activist Mary Ann Sorrentino reflected the feelings of many others when she accused Jackson of poor judgment and a lack of respect for the battles that feminists of the '60s and '70s fought in an article published on Salon.com. "Those of us who drove in the dark of night to deliver or pick up a friend in a back-alley clinic, terrified that that friend hemorrhaging in the back seat of our car might die on our watch, know things that Ms. Jackson clearly cannot fathom . . . We make no apologies. We have no regrets. But the right we were fighting so hard for—which was granted only a short thirty-seven years ago—was based on what the Supreme Court called 'privacy.' . . . Angie Jackson has the right to choose to take RU-486 and then write about her cramps, her bleeding, and the eventual expulsion of the products of conception on the Internet," Sorrentino wrote, "but many of us who have spent our lives on the front lines of the abortion debate also have the right to hate the fact that she chose to do this. At its worst, it is self-serving, exhibitionist, and selfish. At best, it has 'bad judgment' written all over it."[7]

The divide over this issue effectively illustrates two meaningful generational differences. First, while Angie Jackson may have encountered a disproportionate share of attention, her use of social media reflects a growing trend by young pro-choice activists to reach out to supporters and engage in dialogue around a number of reproductive rights issues online. Second, new activists see that the veil of privacy that shrouds real discussions about unplanned pregnancies and experience of surgical and medical abortion has not helped their cause. They are tired of abortion becoming only more and more taboo and invisible. Websites like I Am Dr. Tiller, The Abortioneers, Anti-Choice is Anti-Awesome, and Every Saturday Morning provide places for people to share their experiences, celebrate victories, and vent about setbacks, but they also help to demystify the abortion experience. The sites are virtual replicas of their mothers' and grandmothers' consciousness-raising groups, and perhaps they are more intimate because of the option of anonymity and liberal use of pseudonyms. Younger activists do not always follow the prescribed path set by their older counterparts, but their inventiveness is an asset. It reflects the very spunk and power that the older generation had to have to trigger sweeping cultural shifts years ago.

The new generation is also less encumbered by political ties and limitations. A number of established pro-choice organizations have turned to online channels to spread their message and keep supporters updated with developments, victories, and nascent threats to choice. Yet, because these organizations often must appease donors and political allies as well as supporters and would-be activists, the blogs and discussions found on their sites tend to be less dynamic and engaging than the material found on independent sites.

Is the younger generation too apathetic? Alexa Kolbi-Molinas, an attorney with the ACLU, observes, "I think it's inevitable that those who were there when the right was achieved are going to view, to *experience* reproductive choice differently than those of us who know illegal abortion only as a piece of American history. Every movement, every issue has such a divide. And I think every movement that has achieved some measure of success has to struggle against apathy, especially among those who reap the benefits of that success. Now, obviously, I work with a number of other younger people—mostly women, I have to say—and I see even younger ones getting involved as legal, and even undergraduate, interns and volunteers. It's very clear that the commitment and passion is out there, I don't think there is any doubt about that, but I'm still not sure the criticism—that people in my generation take the right to abortion for granted—is entirely undeserved."[8]

"I feel like I'm constantly surrounded by people who are pro-choice and will do anything for the reproductive health movement," says medical student Megan Evans, "but I don't think I've ever asked this of friends who aren't directly involved in the movement. They ask about it but they're not really ready to hit the streets, or go door to door if needed; they don't want to do it. It's not that they don't care; they don't care enough."[9]

Ayesha Chatterjee of the Eastern Massachusetts Abortion Fund takes a big-picture approach when considering the issue of generational attitudes about abortion. "Most of my peers are acutely aware of the ongoing threat to abortion and are actively involved in the pro-choice and reproductive justice movement," she says. "I know there is a growing debate on whether, and to what extent, young women in the US take their right to abortion for granted. If indeed they do, I believe it is crucial to understand why—the experiences that inform their attitude, activism, and decision to step aside—and reach out to them as potential allies, not adversaries. Being a 'post-*Roe*' woman myself," the India-born activist continues, "who also grew up in a country where abortion is legal but inaccessible to the majority of women, I think we need to first recognize that the tone of our social and political dialogue may differ at times, and then focus on the commonalities—from financial realities to physical barriers to access—that can bring us together in a cohesive movement that draws from all of our experiences and propels us forward in collective action."[10]

As Ayesha points out, it's useful to understand why younger men and women may not think that their reproductive rights are threatened. Part of this assumption may be a result of the pro-choice movement's success, that legal abortion is available throughout the country. After all, growing up with this right makes it hard to imagine that things could ever be different. Some activists also wonder if their peers are less concerned with protecting the right to choice simply because they are unaware of the extent to which that right is already being curtailed—something that they themselves were once unaware of, too.

"I feel that especially older feminists say that younger feminists and younger women in general don't understand, and they take legal abortion for granted," says Roula, a young activist. "There was even that article in the *New York Times*[11] about the next generation of clinic managers, [asking] where are they? Well, everybody *I* worked with is young and excited, so I don't know how I feel about these statements. But if they're true, I kind of don't blame people. I didn't know how important it was to me until I started reading and talking about and learning people's actual experiences with the need for abortion. It's not like it's easy to understand just by reading the politics of it; you get a sense of it, but it's still easy to make these vapid pronouncements of how 'I agree with this but I don't agree with that.' Only when you've come to a point where you've actually met people who've needed X, Y, or Z, and could not access it, do you realize that this is not like having a personal preference about ice cream flavors."[12]

"Until I actually got involved in Planned Parenthood, I don't think I recognized what the limitations were for women seeking abortion," medical student Shannon Connolly admits. "I just assumed abortion was legal, anybody could have an abortion if they needed it. It's not really a problem. I knew that people had their various moral beliefs, pro or against abortion, but I never realized that there are women in America who want abortions who can't have them."[13]

"I remember having these conversations with friends in high school and college about what we would do if we were ever pregnant and almost everyone said they would get an abortion," medical student Melissa Weston tells me. "We talked about whom we would go to, who would drive us, where we would go, how we would get the money, and how we might feel afterward. Sure, we knew that barriers existed and that fears would arise, but never about the possibility of dying because we didn't know if the person we went to knew what they were doing. Never about being arrested or harassed while in the hospital after a botched procedure."[14]

"Until I became an Abortioneer, it had never occurred to me that I'd have to find a way to pay for it, that I might not be able to find a provider in my town, or that if I did they might not accommodate my gestation, and that people might physically try to stop me from getting an abortion," says Anti-Anti. "When you're not pregnant, abortion is just this distant possibility. You know it's there, and it just seems so easy: if I have an unwanted pregnancy, I can just get an abortion! Wrong."[15]

"I absolutely think most people are not aware of what the realities are in terms of barriers to access," law student Kyle Marie Stock agrees. "They aren't worried about *Roe*, they're not worried about *Carhart*, they're not worried about any of these Supreme Court cases that have chipped away at this right. They don't see it as an immediate threat. When South Dakota had that outright ban [under consideration] most people were like 'eh, whatever, no big deal,'" Kyle says, referring to the 2006 ballot measure that would have outlawed virtually all abortions in South Dakota, except in cases where a woman's life was threatened.[16] "And I'm like no, you don't understand, they did this on purpose so that someone would sue them and then they would take it to the Supreme Court. This isn't going to just affect the people in South Dakota—and even if it did, that's horrible and we should really pay attention to that," Kyle points out. "[People] also take access to birth control and access to emergency contraceptives for granted in a lot of cases. This is not a stand-alone issue; it's all interconnected. The reality is that rich women are always going to be able to get an abortion—whether it's legal or not, people with means will be able to access it. It's the marginalized communities that are going to be most affected by any of the restrictions on abortion."[17]

Technically Legal and Practically Devastating

As seen above, while much discussion about the generational divide centers around fear that *Roe v. Wade* could be overturned, most young people involved with protecting abortion rights see this as a limited scope. Many of the barriers women face in obtaining an abortion are not formal legal barriers. And to a lot of women, these informal barriers can be just as daunting as waiting periods and mandatory counseling scripts, and their repercussions can be just as far-reaching as if abortion were outlawed altogether.

"I am worried about *Roe v. Wade* being overturned, but I am more worried about the barriers to access faced by women every single day in spite of the fact that abortion is legal," says reproductive rights attorney Rebecca Hart. "For a certain subset of women, abortion will likely always be accessible—women who have financial means, women who live in urban areas, women who are not part of historically marginalized groups. To me, the fight to keep abortion legal and accessible is alive and well."[18]

There is no law saying that, as of 2005, 87 percent of counties in the US—and 97 percent of rural counties—must lack an abortion provider.[19] That's just the reality. Likewise, there is no law saying that low-income women are unlikely to have access to reliable transportation—that's just another reality. And those two realities combine to make it pretty difficult for a woman who needs an abortion but lives one hundred or even fifty miles from the nearest clinic and doesn't have a car. For a lot of women, the distance doesn't even have to be that great to be daunting. Say you live in the Atlanta suburbs, don't have a car, and can't afford the cost of multiple cab trips. Your nearest clinic might only be ten miles away, but without affordable transportation, it can take hours to get there.

Now multiply all that hassle not just twice—getting there and back on one day—but four times, if you live in a state that has a mandatory waiting period and requires that you come into the clinic for counseling and/or a required ultrasound. That's yet more money spent on transportation, and if you have a job, that's another half day at a minimum to take off work. And if you don't have a job because your children are too young for school and you can't afford daycare? Then you need to arrange at least two days worth of childcare.

Courtney Lewis, an attorney who lived in Alaska at the time of her interview, echoes the issue of restricted access. "Rural women do not have easy access to an abortion provider," she points out. "It's come to my attention more since I've lived in Alaska. So much is off the grid; it's not connected to the road system. A woman in rural Alaska might have to fly into Anchorage, and if she is beyond her first trimester, she might have to then fly to Seattle. It's expensive and not feasible."[20]

All of these problems can pale in comparison to finding out that your pregnancy is more advanced than you thought. According to Planned Parenthood, a first-trimester abortion at one of its clinics can run anywhere from $300–$950.[21] After twelve weeks, the price generally increases by about $100 per week, and it's not uncommon for late second-trimester and third-trimester procedures to cost at least several thousand dollars, and usually more.

Dana Weinstein found this out after the child she was carrying was diagnosed with extremely severe defects. Dana and her husband received the news in the summer of 2009, shortly after Dr. Tiller was murdered. The hospital where Dana was treated had always referred their late-term terminations to his clinic, and Dana's was the first case the staff had had after his death. After some research, she was sent to a doctor over 1,600 miles from her home.

"I feel like there are going to be other women who are in the situation, women who don't want to be in situations, and they absolutely should have the right and quite frankly the ease. . . . I didn't have the ease. I had to travel out of state; I had to pay personally $17,560 out of my own pocket, and to add that to the already horrific time and horrific stress of the situation, it's just cruel and unusual punishment,"[22] Dana says.[23]

Again, none of the barriers that Dana and her family faced were the direct result of legal restrictions of abortion rights. They were just the reality that she, like thousands of other women, had to contend with. The new generation of pro-choice activists see these barriers, and often question whether the hawk-like focus on the future of *Roe v. Wade* may be distracting attention away from the local and regional struggles happening at this very moment.

A Common Conversation

"Everyone needs to understand that we are in this together," says Planned Parenthood of Utah's Melissa Bird. "If we don't get together and start being the squeaky wheel, they will chip away at abortion and eventually, we will all be asking for permission to use the pill. This is unacceptable to me. That is not the world I want to live in, and I refuse to give up. One of my friends said to me once, 'Good public policy should be like good sex. Deliberate, slow, focused, and make sure no one gets hurt.'"[24]

"My philosophy has been simple for a long, long time," physician Wayne Goldner tells me during a phone conversation in July 2009. "Every time a person tries to make me feel guilty for doing abortions, [I ask] why aren't the women's groups [making] somebody feel guilty for *not* doing abortions? Why aren't they picketing offices that *don't* [provide] abortions? There [are] many women's groups who are competing for diminishing funds, attempting to support themselves, trying to accomplish things and, often, not getting much done. I do think that the women's organizations need to start joining forces more. That's the problem," he continues, "nobody really cares or notices the problem until you're telling it to them. And they just assume that if they have an unplanned pregnancy, they'll find somebody or something. Right now, [there's] still a safety net, but one day soon, people are going to start looking and go, whoa, there's nobody. If we don't learn from history, we are doomed to repeat our mistakes."[25]

As the director and owner of an abortion clinic, June Ayers has a very personal stake in the future of legal abortion, and her concern is palpable when we speak in the summer of 2009. "The thing is, now people accept it as a given and it's not. After thirty-six years now, it is still not a given," she says fiercely. "It could be snatched away, and what are we going to do; I mean, then we have this groundswell of people who go, what the heck happened? The problem is that people should be paying attention to that now because it doesn't only affect abortion rights. We're talking about the same people who picket me that don't believe in birth control—they're for taking away people's right to birth control, too. We need to get the message out now."[26]

"Having grown up pro-life, I have a unique ability to really understand the other side, [to] really try hard to continue to try to walk in their shoes [and] understand what it's like for them, so that you can frame your own message," medical student Rozalyn Love says. "Our first MSFC meeting, I made sure the title sounded very neutral: 'Reducing Abortion'—in huge letters—'Through Reproductive Health Education.' A lot of folks actually thought it was the Christian group on campus who are adamantly against abortion. We talked a lot at that meeting about coalition building, and how most of us are somewhere in the middle, and this is what our patients, no matter what choice they make, deserve and need. [People] were shocked to learn that we would be advocating fewer abortions, just a different way to get there. . . . And people who I knew were very pro-life [asked] can we have a conversation about this, because I'm hearing things I've never heard before and realizing maybe I don't know as much as I thought I did, and I'd like to know more. Promoting that discussion is key; without any discussion, we're not going to make progress."[27]

"I think the biggest problem with politicians, with politics, with every movement in this country is that people aren't able to take themselves out of their experience," activist Alexis Zepeda says, raising her voice as a bus roars down the street past our café table. "And sometimes it's just as easy as telling people these women's stories to let them know the actual reality of people's lives on the other side of the city, or the other side of the country. And that's on us, on people who are already in the movement, to reach out to people. I find that the most resonant piece is the economic justice piece, because it's so fucking wrong that people have to call [an abortion fund] for assistance and talk about their lives like this. I feel like that's one thing the movement hasn't really done, which is essentially mount a giant PR campaign focusing on the economic realities."[28]

"There [are] so many more factors and particulars of each story that if you are being sympathetic or even open to hearing someone's story, you realize that this is never an easy decision," law student and Lilith Fund volunteer Kyle Marie Stock points out. "There's always a host of factors that go into thinking about it. The clinics [that the Lilith Fund works with] are going to give people counseling, they're going to make sure they're secure with the decision; they're going to treat the person respectfully. I think that is really lost in the discussion, that even people who are funding abortion are really aware of people's feelings on the issue and we want to make sure that there's support throughout the whole process. People don't get to that level of discussion often, though, because so often it's like 'oh, you're pro-choice, well you're horrible.'"[29]

How can we change the conversation, then, so that level can be reached? Kyle has one suggestion: "I think that we as activists are failing to [put] real faces and real stories with this issue."

This mantra, of putting a real face on abortion and taking away the veil, is repeated by many young activists who are frustrated with how taboo the subject remains. "A very important change is being able to say the 'A' word in public," Anti-Anti points out. "You never think about those things, because they seem so small. But it's very telling about the stigma that surrounds abortion and pervades the movement. You can't just blurt it out in public. But now that I'm confident that I love abortion and will do whatever to defend it, I have no problem. It's funny because I still feel weird saying 'breasts' and 'vagina.' I guess I'll have to work in a gynecology office before I can say them comfortably. But I've been shushed before for saying 'abortion' in public. I just don't care anymore who hears me."[30]

The pro-choice movement has played a vital role in not just protecting women's rights to reproductive autonomy but in furthering those rights. Individual victories are won every day, whether in the form of securing grants for a local fund, talking to a young woman about what form of contraception is best for her, or helping a woman brainstorm ways to afford her abortion.

These victories, however, are not enough. As long as women benefit from the sacrifices of so many but do not even tell their closest friends that they have had an abortion, and as long as men also remain silent about the role that abortion has played in their own freedom of choice, the pro-choice movement is forever destined to operate on the offense. Until individuals are able to engage in difficult conversations about the ways in which life is enriched by the right to decide when or whether to have children, true reproductive freedom will remain out of reach. By remaining silent about the role that reproductive choice and freedom have played in their lives, pro-choice individuals are unwittingly contributing to the idea that abortion is something to be ashamed of, and they are helping to perpetuate the anti-choice narrative that abortion is always a negative decision.

Reproductive rights affect people's lives even if they're male, if they've never had an abortion, or if they've never known anyone who had an abortion. The simple fact is that everyone benefits from the freedom of choice because that freedom means all citizens are able choose when or if to become a parent; and in turn, that means individuals have the ability to go to college or graduate school, pursue whatever careers they want, and only stay in a relationship if it is healthy for them. Choice benefits society as a whole because it ensures that everyone is able to make the best decisions for themselves and their families.

"Policy [is] really important and really crucial but empty of that human character, that quality where you can see and hear and feel more about people's real lives and their real existence," Alexis Zepeda says. "Unless you're a total soulless asshole, [when] you hear some of the details of the people's stories you have to feel compelled to do something. Women's stories will always win the debate, always."[31]

Activists, attorneys, and providers can and do tell those stories in eloquent and compelling terms, but there is another, equally crucial population whose voices matter. "We need our patients, who we do everything for, to stand up for us," Steph Herold says during our first interview in the summer of 2009, when she is working as a clinic counselor. "We don't need them to tell their abortion stories to everyone they know, although of course that would be great. We need them to fight for abortion access in whatever way makes sense to them. If one in three US women has an abortion by age forty-five, where are these women? Why don't they stand up for us? There's obviously a lot of silence and stigma around abortion, but doctors are being killed. If you want access to this procedure, if you want abortion clinics to be places where women get safe and compassionate care, patients need to start having our backs.

"We have a little form that we give patients when they come back for their follow-up to write how their experience was, how the staff treated them," Steph continues. "One of the questions is, 'Has this changed your view on abortion, and what would you have done about your pregnancy if abortion wasn't legal?' And most people say, 'I would have tried to have an abortion anyway.' That is what scares me and gets me to work every day. This is important."[32]

This urgency is something that the new generation of pro-choice advocates share with the second-wave feminists of the 1960s and 1970s. The struggles are different; the earlier generation was fighting to legalize abortion, whereas today the challenge is to keep what is legal on the books accessible and affordable in real life. And the ways of achieving those goals are different too, as younger activists increasingly turn to social media and choose to work outside of established pro-choice organizations to affect positive change. But the tenacity, dedication, and passion have not diminished from one generation to the next, and there are many lessons that each generation can teach the other. While the blueprint of grassroots activism and messaging that the second-wave activists wrote needs to be updated for today's social and political climate, it is still instructive to be aware of what approaches were successful in the past—and which were not. For their part, second-wave activists would do well to take a page in social media engagement from their younger cohorts and remain just as open to new ideas and opinions as they once wished their elders were with them.

CHAPTER SEVEN

I WENT TO THE MARCH FOR LIFE, AND ALL I GOT WAS THIS LOUSY FEAR OF CHOICE

The March for Life is held in Washington, DC every year. In previous years, I had been caught off-guard by random sightings of protestors wandering through my neighborhood, holding large photographs of fetuses in one hand and maps in the other. In 2011, I decided to see the event firsthand. I went to the National Mall and wandered around for an hour, reading signs and listening to speeches. One handmade, double-sided sign caught my eye for the sheer number of pink hearts decorating the edges and its enthusiastic message: one side read, "I beleive [sic]: (1) in God (2) You are a child of God (3) God forgives—come to Him (4) God loves, embraces, adores, smiles, on Life (young to old)"; the other side continued, "More things I beleive: (1) You are loved (2) URLUVD (3) a drawing of a sheep with the word 'ewe' + R + heart drawing + ed (4) See number 1." Other signs, though less exuberant, featured correct spelling and less text-message-style communication, and mainly featured pictures of fetuses with variations on the idea that abortion harms women.

The participants I saw were overwhelmingly white, although there were Hispanic and African American protestors there, too.

There were lots of children and young adults, and while the crowd seemed pretty evenly split between men and women, the speakers I heard were almost all men. They went on at length about what was best for women and children, although the crowds around me seemed pretty distracted at times, and at various points I couldn't hear the speakers' voices over the conversations on the ground.

What I did hear, both from the stage and more casual conversations, presented an idea of abortion and women's health that was so clearly at odds with reality, it would have been funny if it weren't terrifying. These were people who really did believe that a fertilized egg should have the same rights as a person, that Planned Parenthood clinics were deliberately committing genocide, and that abortion care is comparable to the unimaginable cruelty of the Holocaust. While these protestors likely represented the most extreme of the anti-choice movement, the fact remains that they are also highly visible, quotable, and determined to tell women what to do with their bodies.

The anti-choice movement has less trouble than the pro-choice movement in getting its message across because nuance is not something that exists in the anti-choice universe. Embryos and fetuses are unborn children. Women are mothers. And abortion is the murder of a child.

"A lot of times I hear the pro-choice ideology being put in terms of, it's my body, it's my choice," Shaundell Hall, a medical student and member of Medical Students for Choice, points out. "But when someone is thinking that an embryo or fetus is a person and entitled to the same rights as people walking around, then [the question becomes,] how important is privacy versus homicide?"[1]

This emotional language and single-minded focus has success-fully set the tone of the national abortion debate. This is evident in the very terms that the media—be it liberal, conservative, or neutral—use to describe the opposing sides: pro-life versus pro-choice. Equating life with choice is troublesome to many people, but in the case of these terms, it's a false equation.

"Pro-life" is an inaccurate and misleading term because it sets up a false equivalency: supporting abortion does not mean that you support death. The linguistically and logically honest pairing is "pro-choice" and "anti-choice," two terms that do mean the opposites sides of the same idea. At its root, that is what the abor-tion debate comes down to: whether women have the choice to make their own decisions (and even the anti-choice contention that it's about choosing life for a fetus still hinges on that idea of choice). But since "anti-choice" is less emotionally manipulative than "pro-life," it is small wonder that the anti-choice movement has been so vociferous about using very specific terms to describe itself and its message. The success of anti-choice messaging can be seen in the language around many abortion debates, such as the manipulative term "partial-birth abortion."

The language that is used when the public hears about abortion is important, and it plays a large role in the way women experience their own choices.

Why Abortion Matters

Abortion is the meeting place between women's bodies, sexu-ality, and privacy. Any of these topics are potentially divisive and controversial issues in themselves; taken together, they represent a powder keg of conflicting ideas and beliefs about the extent to which an individual's rights dovetail with larger societal expectations. In theory, an abortion is something that every adult woman has the right to undertake autonomously, without the interference or input of her parents, partner, friends, employer, religious leader, or elected political representative. And while that right would seem perfectly in keeping with this country's long and proud investment in the idea of personal freedom, it directly contradicts another cherished American ideal, one steeped in a Christian tradition: the sanctity of the family, especially motherhood. Having a child is considered one of the most normal and natural biological impulses for both men and women. The idea that not everyone feels that impulse, or is able to act on it, goes against the central and romanticized idea of the family as the cornerstone of American society. It challenges the very identities and roles that make up who we are imagined to be as human beings.

This is a shutdown argument—either one agrees with these assumptions or one doesn't, but it's difficult and frustrating to argue them on the sound bite level at which so much of the popular abortion debate has played out. These are deeply ingrained thoughts and values that are held to one extent or another by the majority of American citizens, but the controversy and contention comes in when people are absolutely unwilling to either consider someone else's viewpoint or, perhaps more importantly, concede that what an individual chooses to do with her or his body is a personal choice.

It is interesting and instructive to look at how another mainstay in the culture wars has been able to turn once-vehement opposition in a more accepting direction. The LGBTQ rights movement is also about sexuality, privacy, and—though to a lesser extent—women's bodies, but it has made more headway in the realm of legal protections and cultural acceptance for two reasons. First, it has been able to successfully show the general public that being gay is not a choice—and when something's not a choice, it's a lot easier to wrap one's head around it. When something is a choice, the cultural conscience feels the need to judge in one direction or another, and the enlightenment sensibility of America expects individuals to make the "right" choices.

The second reason is that having an abortion is something a person *does*; whereas being LGBTQ is something that a person *is*. And because of this, keeping one's sexual identity in the closet is a very different proposition than keeping an abortion in the closet. It is much more imperative for each individual LGBTQ person to decide for him- or herself the extent to which they want to be open about that aspect of themselves than it is for a woman to decide to what extent she wants to publicly talk about a past medical procedure. While we all might want "everyone else" to talk about their abortions and not want to do it ourselves, coming out of the closet much more closely aligns the personal risks and personal benefits with the risks and benefits to the nation of approaching sexuality in a more open-minded way and becoming a more tolerant person. It makes the issue visible, and, eventually, understandable, even in the face of bigotry and hatred.

This is not to say that homophobia has been chased out of the US—far from it. However, the effort to mainstream LGBTQ identities, and include alternative sexualities within liberal family values, has seen incredible advancements in recent years. Meanwhile, abortion remains taboo, even in liberal circles, because it is still seen, by and large, as a choice that is best never to make.

Focus on the Fetus

The fanaticism and relentless moralizing seen at the Right to Life March drives the anti-choice movement as a whole, not just its most dogmatic supporters. Herein lies the heart of this stubborn culture war. The 2008 Republican Platform stated that, "Faithful to the first guarantee of the Declaration of Independence, we assert the inherent dignity and sanctity of all human life and affirm that the unborn child has a fundamental individual right to life which cannot be infringed. We support a human life amendment to the Constitution, and we endorse legislation to make clear that the Fourteenth Amendment's protections apply to unborn children. . . . We all have a moral obligation to assist, not to penalize, women struggling with the challenges of an unplanned pregnancy. At its core, abortion is a fundamental assault on the sanctity of innocent human life. Women deserve better than abortion. Every effort should be made to work with women considering abortion to enable and empower them to choose life."[2]

Concentrating on the fetus rather than the woman allows the anti-choice movement to sidestep accusations of misogyny. It removes the act of sex from the question entirely. It also removes gender from the discussion, at least in terms of who's doing the talking: it's marginally more palatable to hear a man (and the large majority of anti-choice leaders and politicians are men) talk about a beautiful living fetus than it is to hear him tell women what they should do with their bodies.

It is no accident that the anti-choice argument boils down to the unborn. Fetuses are all potential, not actuality, but this only makes it easier to romanticize an unborn child. The anti-choice movement's focus on the fetus allows opponents of choice to exploit the positive connotations of pregnancy and parenthood—love, family, and the human potential to cure cancer or write the next great American novel—at the same time as it ignores the more sobering aspects, like socioeconomic disparities, health concerns, inadequate insurance, and unsupportive workplace policies. After all, in the world of the unborn, none of this yet exists.

Everyone holds sacred the beauty of family. We all have mothers and fathers, sisters and brothers, daughters and sons. It is easy to manipulate the sentiments of just about any human being, when you question whether the people they love deserved to live upon their conception.

Still, you can't point to the fetus forever, especially when it is surrounded by a whole other human being. The issue of the woman has always been troublesome for anti-choice leaders. How to present the movement as loving and respecting women, even serving to guard and protect them? It's not too surprising then that the concept of "post-abortion syndrome" has captured the imaginations of the anti-choice movement.

While the literature does not support the existence of post-abortion syndrome and the American Psychological Association does not include it as a diagnosis, it has become nothing short of proven

fact in the anti-choice mind. In a 2007 article for the *New York
Times Magazine*, Emily Bazelon spent time with Rhonda Arias, an
"abortion recovery counselor" at a prison who had had four abortions herself. Arias struggled with years of drug and alcohol abuse
and attempted suicide—all problems that she believes stemmed
directly from her abortions. Arias began to see a larger pattern
all around her: "In America we have a big drug problem, and we
don't realize it's because of abortion."[3]

It is tempting to dismiss Arias's statement as pure hyperbole, a
grandiose attempt to boil years of regrettable and painful behavior
down to a single choice made within those circumstances. However, the ease and conviction with which Arias and others in the
anti-choice movement blame abortion for a whole host of personal
problems is not hyperbole. They are serious about what they see
as the disastrous effects of abortion on women's lives. Not only
does this perspective take personal responsibility out of the equation, it also portrays the pro-choice movement as a sort of demonic
and manipulative force that only sees the financial reasons for providing abortions and ignores grave complications to the individual
and family.

That this line of thinking also casts women as weak-willed, and
unable to fully accept or account for their decisions, is especially
interesting, given the extent to which anti-choice women embrace
the "abortion hurts women" narrative. As opposed to the rest of the
anti-choice movement, when it comes to this approach, women's
faces often appear in leadership. Theresa Burke, a pastoral associate with Priests for Life, founded Rachel's Vineyard, an organization that bills itself as the "largest post abortion ministry in the

world."[4] The executive director of Priests for Life, Janet Morana, cofounded the Silent No More campaign along with Georgette Forney, president of Anglicans for Life. Their campaign seeks to raise awareness about the "damage" that abortion causes.[5] And women with personal experience of abortion serve as state leaders for the anti-choice organization Operation Outcry, which collects and publicizes testimonies.

There's a pattern in many of the personal stories on the Operation Outcry and Silent No More websites. Invariably, the woman says that a partner or parent pressured her to have the abortion; that the clinic employees were dismissive and uncaring; and that in the months and years following the initial abortion, she turned to alcohol, drugs, and/or promiscuity—often leading to more abortions—to deal with her pain and confusion. These narratives neatly tie up a grab bag of personal stressors and extenuating circumstances into a tidy package where abortion is the beginning, middle, and end of a woman's problems—with the strong implication that if one woman could have such a horrible experience, then every woman is at similar risk for a lifetime of misery, addiction, and regret. That these women seem to feel a duty to prevent other women from even entertaining the idea of choosing to have an abortion—that they would deny other women the same right that they exercised—echoes the arrogance of the anti-choice movement at large. Assuming that one person knows what is best for a complete stranger, or that the very specific circumstances of their own life can be extrapolated and writ large onto someone else's life, is a very specific kind of pandering and patronizing. Significant sums of money (Priests for Life took in over $10 million in contributions in 2010[6]) are now spent every year promoting the idea that years of pain and confusion can be explained by one single act, apart from and untouched by anything else that occurred in that woman's life previously or since. This stunningly simplistic explanation is attractive, because it leads to an equally simple solution: apologize and atone for the act, and life will get better.

These organizations claim to be about healing and helping women, but the focus on the fetus remains front and center. That is, after all, what every story and testimony revolves around: the very fact of the pregnancy itself. This entire wing of the anti-choice movement is just one more example of how central the idea of unborn children is to the success and emotional power of anti-choice beliefs, and it also serves to underscore a key difference between the mainstream pro- and anti-choice movements. The pro-choice movement generally keeps its focus squarely on the woman who will be affected by reproductive rights restrictions; when children are mentioned, it is almost always in the context of the existing family or fatal fetal defects. And while it makes sense that the pro-choice movement, which came about in large part to protect and defend women's rights, would spend most of its energy working on behalf of actual women, this emphasis has left the movement open to charges that it is anti-child and anti-family.

I remember a button that my mother had when I was young, three words in white font on a magenta background: "Pro-Child, Pro-Family, Pro-Choice." To me, that seemed to sum up the entire pro-choice argument very succinctly: it was not about being anti-children, it was about supporting families, children, *and* choices.

This was also a refrain that often ran through my head during the first few months of my own pregnancy. My husband and I had talked for years about whether and when to have a child, and we deliberately waited until we felt we were as secure as possible financially, emotionally, and as a couple to even think about bringing another person into our lives.

Yet, while we were excited at the news that I was pregnant, we were also caught off guard by all the other emotions we felt, ranging from fear to ambivalence and even to second thoughts. It took many long and honest conversations about all the ways in which our lives were going to change for us to both feel that we had made the right choice in deciding to have a child, and even then, we approached each new diagnostic test with the knowledge that if the news was grim, we would have to have even more difficult conversations. The first few months of my pregnancy coincided with the furor over Virginia's proposed transvaginal ultrasound law and its aftereffects, and at each ultrasound appointment I thought about how devastating it would be to be forced to look at the images of a pregnancy that, for whatever reason, needed to be terminated.

Our emotional maelstrom subsided after several months as the pregnancy progressed normally and we had the time and space to wrap our minds around becoming parents. But my experience taught me that no woman should ever be judged for deciding that she cannot continue a pregnancy. Whether it makes perfect sense on paper to become a parent, or whether it objectively looks like the worst idea in the world, the choice to have a child belongs only to the woman—and, in many but far from all cases, the man—who are responsible for the pregnancy occurring in the first place. To claim otherwise is to blatantly disregard the importance of ensuring that every child is a wanted and desired one and will receive the love, support, and attention that it deserves. I am grateful that I became pregnant when I wanted to, and I continued that pregnancy because I chose to. And I am equally grateful that there will be absolutely no doubt in my daughter's mind that her father and I had her because we wanted to, not because we had no choice in the matter. That is a certainty that she—and, indeed, every child—deserves to have.

And this is a certainty that most people, compassionate people who can't help but respond to appeals to the fetus and the sanctity of family, would want for all children in the world. Yet this is a point that the pro-choice movement seems to talk about only in response to direct anti-choice attacks. Pro-choice messaging is fearful of the angelic unborn child that the anti-choice movement has so carefully constructed, with all its tiny fingers and toes intact. The culture war sits at this crux of human attachment and is stuck there. Discussing how to create a world where "life" is truly wanted and supported is lost in rhetoric that idealizes the unborn, without context, and pities the woman, with every context in the world parceled down to her decision to abort.

The Crisis Pregnancy Clinic Guide to Procreation

The anti-choice narrative of pregnancy was one that my husband and I encountered firsthand when we visited a crisis pregnancy clinic. I had heard stories about the clinics, which advertise free pregnancy tests abundantly on city buses and on college campuses and purport to be caring resources for scared, pregnant women.

Crisis pregnancy clinics, or CPCs, are notorious for using a variety of tactics to persuade women to continue their pregnancies, from offering free diapers and warning of the risks of abortion to giving false ultrasound information so a woman may think her pregnancy is too advanced for abortion to be an option. In some extreme cases, CPCs violate patient confidentiality to tell a woman's family or partner that she is pregnant with hopes that they may curtail her plans. CPCs deliberately choose innocuous names like "A Woman's Choice" or "Pregnancy Clinic," and though the vast majority of clinics are not staffed by licensed medical professionals, they do not make that information clear.

I'd long been curious to see firsthand what these CPCs were like, but one thing had always stopped me: I wasn't pregnant, and I am completely unable to tell a lie with a straight face. But now that I wouldn't have to fake it, I asked my husband if he'd be willing to go with me to a CPC. We found a list of locations in the Washington, DC area and chose a clinic located in a politically progressive neighborhood we were very familiar with. On our way there, we rehearsed our story: I believed I might be pregnant, had heard about their clinic, and wanted to get some advice about what to do if the test was positive.

The woman my husband and I met with at the clinic never introduced herself to us and did not wear an ID. I didn't realize this until we were well into our session, at which point I was too busy thinking of appropriate responses to her questions, and queries of my own, to figure out how to tactfully say, "By the way, what's your name?" She was polite and personable, both when I met with her one-on-one for the intake interview and when my husband joined us after I took the pregnancy test.

The intake interview was pretty low-key. I was never asked for any identification, but I did have to provide my name, address, and phone number. Questions about my religious preference, employment status, and marital status followed, as did questions about my thoughts on abortion, parenting, and adoption; who would help me care for a baby; and whether my parents would be supportive. The woman laughed at this question, noting that since I was a married adult, that might not be a concern. At the end of the interview, I was asked to sign the intake form. I read the fine print above the signature line, which stated both that the people at the CPC were trained crisis counselors and that none of them were licensed counselors. Despite the lack of licensing, they were still referred to as "counselors."

The pregnancy test itself was even more do-it-yourself than a drugstore test. I went into the small, clean bathroom, urinated into a cup, and then went back into the equally clean and well-organized room where the woman waited. My husband was allowed to come in at this point, and he sat next to me on the couch as I carefully filled a dropper with urine and placed six drops into the pregnancy test. The woman covered the test window with the wrapper and filled my husband in on our previous conversation for four minutes, then said we could see the results. Upon seeing the positive sign, the counselor said, "Well, congratulations!"

During the intake interview, I had explained that my main concern if I was pregnant was that I was on a range of medications for chronic pain conditions (which is true), and I was concerned about the effects of those medications on a developing fetus. The woman had said straight-out that the clinic was not "abortion-minded," and I made it clear that I just wanted information about all my options. After the positive test result, both my husband and I reiterated our concern; the woman said that they weren't medical professionals, repeated the not "abortion-minded" line, and gave us a wealth of information about abortion and adoption. Before we left, she showed us all the toys, baby clothes, and maternity clothes that were available for those who needed them. She said she hoped we would make the right decision and that she'd be praying for us. There was a little more talk about religion than either my husband or I expected, but otherwise she was charming and polite throughout the whole appointment.

I have to admit, the entire experience was a lot less inflammatory than I had expected. My husband thought that I intimidated the woman, since I wasn't like the usual person who showed up looking for help. Both the questions I was asked and comments that the woman made indicated that this clinic worked primarily with young, single women and teens who were concerned about affording diapers and baby clothes. As a married, white, adult woman who didn't mention finances as a pressing concern, I probably didn't fit the standard profile for this CPC. Whether it's true that I intimidated her, I was kind of disappointed that my first attempt at undercover journalism had yielded such muted results.

Then I got home and began to read the various pamphlets that the woman gave us and that my husband picked up in the waiting room—a small mountain of information on topics ranging from condoms to adoption to abortion. Most of the adoption material was produced by organizations that seemed dedicated simply to providing good placements for children, although one pamphlet was credited to Bethany Christian Services, an organization whose website links to crisis pregnancy clinics.

Some of the most interesting material had nothing to do with abortion. The pamphlet "Condoms: What's Still at Risk?" presented grim statistics about condom use: they don't reduce the risk of HPV infection, only reduce the risk for chlamydia and gonorrhea by half, and approximately three out of every twenty couples using condoms "end up pregnant anyway within the first year of use." There were only two ways to truly protect yourself, the brochure concluded: abstain from all sexual activity, including oral sex, or practice "lifetime faithfulness" to a single, uninfected partner.[7]

Curious about the Medical Institute for Sexual Health, which produced this pamphlet, I went to their website. Information about the organization itself was scarce; the mission statement consisted of one sentence: "To empower safe, healthy living by communicating objective and scientific sexual health information." The section detailing what the organization does was more verbose: "The Medical Institute for Sexual Health (MI) was founded in 1992 by Joe S. McIlhaney Jr., MD, a prominent obstetrician/gynecologist and infertility specialist. . . . MI is the leading organization in the United States studying the science involved with the sexual behavior of adolescents and young adults and the impact that behavior has on the spread of sexually transmitted infections as well as the emotional and physical implications. MI is the only organization in America that is backed by a highly qualified team of nationally recognized MDs and PhDs dedicated to providing science-based sexual health information."[8]

That last statement seemed like a bit of a stretch—really, the *only* one in America?—but grandiose claims aside, it's also worth noting that Dr. McIlhaney Jr., is a fan of abstinence-only education, having testified before Congress about his belief that so-called "abstinence plus" programs, which teach not just about abstinence but also contraception use, are not as effective as programs which simply tell teenagers not to have sex.[9] However, a study undertaken by Advocates for Youth, a nonprofit organization that focuses on adolescent sexual and reproductive health, found that teens who receive comprehensive sex education are 50 percent less likely to "experience pregnancy" than those that receive abstinence-only education, and that comprehensive programs help increase the use of contraception, delay the timing of when an adolescent first has sex, and reduce the number of sex partners.[10]

MI's clear bias means that its statistics about condom safety should be taken with a giant grain of salt. There is no indication that a distinction is being made between data on perfect use, which is the effectiveness of a method if the directions for its use are followed every time the user has sex, and typical use, which looks at the actual use of the method, and includes incorrect and inconsistent use.[11] This distinction is important, because when women and men practice "perfect use," the risks of HPV infection, unintended pregnancy, and contracting chlamydia and gonorrhea drop dramatically; for example, the first-year contraceptive failure rate for condom users who practice perfect use is only 2 percent.[12]

That's a pretty huge difference, and it makes me wonder if CPC clients would be better served by receiving information about how to achieve perfect contraceptive use, as well as how to talk to your partner about the importance of using contraception every time you have sex, and information on the different types of contraceptive methods that are available to men and women. After all, people come to a crisis pregnancy clinic because they're already having sex; information about how to best protect themselves and their partners would be much more useful than material that exaggerates the risks of condoms and castigates anyone who doesn't practice abstinence.

Instead of carrying any factual information like that, though, the CPC did offer another abstinence-promoting brochure, this one titled "Sex Was Never Meant to Kill You." Produced by Why kNOw? Abstinence Education, this bright green, pocket-sized pamphlet is not subtle. Having sex is equated with "giv[ing] into the pressures and indulg[ing] your desires,"[13] with results that included low self-esteem, bitterness, depression, and rejection. Saving sex for the wedding day, however, results in the "ultimate freedom: physically, mentally, emotionally, and spiritually."[14] Readers were advised not to "frequent intimate places" or "date MORONS!" (capitalization theirs).[15]

Originally a division of a crisis pregnancy center in Chattanooga, Tennessee, Why kNOw? was a curriculum used for middle school and high school students. A review of the 2002 edition of this curriculum by the Sexuality Information and Education Council of the United States (SIECUS) found numerous problems with the material and concluded that, thanks to its negative messaging (including using language that implied that victims of abusive relationships were to blame for their abuse), distorted information regarding STDs and condoms, promotion of biases, and portrayal of one worldview based in Judeo-Christian religion, the curriculum was inappropriate for use in public schools.[16]

This material also has the distinction of being reviewed in Rep. Henry Waxman's 2004 report on abstinence-based education, "The Content of Federally Funded Abstinence Only Education Programs." The Waxman report concluded that Why kNOw? contained errors and distortions of public health information. One blatant example of this was their contention that "[t]wenty-four chromosomes from the mother and twenty-four chromosomes from the father join to create this new individual."[17] It doesn't take much more than a high school biology class to know that human cells actually contain 23 chromosomes from each parent.

The images of fetal development included in another booklet were scientifically accurate, but given that the ostensible point of the material was to be an "abortion education resource," one could be excused for wondering what the point of these full-color, close-up images was. When I flipped to the last page, I saw that the pamphlet was produced by Care Net, "a Christ-centered ministry whose mission is to promote a culture of life within our society in order to serve people facing unplanned pregnancies and related sexual issues" and whose vision is "a culture where lives are transformed by the Gospel of Jesus Christ and every woman chooses life for herself and her unborn child."[18]

The other abortion-related material that we received was produced by Focus on the Family, an anti-choice Christian organization; Life Dynamics Incorporated, another anti-choice group; the CPC itself; and one pamphlet written by Vincent Rue, the man who coined the phrase "post-abortion syndrome." These pamphlets variously contended that "abortion is no solution at all,"[19] that "many women who choose abortion go against their own sense of right and wrong"[20] and that abortion could lead to "thoughts of suicide."[21] A pamphlet about medical abortion painted a dreary picture of a young woman, her dreams dashed, alone and traumatized after choosing abortion. Another fact sheet casually mentioned that "it takes around ten years for women to recover emotionally"[22] from abortion.

One pamphlet claimed that abortion makes women infertile,[23] despite the fact that scientific studies have shown that there is no proven relationship between abortion and subsequent infertility.[24] The abortion resource booklet heavily implied that there was a connection between abortion and breast cancer, even though an extensive review into the subject conducted by the National Cancer Institute in 2003 found that there was no correlation between induced abortion and an increased breast cancer risk. Furthermore, the NCI also concluded, "Considering the body of literature that has been published since 2003, when NCI held this extensive workshop on early reproductive events and cancer, the evidence overall still does not support early termination of pregnancy as a cause of breast cancer."[25]

We also came home with a pamphlet called "Patient Rights for the Woman Who is Seeking a Legal Abortion." I began to read this material with great interest, lulled by the benign-sounding title into thinking that, finally, here was some neutral information that focused on women's health and safety. Instead, the text was all about what women should watch out for when it comes to abortion providers. Are they licensed? Do they have malpractice insurance? What about a history of medical malpractice? A "post-abortion checklist" included questions like, "Were you physically or emotionally injured as a result of your abortion?" and "Did anyone tell you that you couldn't change your mind about the abortion?" Readers of the pamphlet were exhorted to not "allow anyone to destroy this document or take it away from you" and to not allow the doctor to perform an abortion until he or she completed a section of the form that asked for the name of their malpractice insurance company, policy number, and policy limit, among other information.[26] Unsurprisingly, the anti-choice group Life Dynamics Incorporated produced the pamphlet.

I knew going into this CPC that I would not receive any pro-choice information. But I was still shocked at just how factually inaccurate and misleading the abortion information actually was. Just because a clinic is "faith-based," as the woman I met with pointed out—to say nothing of not "abortion-minded"—does not give it the right to provide women and their partners with lies. If I actually had been a scared teenager or young woman who had little idea of what my options were, reading about the purported risks of abortion would have terrified me and made me think that an abortion was the worst choice a woman could ever make. I would not necessarily have thought to question the validity or accuracy of those pamphlets and brochures; after all, they were provided by a clinic that advertises itself as providing accurate information and compassionate care. The very fact that they were faith-based might even cause me to put more trust in their materials; after all, that term has connotations of support, respect, and understanding—not judgment and fear-mongering.

As I read over the material, my mind kept wandering back to something that the woman told me as she handed us the pamphlets. If a woman or girl wanted, she said, the staff would read over the material with them and talk about it. The idea that someone who calls herself a counselor when she's not even licensed would go over this inaccurate information with a scared and confused woman seemed further evidence of how badly the clinic was abusing the trust of those it purported to care about.

If this CPC and the thousands of others that operate in the United States really want to give women and men accurate information about abortion, they have reputable and neutral sources to turn to. Of course I don't expect a CPC to hand out pamphlets from Planned Parenthood, but both the American College of Obstetricians and Gynecologists and the National Institutes of Health have fact sheets and other materials about abortion that are neither pro- nor anti-choice. Instead, these documents are straightforward and accurate and simply explain what an abortion is, why a woman may choose one, and what a woman can expect before, during, and after the procedure.

Individual communities are beginning to question the tactics of CPCs, with mixed results. In 2010, the city council of Austin, Texas, unanimously passed an ordinance requiring CPCs to post signs saying that they neither offer nor refer clients to birth control or abortion services.[27]

The Austin ordinance is currently the only one of its kind, though not for lack of trying. A similar measure was passed in Baltimore, Maryland, in 2009, but was struck down in 2011 on the grounds that it violated the First Amendment. New York City has also attempted to regulate its CPCs, but in July 2011 a federal judge barred a law that would have required crisis pregnancy clinics to disclose information about their services, including whether a licensed medical provider was on site.[28]

Misleading information and deceptive advertising practices are not the only reasons to be concerned about crisis pregnancy clinics. A 2010 clinic violence survey from the Feminist Majority Foundation found that 57 percent of abortion clinics reported proximity to a CPC, and that 32 percent of clinics that are located near a CPC experienced higher rates of severe violence, compared to 11.3 percent of clinics that are not near CPCs.[29]

A number of violent anti-choice extremists have volunteered with or run crisis pregnancy clinics. Scott Roeder, the man who murdered George Tiller, was a "sidewalk counselor" for a CPC near Dr. Tiller's clinic in Wichita; James Kopp, who murdered Dr. Barnett Slepian and is suspected of attempting to kill four other doctors, founded a CPC in San Francisco.[30] For years, Operation Rescue has urged its supporters to volunteer at their local CPCs,[31] some of which take a very active role in targeting abortion providers.

And those protestors frequently carry signs that display graphic—and often misleading—images of bloody fetuses and close-ups of fetal hands and feet. While these striking images attract attention, they have also been criticized for claiming to show fetuses at one gestational age when their size and stage of development indicates another age altogether—for example, claiming that a photo of an eight-to-ten-week fetus is actually showing a six-week fetus, or that a fetus is ten weeks when it is really between twelve and fourteen weeks.[32] Promoting the idea that a six-week fetus has recognizable facial features or hair is manipulative both on a visceral level and in terms of the larger abortion debate, given how large a role fetal development plays in reproductive rights law.

There is also the fact that a large number of anti-choice images depict fetuses from the later stages of pregnancy, which gives the misleading impression that a high number of abortions are performed after the first trimester, when really the opposite is true.

The origins of these pictures are often murky as well. While those in the anti-choice movement who photograph fetal remains tend to claim that they found the remains in trash bins outside of abortion clinics, there is often no way to certify that the fetuses were actually aborted, as opposed to being the result of a miscarriage.[33]

An Anti-Choice View of the Universe

Just as they disregard the realities of many women's lives while claiming to be guardians for helpless women, anti-choice activists also disregard racial and socioeconomic disparities but claim to be the guardians of helpless racial minorities. In February 2010, billboards were erected in predominately African American neighborhoods in Atlanta, each featuring an image of a sad-looking black child with the text "Black Children are an Endangered Species."[34] Sponsored by the anti-choice Radiance Foundation and Georgia Right to Life, the billboards' appearances coincided with a proposed bill called the Prenatal Nondiscrimination Act, which would make it a felony to provide coerced abortions on the basis of sex or race.[35]

Pro-choice activists wasted no time in opposing both the billboard campaign and the bill itself, exposing both as an attack on black women's autonomy and emphasizing the campaign's negative messages about black women. "Either we were dupes of abortion providers, or we were evil women intent on having abortions—especially of black male children—for selfish reasons," Loretta J. Ross, the national coordinator of SisterSong Women of Color Reproductive Health Collective, wrote in an article about how her organization and others responded to the campaign.[36] "We repeatedly asserted our own agency as black women who are trustworthy, informed, and politically savvy. We insisted that whether black women were pro-choice or pro-life, we were united in believing that black women could reasonably decide for ourselves whether to become parents."[37]

This messaging proved powerful, especially when combined with the goals of reproductive justice activists: to reduce the number of unwanted pregnancies in the black community and remove barriers "that interfere with personal decision making."[38] The original bill never passed out of a House committee,[39] and a revamped bill was again defeated at the end of the 2010 legislative session.[40]

Approximately one year after the Georgia billboards went up, another was erected in New York City's SoHo neighborhood. This one featured a picture of a young black girl and the text, "The most dangerous place for an African American is in the womb."[41] Unlike the Georgia campaign, this billboard wasn't tied to any proposed legislation in New York; and thanks to a swift public outcry, it was soon taken down. Perhaps no reaction was more personal than that of the mother of the girl pictured on the billboard, who had never been approached for consent. She eventually filed a lawsuit against Life Always, the organization that sponsored the ad, calling it racist and the use of the girl's image defamatory.[42]

Rather than be deterred by these setbacks, the anti-choice movement instead set its sights on the federal level. In late 2011, anti-choice Republican Congressman Trent Franks of Arizona sponsored the Susan B. Anthony and Frederick Douglass Prenatal Nondiscrimination Act of 2011, which would criminalize abortions performed on the basis of race or sex and could imprison doctors who failed to determine whether fetal race or gender was part of why a woman wanted an abortion.[43] Franks and other Republican supporters defended the use of Anthony and Douglass's names in the title by saying that the bill would protect women and minorities.[44]

Protect them from what, exactly? Sex-selective abortions are extremely rare in the US. The majority of abortions are performed before the woman even knows the gender of the fetus. A tiny number of abortions—3.8 percent—take place between the sixteenth and twentieth week of pregnancy, and 1.5 percent occur at the twenty-first week or later.[45] According to the American Pregnancy Association, while it may be possible to determine the sex between the eighteenth and twentieth week of pregnancy, nothing is 100 percent certain until birth.[46] Given the medical realities both of when abortions are performed and when sex can be determined, it seems highly unlikely that women are choosing to have abortions due to the sex of the fetus.

The implication that women have abortions because of the race of the fetus, and that women of color need special oversight when it comes to making their own health choices, is equally insulting and ill informed. As Debra Ness and Andrea D. Friedman, the president and director of reproductive health programs, respectively, at the National Partnership for Women & Families, pointed out in their December 2011 Congressional testimony, "This legislation undermines the rights of individual women to make their own personal and private health decisions, in particular whether and when to bear a child. Even worse, it particularly harms women in those communities the bill is purportedly aimed at helping."[47]

The bill—renamed the Prenatal Nondiscrimination Act, or PRENDA—threatens five years in prison not just for any doctors who perform an abortion if they know it was sought for reasons relating to gender or race, but also for anyone who goes with the woman across state lines to get an abortion for any of those reasons.[48] So, not only would physicians have to question patients about their race, the race of their partners, and their reasons for getting an abortion, but a woman's family or friends would have to interrogate her as well, to be sure they weren't unwittingly committing a crime. Physicians, counselors, nurses, or other medical professionals would also be required to report any suspected violations, which could create an atmosphere of suspicion and mistrust among medical professionals.[49] PRENDA also allows a woman, or her spouse or parent, to sue a physician for performing an abortion if they suspect he violated the law; and it allows both those parties and an attorney general to obtain an injunction against the doctor, so he can no longer provide abortions.[50] It's not difficult to see how these stipulations could be misused by an estranged husband angry that his wife got an abortion, or a parent who disagrees with her daughter's choice—or an anti-choice attorney general.

In addition to interfering with both the professional relationship between patients and medical professionals, and the private conversations between women and their support networks, PRENDA could also have a chilling effect on health clinics in minority communities. If physicians and other medical professionals are going to be under such scrutiny for having women of color as patients, it stands to reason that they may become reluctant to serve these communities, for fear of the possible legal and financial repercussions if they are even suspected of violating PRENDA.

This bill, like all the other legislation that purports to care about women of color, fails to offer any reasonable and rational approaches for lowering the rates of unplanned pregnancy, and completely ignores the complex and interconnected factors that contribute to those rates in the first place.

It is true that there is a higher number of unintended pregnancies reported in the black community: 67 percent, versus 40 percent among white women, and 53 percent in the Hispanic community.[51] However, black women have a lower abortion rate than white women—30 percent versus 36 percent, with Hispanic abortion rates at 25 percent.[52] Obviously, these numbers point at a wealth of social issues, some of which Susan Cohen addresses in *Abortion and Women of Color: The Bigger Picture*. Cohen suggests that higher unintended pregnancy rates for black women reflect the difficulties of minority communities in accessing quality contraceptive services: not only may there be a lack of health clinics in these communities, but there may also be financial limitations that make it more difficult for women to afford prescription contraceptives, which tend to be more effective and more expensive.

In 2002, the Institute of Medicine reported that overall, minorities are less likely than whites to receive needed medical services.[53]

Dr. Willie Parker offers a few more theories about the disparate rates: "The social aspect of African-American women being less likely to marry, and therefore being in social circumstances where . . . partnering situations turn out to be less stable, resulting in sexual activity [that] tends to be more spontaneous and less intentional with regard to contraception use. So, we have these less stable social relationships, at least sexually, and you have lower rates of contraceptive access and use."[54]

If those behind the race campaigns and proposed legislation really wanted to support women, perhaps they would actually address these factors. Maybe they would look at the role that poverty, diminished education opportunities, and fragile or nonexistent social support programs have in contributing to unplanned pregnancy rates across the board, not just in minority communities. If they really wanted to help women and children, they would actually support the work that Planned Parenthood and independent health care clinics do to provide basic health care, contraception, and critical services in low-income communities. Maybe then they would stop singling those facilities out in the same way that they claim such centers target low-income communities. "Any clinic anywhere in DC is in a black community," Dr. Parker observes dryly, adding, "I see a lot of mischief being done."

Mischief, indeed. The kind of mischief that plays on pervasive social stereotypes and misogyny to promote the fallacy that women of all races are unable to make their own decisions, and need the helping hand of government—but only when it restricts reproductive health services. The kind of mischief that eschews difficult questions in favor of once again venerating motherhood at all costs and perverts the language of both the civil rights and women's rights movements to do so. And the kind of mischief that will have company, if Trent Franks and his ilk have their way: in February 2012, the House Judiciary Committee approved the Pre-natal Nondiscrimination Act.[55]

The protestors I saw at the March for Life carried signs and cheered for speeches that put forth one very narrow view of life: a view that has no room for the questions and doubts and decisions that every person must grapple with at some point in his or her life. In a way, the anti-choice movement promotes a utopian view of the world, where every child is wanted and healthy, where every woman has a supportive partner and employer, and where every man becomes a father exactly when he is ready and no sooner. It's hard to argue with this overall picture because that's the kind of world that a lot of people want to see, regardless of their beliefs about abortion. But where the anti-choice movement becomes dangerous is in its stubborn refusal to allow for the challenges that real "life" presents.

It's up to the pro-choice movement—and really, anyone who values the freedom to choose when and if to have a child—to push not just for policies that are realistic but also for a greater under-standing of just how common the choice of abortion is, and just how many good and compassionate reasons there are for making that choice.

"I'll never forget going to the Supreme Court when they were considering the partial-birth abortion ban," Alexis Zepeda says, referring to *Gonzales v. Carhart*.[56] "The chant that gave me chills and that always gives me chills whenever I say it or hear it is 'Five-four, four-five, these decisions change our lives.'" Alexis holds out her arms toward me. "Please note," she says, "the hair on my arms is standing up. It's so important, it's forty years of a legacy."[57]

CHAPTER EIGHT

ON DEMAND AND WITHOUT APOLOGY

"What's the problem with national organizations that I see here?" Bess,* an activist, asks. "It's a problem of having too much perspective. Every now and then you just have to say, damn the torpedoes, I'm suing Nebraska. The waiting periods, parental involvement, mandatory state-written 'counseling' scripts, ultrasounds, waiting-room signs, questionnaires, banning 'gender and race-selective abortion,' all these ridiculous things are just sliding by, and no one comes out saying, 'Wait a second, maybe one of these is okay, but—undue burden test please?' Instead we're all, 'Thanks for the new law, dudes! It's awesome that you didn't *totally* repeal *Roe*! Keep up the good work and we will enable you to keep strangling us!'"[1]

Bess is not alone in her frustration. "The kind of barriers that are now put between women and their right to abortion would've been unthinkable twenty-five years ago," law student Kelsey Collier-Wise says. "And honestly, I think we have our own movement to blame for that. National organizations have been too willing to compromise on things like minors' rights and funding, and they've

---

* Not her real name.

embraced anti-abortion language that's made it seem like restrictions are reasonable. Unless we change directions, I am afraid that abortion is going to end up legal for all and available to none."[2]

Like a lot of people, filmmaker Angie Young thought that the 2008 election of Barack Obama would mean that abortion rights would be protected. "But Obama won, and I still don't think anything is certain," she tells me during the summer of 2009. "While Obama did overturn the global gag rule as one of his first orders in office,[3] I still feel like a lot of pro-choice ground continues to be sacrificed in the name of appealing to the 'center.' And the more ground we lose, the more we allow abortion to be painted as a terrible, despicable 'choice' that we must be loath to make and feel guilty for for the rest of our lives, the more we sell ourselves out and pave the way for losing more rights. [We need] to come together and stop pandering to the right and make our side strong again. Abortion on demand and without apology needs to be resurrected as a slogan. As famous suffragette Abigail Allen once said, 'We need to be radical, radical to the core.'"[4, 5]

"I give these organizations credit because it seems like we're getting fired at from all sides," activist Steph Herold says. "I just wish there was more thought going into [our actions] before this happened, before there were a record number of abortion restrictions passed. It reminds me a lot of what happened with health care, where the abortion rights movement got royally screwed and kind of knew about it beforehand but [hoped] it wasn't going to happen. And when it did, there was nothing we could do about it. It just feels like we're very powerless."[6]

In an article for the website Feministe, Steph explores the current reality of the pro-choice movement. "It's time for the pro-choice movement and our allies to admit some failures," she writes. "Somehow, despite the proliferation of national and local feminist organizations, we haven't gotten nearly as far as we should have."[7]

"It's time we take a page out of the AIDS activist ACT UP hand-book," Steph proposes in the same article. Formed in response to the AIDS crisis, the grassroots and direct-action-oriented ACT UP (AIDS Coalition to Unleash Power) was extremely vocal and unapologetic in demanding help for AIDS patients. "It's time we started demanding instead of asking politely," Steph continues. "When prices for AIDS medication went through the roof, ACT UP members infiltrated and chained themselves to the Stock Exchange. When *Cosmopolitan* published a scientifically bogus article saying that if you have hetero sex you can't get HIV, ACT UP shut down *Cosmo*'s building.... ACT UP is just one piece of the gay rights movement, and even they were far from perfect. And yet, no matter how much you gripe or gloat about the gay rights movement and the big [organizations] associated with it, they're winning their culture war."

Established pro-choice organizations such as Planned Parent-hood, the Center for Reproductive Rights, NARAL Pro-Choice America, and the National Abortion Federation (NAF) must bal-ance the interests of their supporters, donors, political allies, and the women whose rights they work to safeguard. This is a difficult balancing act even in the best of times, and the recent economic crisis has made it difficult for many organizations to maintain the levels of funding and donor support that they depend on.

While these established organizations are adept at using

their platforms to draw attention to reproductive rights issues, it often seems that they don't know how to best harness that attention—and energy—once they have it. The websites of Planned Parenthood (and its action center), NAF, and NARAL all offer suggestions for ways that individuals can get involved, including volunteering as a clinic escort, signing up for the organization's e-mail alerts, becoming a member, donating money, and contacting politicians. Each website also offers a way for people to share their own stories with the organization, and NARAL has tips for how to have conversations about abortion and reproductive health.

These are all useful suggestions and resources, but they pale in comparison to the dynamic and personal actions independent activists are engaging in on websites like The Abortioneers and Every Saturday Morning. These sites offer more of a real-time, real-world perspective on what speaking out about choice really entails, as well as plenty of relatable examples of just why reproductive rights matter. The mainstream organizations would do well to capture even half of the passion and forthrightness expressed not only on those sites but also Feministe, Feministing, Abortion Gang, I Am Dr. Tiller, Anti-Choice is Anti-Awesome, and Feminists for Choice (a website that I both write and edit for).

But while Planned Parenthood, NAF, NARAL, and other organizations all have websites, blogs, Facebook pages, and Twitter feeds, there seems to be a marked reluctance to allow their staff to engage in this kind of direct outreach and dialogue, and even to hire on people who are already engaged in this work on their own time.

In another Feministe article, activist Steph Herold recalls her excitement at moving to New York and looking for a job. "Over the course of a few months, I landed interviews at many of the big pro-choice organizations here," she writes. "I interviewed for jobs at these places that fit my experience, jobs at which I could've kicked ass. But each interview ended with some version of this: 'I'm sorry, but you are too radical/too much of an activist to work for us.' At one particular organization, a senior executive looked me in the eye and said, 'If you work here, you have no voice on reproductive rights.' . . . These requests were not implied. They were said to me in no uncertain terms."[8]

Steph touches on some of the reasons for this response, ranging from unfamiliarity with online media to a concern about offending donors. In my experience these are all valid concerns, and they all speak to just how entrenched traditional organizations have become. It's as though any communal memory of how hard activists had to fight in the 1960s and 1970s, how they had to be creative and risk upsetting their elders and commit to this work twenty-four hours a day, seven days a week, has been erased in the intervening decades. It's a peculiar kind of close-mindedness for pro-choice organizations to adopt, particularly given how the movement was built on the sheer chutzpah of so many young women. As Steph puts it, "There is something perverse about not wanting to hire people who are so committed to the movement that they work in it in their spare time."[9]

Equally perverse, to borrow Steph's word, is not knowing what to do with the people you have hired. My friend Stan,* who worked for a large pro-choice organization, says, "For a

---

* Not his real name.

movement that draws such talented people, we waste so much. Thinking about dozens of friends in the movement, I don't think I know anyone who considers herself to have a strong mentorship or professional development program. If you get along with your boss or peers, that's great, but it's incidental to how these [organizations] are run. Many of these institutions are large but are still run as if they were a three-person shop. Indeed, some of these groups are run by their founders, something that makes little sense decades later.[10]

"These orgs are still very command-and-control driven from the top down," Stan continues. "So ideas don't bubble up but are dictated downward. I was asked to do a lot beyond my job description and yet I didn't really have expanded responsibility. It wasn't until I left the organization that I realized how badly it was run and how unhappy I was there. It's not as though I'm unfamiliar with consciousness raising or the idea of connecting my personal struggles with larger political concerns—I just was committed to making things work for me even long after it stopped making sense. And in truth I had been miserable and ineffective. And so were so many close friends, both at my own organization and others."

During the twelve months that I worked in NAF's communications department, *Newsweek* published an article about younger pro-choice activists. I e-mailed the writer on my own time to praise her piece, and I mentioned that I was examining some of the same subjects for this book.

Several e-mails later, I was invited to take part in an e-mail roundtable for the magazine, to be published as a follow-up to the initial article. I had mentioned that while this book was an independent project, I did work at NAF, and the journalist asked if I could discuss some of the organization's work for the piece.

When I asked my supervisor, I was told no, in no uncertain terms. The only person that could do that, she told me, was our executive director. Indeed, I couldn't even be identified as a NAF employee in the article. Never mind that my comments could theoretically be reviewed before being submitted, or that this could be good publicity for the organization. In the end, I participated as an independent author, not an employee. That experience hastened my decision to make that one-time distinction a permanent reality, and I left NAF six months later.

I doubt that NAF is the only organization that exercises such tight control over who can speak to the press, or that I was the only employee at NAF who butted up against this particular policy. But that mentality seems part of Stan's observation that ideas are "dictated downward" and that organizations are not taking advantage of their employees' commitment and genuine desire to further their message.

And quite frankly, it's asking a lot of any one person to be the only one responsible for disseminating her organization's message. If the established groups were willing to let their employees take more of a role in discussing their work with the press, the message could be spread that much more widely. Of course, employees would need to be trained as to how to do press interviews and most effectively discuss the issues and positions—but I doubt that it would take too much additional work to ensure that communications, policy, and legal staffers, for example, would be able to stay on message and intelligently represent their organization.

That said, there are some real benefits to working at an established organization. They offer a wealth of institutional knowledge and have a great deal of practical know-how, particularly when it comes to reaching out to donors and working within state and federal legislatures. There are also benefits from a more nuts-and-bolts viewpoint, as Serena Freewomyn, the cofounder of the Abortion Access Network of Arizona, found through her volunteer work with a well-known pro-choice group.

"One of the big advantages of volunteering with [the organization] is that the volunteer roles and expectations are very clearly defined. The volunteer supervisor does a good job of telling you exactly what you'll be doing during a shift. We always have specific talking points. And the training opportunities have been good. I feel like I've grown professionally during my time as a volunteer, mostly because I've taken advantage of every training opportunity that has been available."[11]

Stepping into a role where your expectations are clearly defined and there are ample opportunities is particularly important in the pro-choice field where a lot of the volunteers tend to be younger and have had limited exposure to the specifics of the issue. Working for a well-established organization means that you can focus all of your energy on the work itself, and this is a factor whose importance cannot be overstated.

Some pro-choice organizations, like Medical Students for Choice (MSFC), have found a way to combine the necessity of independent work with the usefulness of having a solid internal framework. The organization operates on a grassroots-driven model, where individual chapters are led by students and supported by MSFC's staff to achieve the organization's goals.[12]

This kind of model is one that it may behoove other organizations to study more closely. As reproductive justice activist Steph Herold observes, some of the problems facing the movement may stem in part from "the larger pro-choice movement not focusing on where the energy is. A lot of grassroots people doing really excellent organizing work are organizing under the framework of reproductive justice. It's focusing on young people, it's focusing on women of color, it's focusing on the gender-queer community. Engaging at that level would take a tremendous framework shift for them, I think."[13]

Serena Freewomyn has experienced disconnect even within a local chapter of a much larger organization. She admits that, as much as she enjoys her volunteer work, it has been a challenge to work within a more "corporate" framework. "I understand why they do things the way they do. However, that corporate model does not respond well to criticism. I expressed some concern that our trainings were not LGBT friendly. We had watched a video produced by [the organization] about the history of the birth control pill, [and] it was a very hetero-normative discussion. I gave suggestions about how we could bring a discussion of transgender health care into our activism. My concerns did not progress beyond my discussion with my volunteer supervisor, primarily because this did not fit the list of priorities handed down from the top of the food chain."[14]

There are genuine and distinct aspects of the abortion issue, and every activist has his or her own pet cause within this larger framework. Some think that increased access to abortion itself is the most important part to focus on, while others advocate increased sex education and contraception access. Still others are tightly focused on repealing restrictive laws on either the state or federal level, while others insist that the movement should focus more on poverty, or the rights of people of color, or safeguarding *Roe*.

So it's easy to understand that organizations have their lists of talking points or priorities and might not have the most open mind about deviating from them. Yet, that rigidity is increasingly problematic and outdated. It smacks of a kind of myopia that insists that past practices are best practices, and it keeps the organizations' leaders from being able to nimbly respond to, or even head off, increasingly creative attacks from the anti-choice movement.

Changing Minds, One Tweet at a Time

During the 2011 election season, voters in Mississippi were asked to vote on a personhood amendment, which would define life as beginning at the moment of conception and effectively ban all abortion in the state. Despite predictions that the amendment had enough support to pass, voters shot it down by a decisive margin.[15] This defeat can be attributed to many different things: the months of work by local activists, governor Haley Barbour's public reservations about the initiative, the vague and confusing wording of the amendment itself, and the eleventh-hour push by mainstream organizations all contributed to the result at the polls.[16] What struck me the most, though, was the work of concerned women and men in the state who, unburdened by the concerns and expectations of national groups, worked quickly and nimbly in their communities to educate those around them.[17] This kind of grassroots action stands in sharp relief to how too many larger groups work, and it makes me wonder if those organizations are really going about their work in the most meaningful way and truly harnessing the power and energy of their supporters and employees.

The response to the Susan G. Komen Foundation/Planned Parenthood controversy is equally instructive. In January 2012, the Komen Foundation—one of the country's largest breast-cancer awareness and advocacy organizations—announced that it would no longer provide funding to Planned Parenthood clinics for breast cancer screening and education services.[18] The Komen Foundation's official reason was that the organization had a new rule that prohibited it from making grants to organizations that were being investigated by state, local, or federal authorities; and since Planned Parenthood was the subject of an inquiry from Republican Representative Cliff Stearns, it was deemed ineligible for Komen's funding.[19]

Reaction to the Komen decision was swift, loud, and powerful. The news broke on January 31, and Planned Parenthood put out a press release the same day expressing their "deep disappointment" in the move and announcing that they had established a Breast Health Emergency Fund to ensure that its centers could continue to provide the services that Komen had supported.[20]

Planned Parenthood also sent e-mails out to their members, as did progressive organizations like CREDO and MoveOn.[21] New York mayor Michael Bloomberg announced that he was donating $250,000 to Planned Parenthood,[22] and twenty-six Democratic senators issued a letter to Komen, urging the organization to rethink their decision.[23]

As powerful as the response by organizations and politicians was, however, the Komen uproar also made it clear how influential social media has become. Thousands of women and men turned to Facebook, Twitter, blogs, and the comment sections of online newspapers to express their support for Planned Parenthood and share their stories of health services that they had received from their local affiliates. Activists completely unaffiliated with Planned Parenthood set up websites in support of the organization and contacted Komen corporate sponsors to protest their affiliation with the group.[24]

All in all, the uproar represented a new kind of synergy between the old and new forms of activism. Supporters were mobilized by news stories and official press releases, which likely helped shape their thinking about the decision and what next steps they could take. But instead of just sending checks to Planned Parenthood and renewing their membership—which thousands undoubtedly did as well—they used social media to spread the story, call on Komen to reconsider, and discuss the issue in their own communities. Over 1.3 million Twitter posts about the story were sent in the week after the decision was made public, with more than 460,000 in one day alone.[25]

Both forms of activism drew quick results. Within four days, Komen announced that they would not be pulling funding from Planned Parenthood.[26] Komen's anti-choice senior vice president of public policy, Karen Handel—who was largely credited with the decision to pull the funding—resigned from the organization.[27] And the fallout continued through 2012; the Komen Foundation's annual Race for the Cure events drew fewer numbers of participants than expected, and Komen founder and CEO Nancy Brinker resigned her position in August, though she will remain a board member and continue to work with the organization.[28]

The Komen controversy isn't just an example of a high-profile public relations nightmare. It's evidence of the power of quick, unencumbered grassroots actions. "I think the Internet is a powerful strategic tool going forward, as a way of quickly explaining to women what's at stake in their lives about a particular public policy issue and how it affects them, whether it's a Supreme Court decision or a state, local, or congressional action," says Judith Lichtman, senior advisor at the National Partnership for Women & Families, as she reflects on the Komen fiasco. "You have vehicles today for speaking directly to your constituents and having them be heard. The thread between advocacy groups speaking to women and women taking action is a much more direct link today than it was probably ten years ago or even five years ago, in feeling empowered to take action and to be heard."[29]

This is a power that Todd Stave, the landlord of a Maryland abortion clinic, tapped into when he decided that he was tired of being harassed by anti-choice protestors. Though Stave is no stranger to their various tactics—his father first operated the clinic, which has been firebombed, and the family's home had been a protest site—he felt that a line was crossed after a group of protestors came to his daughter's middle school in the fall of 2011, carrying signs with his name and contact information on them.[30]

As harassing phone calls began pouring into his home, Stave's friends asked how they could help. So Stave collected the names and phone numbers of those callers and asked his friends to call

them and calmly and respectfully convey the message that while
the Staves thanked them for their prayers, they neither could nor
wanted to terminate the clinic's lease, and that the family supported women's rights. This tactic proved successful, not just in
terms of the support that the Stave family received but also in the
effect that the campaign had on anti-choice protestors. "Eighty
percent of the people are not going to do this anymore," Stave
said in an interview. "Twenty percent of the people will always be
there. . . . 80 percent of the people are going to go away once you
reveal who they are, once they're no longer anonymous, once they
realize there's going to be a reaction to their action, they're not
going to do it anymore."[31]

The experience led Stave to found Voice of Choice, a group
which now has thousands of volunteers (including myself) willing
to help doctors, clinic owners, and landlords who are experiencing
similar forms of harassment.[32]

The Next Forty Years

Todd Stave's creative and polite response—and he exhorts all
group members to be polite and respectful when contacting anti-
choice protestors—has won him praise both from other activists
and organizations such as NARAL. But his initiative at tackling a
problem that has bedeviled the pro-choice movement for decades
also highlights the hesitancy of the movement itself to undertake
such activities on a large scale. Indeed, it is much more common to
see established organizations speaking out only when responding
to direct attacks from the anti-choice side, continually playing

defense to the aggressive and offensive strategies of the anti-choice movement.

The pro-choice movement's longstanding alliance with the Democratic Party is equally problematic. The 2009 health care battle made it clear that regardless of their personal beliefs, pro-choice politicians were willing to compromise and settle for much, much less than women deserve when it comes to reproductive health care.

"The inability to separate or to pressure these people who have more or less betrayed us several times now—it feels like an abusive relationship," activist Steph Herold says about the movement's dynamic with the Democratic Party. "The cycle that we keep going through, that we ask them to do something like get abortion care covered in health care reform, and they say, don't worry about it, don't worry about it, that'll happen, and then it doesn't and they're not held accountable."[33]

"I am ready for the Democrats to get off their rear ends and go, to heck with the Republican Party, we are going to shove everything that we can possible shove down your throat," clinic director June Ayers says forcefully. "I'm ready for some aggressive politics on behalf of the Democrats, and I think there are a lot of Democratic people out there who believe the same way. I don't think we should be playing footsie with anybody who isn't on the bandwagon anymore. This is the time to make some changes in the United States, to bring this into the twenty-first century, to move us in a positive direction, to take away that big 'C' of conservatism that makes us want to run back to the '50s. The '50s are over with, okay; we already have been to the moon; there are other things out there and we're losing that. If you keep looking back, you never look forward, and if we're going to be around fifty or one hundred years from now we need to be looking forward."[34]

That includes looking for ways to remind both the movement and its supporters that reproductive rights is an issue that affects men as well as women. "How do I get to tell you what to do with your uterus?" Norman,* a clinic escort on the East Coast, asks before adding with a laugh, "because I'm certainly not going to let you tell me what to do with my balls! I don't understand why more men are not involved," he continues more seriously. "Because it's not just an issue that affects women only. It is a reflection of our society's values: it is a reflection of egalitarianism and freedom in general."[35]

"It really is a family issue and a men's issue and the issue for men in the lives of women of childbearing age," the National Partnership for Women & Families' Judith Lichtman observes. "Men aren't rushing to have nine or eleven children either!"[36]

And this message—that both genders benefit from accessible contraception, comprehensive sexual education, and legal abortion—is an important one to consider and broadcast. Reproductive rights issues are often framed through the lens of how they affect women, but that needs to be broadened to include the consequences for men, as well. Narrowing the scope to just one gender allows for the continued stigmatization and marginalization of these concerns and also fails to take men to task for their own inaction as reproductive rights are restricted and abortion services become harder to access.

---

* Not his real name.

But involving men to a greater degree in the pro-choice move-ment isn't the only change some activists would like to see. "Would there be more enthusiastic activism if we celebrated ourselves every once in a while? There are *annual* gay pride marches in cities around the globe. Why do we only mobilize when we're desperate, when the situation is bleak?" Steph Herold asks in an article for Feministe. "Where is our version of It Gets Better? Where are our radical fringes demanding justice? Why don't we take pride in our movement, celebrate ourselves and our values, and, at the same time, fight like hell and win?"[37]

A lot of young activists—and some older ones, too—are starting to do just that. As more independent organizations and websites find their footing and their audiences, more voices are entering the debate, and a lot of those voices are echoing these concerns. As bleak as the entirety of 2011 and the first few months of 2012 have been for the pro-choice movement—and indeed, have been since the murder of George Tiller and the health care reform compro-mises in 2009—all these defeats and setbacks have had the effect of galvanizing activists into taking more direct action because, quite frankly, there's not a lot left to lose. As anti-choice supporters and politicians find ever-more inventive ways to disparage women for the choices that they make in their personal lives, both women and men are beginning to feel more empowered—and impatient—to take action on their own, rather than wait for guidance from the pro-choice movement's long-time leaders.

Every movement needs a variety of voices. Steph used the example of how ACT UP served as the more extreme side of the gay rights movement, but similar comparisons can be made with the respective roles of Greenpeace and Earth First! in the environ-mental movement. Like ACT UP, Earth First! is the more radical voice, agitating for direct action and garnering lots of media atten-tion. And that, in contrast, makes the demands of Greenpeace—which could seem radical on their own—look a lot more palatable to both the public and politicians. Greenpeace's radicalism, in turn, makes old-generation movements like the Sierra Club and the World Wildlife Fund seem utterly acceptable, even to most conservatives, though both were fringe movements when they started up generations ago.

Today, not one pro-choice organization is asking for abortion on demand or celebrating abortion as a valid and affirming choice. There's no guarantee that either stance will ever catch on with the general public, but discussing where those perspectives fall within the goals of the pro-choice movement help push the conversation forward. Plenty of young activists would like to see these more extreme positions become more acceptable both within and out-side of the movement, and they are ready to make it happen.

Likewise, the local faces of the pro-choice movement need to have more power. Planned Parenthood and NAF have member clinics all over the country, but too often the parent organizations overlook the vital role that these clinics could play in the fight. Local clinics know their communities better than the national offices ever could; they know the stories of the women they serve, they know the faces of the protestors outside, and they know what reasons their patients cite when choosing abortion. These clinics can help influence pro-choice attitudes in a very hands-on way, and that in turn can affect both local and state politics.

But so many established organizations focus their efforts on the federal or state rather than the local level, and this means that local affiliates and member clinics don't always get the support—financial or institutional—that they deserve. It would benefit these parent organizations to devote more funding and support to their affiliates that are on the front lines. Reproductive rights is an issue that affects people on a very personal level, and as important as it is to fight bad legislation, it's even more important to prevent that legislation from being enacted in the first place.

In addition to examining the laws that have contributed to limited access, attention must be paid to the role that citizens play. After all, politicians are only in office through the votes of their constituents, and it is possible to repeal bad laws with enough public pressure and outcry. A great deal of responsibility for the current state of abortion rights lies with a public that stubbornly refuses to get involved in an issue until it directly affects their lives. As the generation that fought for *Roe* ages out of needing abortion care, it falls to their children and grandchildren to stop thinking of abortion rights as something that was settled in the 1970s and to educate themselves about the very real threats and barriers that still exist and are only worsening with every passing year.

It is imperative that the pro-choice movement support this education at every turn, and that's what my picture of the ideal pro-choice movement revolves around: education, outreach, and conversation. A movement that trusts not in the power of politicians, laws, and political parties, but one that trusts in the intelligence and compassion of individuals. A movement that gives its affiliates and clinics the latitude and resources they need to do substantial outreach and educational work within their community. A movement that *starts* the conversation about rights and choices, rather than reacts to the attacks of others, and that is open-minded enough to accept that just as there are thousands of reasons to choose abortion, there are thousands of ways to feel about that choice. The movement can only be strengthened by allowing for and understanding every possible point of view.

Real and lasting change will only come when people decide that it's not okay to judge a complete stranger on the basis of a personal choice, and that it's not okay to elect politicians who want to do that, either. That decision will affect not just who they vote for, but also how they talk about abortion and contraception with their friends, relatives, and children.

Change can be brought about more effectively and rapidly by following the example of young activists who seamlessly integrate pro-choice activism into their everyday lives. For them, reproductive rights is a topic that can and should be brought up in "mixed company," with friends who might never think about abortion rights or partners who have never considered what they'd do in the event of an accidental pregnancy.

In her interview with me several years ago, pro-choice activist Raina Aronowitz mentioned that she brings up abortion "at the bar" when she's out with her friends.[38] This is the kind of inspiring and unapologetic action that younger activists are engaging in all the time, and that is great. Why shouldn't abortion be just one more subject that friends and acquaintances can discuss in casual settings, on casual occasions? Treating abortion like just another conversational topic demystifies it, makes it less of a capital-T topic; it removes that whole "movie of the week" vibe that so many people still associate with addressing controversial and personal subjects. There's a vicious cycle at work here, where the very word "abortion" has become loaded with so much meaning it doesn't deserve, to the point that even saying "abortion" feels daring. This cycle just keeps loading the word with more power than it should have. Saying the word out loud, talking about the action itself in either personal or speculative or political terms, drains it of its power and normalizes the word immensely.

For forty years, the movement has drifted away from the personal and into the political, into the thicket of court battles and ballot initiatives and an increasingly brazen anti-choice movement. For four decades, it's been reacting to attacks on an issue that *Roe v. Wade* was supposed to settle.

It's time for a new approach, and it's time to listen to new voices. It's time to take back the terms of the debate, to be on the offense again and never apologize for supporting the right to choose. And it's past time to remember that all of these actions must begin and end with one simple truth, a truth that the movement cannot allow itself to drift away from any further than it already has.

There is nothing wrong with having an abortion. End of story.

ACKNOWLEDGMENTS

This book could not have been written without the input and insights of the women and men whose stories appear on these pages. My deepest thanks for their candor, eloquence, and grace.

Thanks as well to my extraordinary agent, Penn Whaling; my amazing editor, Crystal Yakacki; Cherry Chevapravatdumrong, David Nelson, and Cara Spindler for their support, friendship, and wonderfully honest critiques; Sybil Breman, for her inimitable Southern hospitality; Judith DeWoskin and Ken Mikolowski, for making writing so fun; and Vince Mareino, for always believing in me, even when he didn't understand.

RESOURCE LIST

The following organizations, books, films, and blogs all proved useful during the researching and writing of Generation Roe. *All information is current as of this writing.*

Organizations

The American Civil Liberties Union Reproductive Freedom Project
http://www.aclu.org/reproductive-freedom

This project of the ACLU helps protect the right to make informed decisions free from government interference about when and whether to become a parent and fights discrimination against pregnant women. The project works to ensure access to abortion care, age-appropriate sex education, and safe and affordable contraception. Its website offers additional information about specific issues and ways to take individual action.

Alan Guttmacher Institute
http://guttmacher.org/

This nonpartisan research group advances sexual and reproductive health in the United States and around the world through social science research, public education, and policy analysis. Research, reports, and additional resources are available on its website.

Backline
http://www.yourbackline.org/

Backline promotes unconditional support for women's decisions, feelings, and experiences with pregnancy, abortion, and adoption. The website offers a number of resources around parenting, adoption, abortion, and after-abortion issues, including its Talk Line and other direct services.

Catholics for a Free Choice
http://www.cath4choice.org
CFC provides a voice for Catholics who believe that the Catholic tradition supports a woman's moral and legal right to follow her conscience in matters of sexuality and reproductive health. CFC has an education and communications program that carries out the research, development, production, and distribution of publications on reproductive health, ethics, theology, and other topics.

Center for Reproductive Rights
http://www.reproductiverights.org
The Center uses the law to advance reproductive freedom as a fundamental right that all governments are legally obligated to protect, respect, and fulfill. The Center promotes access to contraception, ensures access to abortion, supports adolescent reproductive health care, works to guarantee low-income women's reproductive freedom, trains reproductive rights lawyers, and uses legal resources to end violence based on gender or the assertion of reproductive rights.

Exhale
http://exhaleprovoice.org/
Exhale is a community-led organization that addresses the emotional health and well-being of women and men after abortion. Exhale provides support through its national talkline service; offers resources for women and men who want to share their stories; and works with media outlets on issues around abortion well-being and addressing personal abortion stories.

Feminist Majority Foundation
http://feminist.org/

FMF is dedicated to women's equality, reproductive health, and nonviolence. FMF engages in research and public policy development, public education programs, grassroots organizing projects, and leadership training and development programs, and participates in and organizes forums on issues of women's equality and empowerment. The FMF's sister organization, the Feminist Majority, engages in lobbying and other direct political action, pursuing equality between women and men through legislative avenues.

NARAL Pro-Choice America
http://naral.org/

NARAL Pro-Choice America uses the political process to elect pro-choice lawmakers and defeat anti-choice candidates, on both national and state levels with NARAL affiliates. The NARAL Pro-Choice website offers a variety of ideas and information for ways that individuals can make a difference.

The National Abortion Federation
www.prochoice.org

The professional association of abortion providers in North America, NAF offers training and services to providers and offers information and referral services for women and their partners. The NAF Hotline answers questions about abortion, pregnancy, and related issues and helps individuals locate clinics and other resources in their communities.

National Network of Abortion Funds
http://www.fundabortionnow.org/

The National Network of Abortion Funds coordinates one hundred local funds across the country that help women pay for abortion services. NNAF also provides tools for activists; fights for Medicaid coverage for abortion services; and works to remove barriers to abortion for immigrant women, young women, and incarcerated women.

Our Bodies, Ourselves/Boston Women's Health Book Collective
http://www.ourbodiesourselves.org/

OBOS is a nonprofit, public interest women's health education, consulting, and advocacy organization. In addition to publishing the well-known series *Our Bodies, Ourselves*, which presents health and medical information from a feminist perspective, OBOS advocates for women's health in the US and worldwide and is active in public policy and educational efforts.

Planned Parenthood Federation of America
http://www.plannedparenthood.org/

Planned Parenthood operates on both a national and local level, advocating for public policies that guarantee reproductive rights and ensure access to women's health services. Planned Parenthood provides educational programs, promotes reproductive health care research, and provides comprehensive reproductive and complementary health care. Planned Parenthood has several advocacy networks, including programs specifically aimed at college students and Republicans. The website includes information on locating clinics in individual communities.

Religious Coalition for Reproductive Choice
http://www.rcrc.org/

Founded in 1973 to safeguard the right to choice, the Coalition works to ensure reproductive choice through education and advocacy. Of particular focus are the reproductive issues of people of color, those living in poverty, and other underserved populations.

SisterSong
http://www.sistersong.net/

SisterSong Women of Color Reproductive Justice Collective works to strengthen the voices of women of color and indigenous women around issues of reproductive justice. SisterSong educates women of color on reproductive and sexual health and rights and works toward ensuring access to health information, resources, and services.

Books

Abortion Wars: A Half Century of Struggle, 1950–2000, edited by Rickie Solinger.
Twenty-two contributors focus on issues related to reproductive rights.

America's Women: 400 Years of Dolls, Drudges, Helpmates, and Heroines, by Gail Collins.
A wide-ranging examination of women's roles and lives throughout American history.

American Wife, by Curtis Sittenfeld
A novel about the events and decisions that shape the life of a young woman who, after marrying into a well-connected political family, becomes the First Lady.

Behind Every Choice Is a Story, by Gloria Feldt.
Feldt, a former president of Planned Parenthood, shares her own experience as a young mother and the stories of dozens of other women to explore reproductive rights issues.

Dispatches from the Abortion Wars: The Costs of Fanaticism to Doctors, Patients, and the Rest of Us; and *Doctors of Conscience: The Struggle to Provide Abortions Before* Roe v. Wade, by Carole Joffe.
Both of Joffe's books examine the pro-choice movement: *Doctors of Conscience* through the lens of health care in the years leading up to, and following, *Roe*, and *Dispatches* by looking at threats to abortion care and access, including financial barriers, difficulties faced by providers and clinicians, and restrictive state laws.

Gingerbread, by Rachel Cohn

A teenage girl deals with myriad family and relationship issues in this young-adult novel.

How the Pro-Choice Movement Saved America: Freedom, Politics and the War on Sex, by Cristina Page.

An examination of the anti-choice movement, including its political lobbying, opposition to contraception, and threats to privacy rights.

Life's Been a Blast, by Emily Lyons.

In her memoir, Emily—with contributions from her husband—discusses her early life, her work in an abortion clinic, and her recovery after the bombing.

My Life as a Rhombus, by Varian Johnson

This young-adult novel examines abortion and unplanned pregnancy through the experiences of two teenage girls.

Revolutionary Road, by Richard Yates

In this novel, a married couple in the 1950s struggle with the direction their lives are taking and their unhappiness with their surroundings and each other.

Sex Wars: A Novel of Gilded Age New York, by Marge Piercy.

A fictional account of life in post-Civil War America, *Sex Wars* includes a wealth of detail about women's lives, reproductive issues, and the burgeoning feminist movement.

The Abortion Resource Handbook, by K. Kaufman.

This 1997 guide presents a great deal of practical information, including self-care during pregnancy and abortion, avoiding crisis pregnancy clinics, and the judicial bypass process.

The Cider House Rules, by John Irving
This classic novel tells the story of Homer Wells, an orphan who grows up under the care of Dr. Wilbur Larch in 1920s and '30s Maine.

The Girls Who Went Away: The Hidden History of Women Who Surrendered Children for Adoption in the Decades Before Roe v. Wade, by Ann Fessler.
Fessler uses first-person stories to explore the issue of adoption in the years between the end of World War II and 1973.

The Perks of Being a Wallflower, by Stephen Chbosky
This young-adult novel focuses on one year in the life of a teenage boy and his often-intense and difficult relationships with family members, friends, and teachers.

The Story of Jane: The Legendary Underground Feminist Abortion Service, by Laura Kaplan.
Through extensive interviews and historical information, Kaplan—a former Jane member—tells the story of the Jane Collective, a Chicago-area feminist organization that provided abortion care for thousands of women between 1969 and 1973.

This Common Secret: My Journey as an Abortion Doctor, by Susan Wicklund and Alan Kesslheim.
In this memoir, Susan Wicklund explores her path to becoming an abortion provider; discusses the difficulties of being a provider, including extensive travel and safety threats; and offers her perspective on the pro-choice movement and its direction.

Witches, Midwives, & Nurses: A History of Women Healers, by Barbara Ehrenreich and Deidre English.
This ground-breaking work, first published in 1973, examines the myriad contributions that women made to the medical profession and the equally

varied ways in which they were demonized for their work. Particular attention is paid to the witch hunts of the Middle Ages, the Popular Health Movement, and the relation of contemporary medicine to women's rights.

Films

4 Months, 3 Weeks and 2 Days
Set in 1980s Romania, this film focuses on two young women, one of whom needs an illegal abortion.

Citizen Ruth
Director Alexander Payne satirizes both the pro- and anti-choice movements in this dark comedy about a pregnant, drug-addicted woman.

Dirty Dancing
Love, sex, and family—not to mention the titular dancing— are the focus of this film, set in the Catskills in 1963.

Frontline: The Last Abortion Clinic
This 2005 documentary explores challenges to reproductive choice, specifically in Mississippi, where the Jackson Women's Health Organization is the only remaining abortion clinic in the state.

I Had an Abortion
From Jennifer Baumgardner and Gillian Aldrich, this documentary features ten women discussing their own reproductive choices.

On Hostile Ground
This documentary follows three abortion providers—two physicians and one physician's assistant—as they practice in various parts of the country.

The Abortion Diaries

This documentary features twelve women sharing their experiences with abortion.

The Coat Hanger Project

Angie Young's documentary explores threats to abortion rights through interviews with activists, physicians, and pro-choice leaders.

The Shame of Patty Smith

This classic 1962 exploitation movie presents a surprisingly realistic and pro-legalization view on abortion and the options available to women.

Blogs

Anti-Choice is Anti-Awesome

http://antichoiceantiawesome.blogspot.com/

Written by a former clinic employee and current reproductive justice activist, this blog focuses on the pro-choice movement in Canada.

Every Saturday Morning

http://everysaturdaymorning.wordpress.com/

Every Saturday Morning is a group blog written by clinic escorts in Louisville, Kentucky.

Fair and Feminist

http://fairandfeminist.com/

This Texas-based blog focuses on issues of gender, race, and class; consciousness-raising and empowerment; and global and local actions.

Feminists for Choice
www.feministsforchoice.com

A collective of women's rights advocates, FFC explores personal, political, and cultural attitudes around choice and feminism.

I Am Dr. Tiller
www.iamdrtiller.com

A memorial to George Tiller and testimony to abortion providers, Steph Herold's blog gives people a place to share their stories about working in the pro-choice movement.

RH Reality Check
http://www.rhrealitycheck.org/

This website publishes a wide variety of articles, commentaries, and essays on sexual health and reproductive rights issues.

The Abortion Gang
http://abortiongang.org/

Founded by Steph Herold, this group blog is written by young activists dedicated to reproductive justice.

The Abortioneers
http://abortioneers.blogspot.com/

The Abortioneers is a group blog whose writers share their firsthand knowledge of the "ups and downs and ins and outs" of abortion care in various direct service settings (e.g., abortion clinic, patient escorting, emergency fund, and so on), as well as addressing relevant political and cultural issues through the lenses of their experiences.

NOTES

Chapter One: Abortion is Not a Four-Letter Word

1 Renee Chelian, clinic director, in discussion with the author, May 7, 2010.

2 June Ayers, clinic director, in discussion with the author, July 8, 2009.

3 Rachel Benson Gold, "Lessons from Before *Roe*: Will Past be Prologue?" *The Gutt-macher Report on Public Policy* 6, no. 1 (2003): 8-11, accessed September 7, 2012, http://www.guttmacher.org/pubs/tgr/06/1/gr060108.pdf.

4 Emily Lyons, in discussion with the author, July 8, 2009.

5 Ann Fessler, *The Girls Who Went Away: The Hidden History of Women Who Surren-dered Children for Adoption in the Decades Before* Roe v. Wade. (New York: Penguin, 2006).

6 Robert Blake, e-mail message to author, July 30, 2009.

7 "Facts on Induced Abortion in the United States," Guttmacher Institute, August 2011, accessed August 22, 2012, http://www.guttmacher.org/pubs/fb_induced_abortion.html.

8 Rachel, in discussion with the author, July 9, 2009.

9 Vicki, e-mail message to the author, March 18, 2010.

10 Vincent Rue, "Abortion and Family Relations," testimony before the Subcommittee on the Constitution of the US Senate Judiciary Committee, US Senate, 97th Congress, Washington, D.C. (1981).

11 Susan A. Cohen, "Abortion and Mental Health: Myths and Realities," *Guttmacher Policy Review* 9, no. 3 (Summer 2006): 8-11, 16, accessed August 22, 2012, http://www.guttmacher.org/pubs/gpr/09/3/gpr090308.html.

12 "Reproduction and Family Health: The C. Everett Koop Papers," Profiles in Science, National Library of Medicine, accessed April 23, 2012, http://profiles.nlm.nih.gov/ps/retrieve/Narrative/QQ/p-nid/88.

13 The Associated Press, "Study Finds Little Lasting Distress From Abortion," *New York Times*. April 6, 1990, accessed February 6, 2012, http://www.nytimes.com/1990/04/06/us/study-finds-little-lasting-distress-from-abortion.html.

14 Ibid.

15 Ibid.

16 Lawrence B. Finer et al., "Reasons US Women Have Abortions: Quantitative and Qualitative Perspectives," *Perspectives on Sexual and Reproductive Health* 37, no. 3 (2005): 110-18, accessed March 31, 2012. http://www.guttmacher.org/pubs/journals/3711005.html

17 "Facts on Induced Abortion in the United States," Guttmacher Institute, August 2011, accessed February 6, 2012, http://www.guttmacher.org/pubs/fb_induced_abortion.html.

18 Ibid.

19 Steph Herold, in a telephone conversation with the author, January 16, 2012.

20 Bess, activist, in discussion with the author, December 30, 2011.

21 Norman, activist, in discussion with the author, December 30, 2011.

22 David Garrow, "Pro-choice Groups Giving Up Too Much?" *The Christian Science Monitor*, February 23, 2005, accessed February 6, 2012, http://www.csmonitor.com/2005/0223/p09s01-coop.html.

23 Susan A. Cohen, "Insurance Coverage of Abortion: The Battle to Date and the Battle to Come," *Guttmacher Policy Review* 13, no. 4 (2010): 2-6, accessed January 28, 2012, http://www.guttmacher.org/pubs/gpr/13/4/gpr130402.html

24 Jennifer Baumgardner, "Abortion Evolution," Abortion Conversation Project, accessed February 10, 2012, http://www.abortionconversation.com/.

25 "Ruth's Story," I'm Not Sorry, accessed February 6, 2012, http://www.imnotsorry.net/2010/09/06/ruths-story/

26 "Rollyn's Story," I'm Not Sorry, accessed February 6, 2012, http://www.imnotsorry.net/2010/09/06/rollyns-story/

27 "Robyn's Story," I'm Not Sorry, accessed February 6, 2012, http://www.imnotsorry.net/2010/09/06/robyns-story-3/

28 Shannon Connolly, in a telephone conversation with the author June 27, 2009.

Chapter Two: Hands-Off Training

1 Wayne Goldner, in telephone conversations with the author, July 2009.

2 "An Overview of Abortion in the United States," Guttmacher Institute, accessed February 6, 2012, http://www.guttmacher.org/media/presskits/2005/06/28/abortionoverview.html.

3 S. K. Henshaw, "Unintended Pregnancy and Abortion: A Public Health Perspective," in *A Clinician's Guide to Medical and Surgical Abortion*, ed. Maureen Paul and David A. Grimes. (Philadelphia: Churchill Livingstone, 1999), 11–22.

4 Cristina Page, *How the Pro-Choice Movement Saved America: Freedom, Politics, and the War on Sex* (New York: Basic Books, 2006), 58.

5 Leslie Reagan, *When Abortion Was a Crime* (Berkeley: University of California Press, 1997), 8-9.

6 Barbara Ehrenreich and Deirdre English, *Witches, Midwives & Nurses: A History of Women Healers* (New York: Feminist Press at the City University of New York, 2010), 64-65.

7 Ibid., 64-67.

8 "That Girl There is Doctor in Medicine: Elizabeth Blackwell, America's First Woman M.D.," US National Library of Medicine, National Institutes of Health, accessed August 24, 2012, http://www.nlm.nih.gov/exhibition/blackwell/index.html.

9 "Women in Medicine: An AMA Timeline," American Medical Association, accessed August 24, 2012, http://www.ama-assn.org/resources/doc/wpc/wimtimeline.pdf.

10 Ibid., 76-77, 81-85.

11 Leslie Reagan, *When Abortion Was a Crime* (Berkeley: University of California Press, 1997), 10-13.

12 Ina May Gaskin, *Birth Matters: A Midwife's Manifesta* (New York: Seven Stories Press), 74.

13 Ibid., 81.

14 Ibid., 75-76.

15 Justin Diedrich, e-mail messages to author, July 30 and August 2, 2009.

16 Sara Rimer, "The Clinic Gunman and the Victim: Abortion Fight Reflected in 2 Lives," *New York Times*, March 14, 1993, accessed February 6, 2012, http://www.nytimes.com/1993/03/14/us/the-clinic-gunman-and-the-victim-abortion-fight-reflected-in-2-lives.html.

17 "Medical Students for Choice: History," Medical Students for Choice, accessed February 10, 2012, http://www.medicalstudentsforchoice.org/index.php?page=history.

18 "Student Organizing: Chapters," Medical Students for Choice, accessed February 6, 2012, http://www.medicalstudentsforchoice.org/index.php?page=find-start-group.

19 "Spotlight on Specialties: Obstetrics and Gynecology," Careers in Medicine, Association of American Medical Colleges, accessed August 24, 2012, https://www.aamc.org/students/medstudents/cim/choicesnewsletter/august11/256750/salaryscoresandotherstats.html.

20 Emily Bazelon, "The New Abortion Providers," *The New York Times Magazine*, July 14, 2010, accessed August 24, 2012, http://www.nytimes.com/2010/07/18/magazine/18abortion-t.html?pagewanted=all.

21 Megan Evans, medical student, in discssion with the author, June 30, 2009.

22 Louisa Pyle, medical student, in discssion with the author, July 6, 2009.

23 Melissa Weston, e-mail message to author, August 28, 2009.

24 D&C, or dilation and curettage, is a process by which tissues are removed from the uterus. "D and C," MedlinePlus, updated June 16, 2010, accessed February 10, 2012, http://www.nlm.nih.gov/medlineplus/ency/article/002914.htm.

25   Justin Diedrich, e-mail messages to author, July 30 and August 2, 2009.

26   Bhavik Kumar, in a telephone conversation with the author, June 28, 2009.

27   "Texas Adolescent Reproductive Health Facts," Office of Adolescent Health, US Department of Health & Human Services, accessed September 12, 2012, http://www.hhs.gov/ash/oah/adolescent-health-topics/reproductive-health/states/tx.html.

28   Eve Epsey, et al, "Abortion Education in Medical Schools: A National Survey," *American Journal of Obstetrics and Gynecology* 192 (2005): 640-3, accessed April 7, 2012, http://comdo-wcnlb.uc.edu/StudentStorage/Organizations/8_Education.pdf.

29   Ibid., 641.

30   Ibid.

31   Ibid.

32   Ibid.

33   Ibid.

34   Shannon Connolly, in a telephone conversation with the author, June 27, 2009.

35   "Educating Beyond the Classroom: Medical Students for Choice Annual Report 2011," Medical Students for Choice, accessed August 24, 2012, http://issuu.com/medicalstudentsforchoice/docs/msfc_2011anrpt4_final?mode=window&backgroundColor=%23222222.

36   Angel M. Foster, DPhil, AM, Jane van Dis, MD, and Jody Steinauer, MD, "Educational and Legislative Initiatives Affecting Residency Training in Abortion," *JAMA* 290, no. 13 (2003): 1777-8, accessed April 7, 2012, http://jama.jamanetwork.com/article.aspx?articleid=197390.

37   Ibid.

38   "Miscarriage," American Pregnancy Association, accessed August 24, 2012, http://www.americanpregnancy.org/pregnancycomplications/miscarriage.html/.

39   "Second Trimester Pregnancy Loss," *American Family Physician* 76, no. 9 (2007): 1341-46, accessed August 24, 2012, http://www.aafp.org/afp/2007/1101/p1341.html#afp20071101p1341-b4.

40   Lori Freedman, Uta Landy, and Jody Steinauer, "Obstetrician-gynecologist Experiences with Abortion Training: Physician Insights from a Qualitative Study," *Contraception* 81, no. 6 (2010): 525-30, accessed April 7, 2012, http://www.ansirh.org/_documents/library/freedman_contraception2-2010.pdf .

41   "Abortion Access and Training," ACOG Committee Opinion, 424 (2009), accessed April 7, 2012. http://www.acog.org/Resources_And_Publications/Committee_Opinions/Committee_on_Health_Care_for_Underserved_Women/Abortion_Access_and_Training

42   Ibid.

43   Kalli Joy Gray, "House Passes Amendment to Defund Medical Schools That Teach Abortion," *Daily Kos*, May 25, 2011, accessed February 10, 2012, http://www.

dailykos.com/story/2011/05/25/979252/-House-passes-amendment-to-defund-medical-schools-that-teach-abortion.

44 Pete Kasperowicz, "Anti-Abortion Language Approved as Amendment to House Healthcare Bill," *The Hill*. May 25, 2011, accessed February 6, 2012, http://thehill.com/blogs/floor-action/house/163249-anti-abortion-language-approved-as-amendment-to-house-healthcare-bill.

45 "Bill Summary & Status, 112th Congress (2011-2012), H.R. 1216," The Library of Congress, accessed August 26, 2012, http://thomas.loc.gov/cgi-bin/bdquery/z?d112:h.r.1216:.

46 Jennifer Steinhauer, "It May Be a 'Budget Battle,' but Some Skirmishes Have Little to do With Money," *The New York Times*, April 7, 2011, accessed August 29, 2012, http://www.nytimes.com/2011/04/08/us/politics/08riders.html.

47 Frank James, "Planned Parenthood: Fight About Us, Not Abortion Funding," NPR, April 8, 2011, accessed August 29, 2012, http://www.npr.org/blogs/itsallpolitics/2011/04/08/135236230/planned-parenthood-budget-fight-about-us-not-abortion-money.

48 Heather D. Boonstra, "The Heart of the Matter: Public Funding of Abortion for Poor Women in the United States," *Guttmacher Policy Review* 10, no. 1 (2007): 12-16, accessed August 29, 2012, http://www.guttmacher.org/pubs/gpr/10/1/gpr100112.pdf.

49 Mark Egerman, attorney, in discussion with the author, June 4, 2010.

50 Judith Davidoff and Shawn Doherty, "Abortion Foes Ask Van Hollen to Crack Down on UW Hospital," *The Capital Times*, July 7, 2011, accessed February 6, 2012, http://host.madison.com/ct/news/local/on-topic/article_80957882-a8d7-11e0-a3a2-001cc4c03286.html.

51 Deborah Ziff, "UW Hospital: Abortion Language Inserted Into State Budget Could Jeopardize OB/GYN Accreditation," *Wisconsin State Journal*, June 22, 2011, accessed February 10, 2012, http://host.madison.com/wsj/news/local/govt-and-politics/uw-hospital-abortion-language-inserted-into-state-budget-could-jeopardize/article_803d71f6-9c51-11e0-b739-001cc4c002e0.html.

52 "Who Are We," Pro-Life Wisconsin, accessed August 26, 2012, http://www.prolifewisconsin.org/whoAreWe.asp.

53 Igor Volsky, "WI Anti-Choice Group Asks Attorney General to Prevent Med School From Teaching Abortion Procedure to Doctors," *Think Progress*, July 8, 2011, accessed February 6, 2012, http://thinkprogress.org/health/2011/07/08/263501/wi-anti-choice-group-asks-attorney-general-to-prevent-med-school-from-teaching-abortion-procedure-to-doctors/

54 John Celock, "Kansas Abortion Bill: Legislators Push to Allow Medical Residents to Learn Abortion Procedures," *The Huffington Post*, March 5, 2012, accessed April 7, 2012, http://www.huffingtonpost.com/2012/03/05/abortion-bill-kansas-medical-residents_n_1321910.html.

55 John Celock, "Kansas Abortion Bill to Ban Procedure by State Workers Passes House," *The Huffington Post*, March 17, 2012, accessed April 7, 2012, http://www.huffing-tonpost.com/2012/03/17/kansas-abortion-bill-ku-medical-center_n_1355351.html

56 Rachel K. Jones, et al., "Abortion in the United States: Incidence and Access to Services, 2005," *Perspectives on Sexual and Reproductive Health* 40, no. 1 (2008): 6-16, accessed April 7, 2012, doi: 10.1363/4000608.

57 Ibid.

58 Rachel K. Jones and Kathryn Kooistra, "Abortion Incidence and Access to Services in the United States, 2008," *Perspectives on Sexual and Reproductive Health* 43, no. 1 (2011): 41-50, accessed April 7, 2012, doi: 10.1363/43041111.

59 "Facts on Induced Abortion in the United States," Guttmacher Institute, August 2011, accessed April 7, 2012, http://www.guttmacher.org/pubs/fb_induced_abortion.html.

60 Roundtable in OB/GYN & Women's Health, "Medical Education in Abortion," *Medscape News*, November 15, 2011, accessed April 7, 2012, http://www.medscape.com/viewarticle/753192.

61 Michael Winerip, "Where to Pass the Torch," *New York Times*, March 6, 2009, accessed April 7, 2012, http://www.nytimes.com/2009/03/08/fashion/08generationb.html?pagewanted=all.

62 Roundtable in OB/GYN & Women's Health, "Medical Education in Abortion," *Medscape News*, November 15, 2011, accessed April 7, 2012, http://www.medscape.com/viewarticle/753192.

63 Louisa Pyle, medical student, in discssion with the author, July 6, 2009.

Chapter Three: Isolated, Stigmatized, and Romanticized

1 Maura Porto, in a telephone conversation with the author, June 28, 2009.

2 Marciana Wilkerson, in a telephone conversation with the author, June 9, 2009.

3 Jody Feder, "The History and Effect of Abortion Conscience Clause Laws," CRS Report for Congress, January 14, 2005, accessed August 26, 2012, http://www.law.umaryland.edu/marshall/crsreports/crsdocuments/RS2142801142005.pdf.

4 Ibid.

5 Ibid.

6 Julie Rovner, "New Contraception Rule Sparks 'Conscience Clause' Debate," NPR, February 18, 2011, accessed August 26, 2012, http://m.npr.org/news/Health/133877729?singlePage=true.

7 The Associated Press, "Obama Administration Revises 'Conscience Clause' Rules: Contraception No Longer Considered Abortion," *The Huffington Post*, February 18, 2011, accessed February 10, 2012, http://www.huffingtonpost.com/2011/02/18/obama-conscience-clause-abortion-contraception_n_825461.html.

8   Ibid.

9   Samantha Henry, "Deal: NJ Nurses Can Skip Aiding Hospital Abortions," *The Huff-ington Post*, December 22, 2011, accessed February 6, 2012, http://www.huffington-post.com/huff-wires/20111222/us-abortion-nurses--lawsuit/.

10 Megan Evans, medical student, in discssion with the author, June 30, 2009.

11 Kate Palmer, e-mail message to author, August 20, 2009.

12 The Associated Press, "Judge Says Wash. Can't Make Pharmacies Sell Plan B," *USA Today*, February 22, 2012, accessed April 8, 2012, http://www.usatoday.com/news/nation/story/2012-02-22/emergency-contraceptives-plan-b-wash-ington/53211188/1.

13 Ruby De Luna, "Washington to Appeal Plan B Ruling," Northwest Public Radio, March 22, 2012, accessed April 9, 2012, http://nwpr.org/post/washington-appeal-plan-b-ruling.

14 "News Release: State Appeals Court Ruling on Access to Medications in Stormans v. Selecky," Washington State Department of Health, March 21, 2012, accessed April 9, 2012, http://www.doh.wa.gov/Publicat/2012_news/12-031.htm.

15 "Code of Ethics for Nurses With Interpretive Statements," American Nurses Association, accessed April 9, 2012, http://nursingworld.org/MainMenuCategories/EthicsStandards/CodeofEthicsforNurses/Code-of-Ethics.pdf.

16 Ibid.

17 Laura Kaplan, *The Story of Jane: The Legendary Underground Feminist Abortion Service* (Chicago: University of Chicago Press, 1995).

18 Renee Chelian, clinic director, in discssion with the author, May 7, 2010.

19 Willie Parker, physician, in discussion with the author, July 7, 2010.

20 Robin Marty, "Nebraska Passes Parental Consent Law, Requires Notarized Signatures," *RH Reality Check*, May 27, 2011, accessed April 9, 2012, http://www.rhrealitycheck.org/blog/2011/05/27/nebraska-passes-parental-consent-requires-notarized-signatures.

21 LeRoy Carhart, physician, in discussion with the author, January 5, 2012.

22 "Facts on Induced Abortion in the United States," Guttmacher Institute, August 2011, accessed February 6, 2012, http://www.guttmacher.org/pubs/fb_induced_abortion.html.

23 "State Facts About Abortion: Viginia," Guttmacher Institute, accessed April 23, 2012, http://www.guttmacher.org/pubs/sfaa/virginia.html.

24 Laura Bassett, "Virginia Board of Health Passes Strictest Abortion Clinic Regulations in the Nation," *The Huffington Post*, September 15, 2011, accessed September 7, 2012, http://www.huffingtonpost.com/2011/09/15/virginia-strictest-abortion-regulations_n_964789.html.

25 Prue Salasky, "'Emergency Regulations' Threaten Virginia's Abortion Clinics," *Daily Press*, September 13, 2011, accessed February 6, 2012, http://articles.dailypress.

com/2011-09-13/health/dp-nws-abortion-va-0910-20110913_1_abortion-clinics-first-trimester-abortions-abortion-services/2.

26   Editorial, "Targeting Abortions," *The Washington Post*, September 4, 2011, accessed February 6, 2012, http://www.washingtonpost.com/opinions/targeting-abortions/2011/09/01/gIQAS7Fa2J_story.html?hpid=z3.

27   Amanda Peterson Beadle, "Women's Health Advocates Fight Against Virginia's Proposed Regulations Targeting Abortion Clinics," Think Progress, June 4, 2012, accessed October 25, 2012, http://thinkprogress.org/health/2012/06/04/494393/womens-health-advocates-fight-against-virginias-proposed-regulations-targeting-abortion-clinics/?mobile=nc.

28   Dahlia Lithwick, "Another Abortion Showdown in Virginia," Slate, July 17, 2012, accessed October 25, 2012, http://www.slate.com/articles/news_and_politics/jurisprudence/2012/07/virginia_attorney_general_cuccinelli_blocks_health_board_on_abortion_clinic_regulations_.html.

29   Laura Bassett, "Karen Remley, Virginia Health Commissioner, Resigns Over Abortion Clinic Regulations," *The Huffington Post*, October 18, 2012, accessed October 25, 2012, http://www.huffingtonpost.com/2012/10/18/karen-remley-virginia-abortion_n_1982118.html.

30   Ibid.

31   Laura Vozzella, "Virginia Health Board Reverses its Decision on Abortion-Clinic Rules," *Washington Post*, September 13, 2012, accessed October 25, 2012, http://www.washingtonpost.com/blogs/virginia-politics/post/virginia-health-board-reconsiders-abortion-clinic-regs/2012/09/13/d83ecf32-fe05-11e1-8adc-499661afe377_blog.html.

32   Laura Bassett, "Karen Remley, Virginia Health Commissioner, Resigns Over Abortion Clinic Regulations."

33   "Interview: Bonnie Scott Jones," Frontline/PBS, November 8, 2005, accessed February 6, 2012, http://www.pbs.org/wgbh/pages/frontline/clinic/interviews/scott-jones.html.

34   Barry Yeoman, "The New Abortion War," *Glamour*, February 2002, accessed February 6, 2012, http://barryyeoman.com/articles/trapeditorial.html.

35   "Targeted Regulation of Abortion Providers: Avoiding the 'TRAP,'" Executive Summary, Center for Reproductive Rights, August 2003, accessed August 29, 2012, http://reproductiverights.org/sites/crr.civicactions.net/files/documents/pub_bp_avoidingthetrap.pdf.

36   Maryclare Dale and Patrick Walters, "DA: Pa. Abortion Doctor Killed 7 Babies with Scissors," AOLNews, January 19, 2011, accessed April 9, 2012, http://www.aolnews.com/2011/01/19/abortion-doctor-kermit-gosnell-charged-with-8-counts-of-murder/.

37   Ibid.

38   Ibid.

39 Ibid.

40 Ibid.

41 The Associated Press, "Judge: 1 Trial for Philadelphia Abortion Doctor, Staffers," CBS Philly, September 30, 2011, accessed April 9, 2012, http://philadelphia. cbslocal.com/2011/09/30/judge-1-trial-for-philadelphia-abortion-doctor-staffers/.

42 Tara Murtha, "Corbett Signs SB732, Called 'Back-Door Ban' on Abortion in PA," Philly Now, December 23, 2011, accessed August 29, 2012, http://blogs.philadelphi- aweekly.com/phillynow/2011/12/23/corbett-signs-sb732-called-%E2%80%9Cback- door-ban%E2%80%9D-on-abortion-in-pa/.

43 Alexis Zepeda, activist, in discussion with the author, July 1, 2009.

44 Anti-Anti, activist, e-mail message to the author, December 12, 2009.

45 From The Abortioneers, accessed February 6, 2012, http://abortioneers.blogspot. com/.

46 Amanda, attorney, in discussion with the author, June 15, 2010.

47 Erin, activist, in discussion with the author, June 11, 2009.

48 Raina Aronowitz, activist, in discussion with the author, April 6, 2010.

49 June Ayers, clinic director, in discussion with the author, July 8, 2009.

50 Roula, activist, in discussion with the author, June 13, 2009.

51 Sara Skinner, activist, in discussion with the author, May 17, 2010.

52 Kate Palmer, e-mail message to author, August 20, 2009.

53 Shaundell Hall, in a telephone conversation with the author, June 24, 2009.

54 Willie Parker, physician, in discussion with the author, July 7, 2010.

55 Rozalyn Farmer Love, "Why I Will Provide Abortions," The Washington Post, June 7, 2009, accessed February 10, 2012, http://www.washingtonpost.com/wp-dyn/con- tent/article/2009/06/05/AR2009060502006.html.

56 Rozalyn Love, in telephone conversations with the author, August 2009.

57 Dana Weinstein, in discussion with the author, April 8, 2010.

58 Justin Diedrich, e-mail messages to author, July 30 and August 2, 2009.

59 Marciana Wilkerson, in a telephone conversation with the author, June 9, 2009.

60 LeRoy Carhart, physician, in discussion with the author, January 5, 2012.

61 Louisa Pyle, medical student, in discussion with the author, July 6, 2009.

62 Rozalyn Love, in telephone conversations with the author, August 2009.

63 Shannon Connolly, in a telephone conversation with the author, June 27, 2009.

64 Melissa Bird, e-mail message to author, September 10, 2009.

65 Katie Groke Ellis, e-mail messages to author, August 19 and 27, 2009.

66 Adrienne Kimmell, e-mail message to author, August 20, 2009.

67 Steph Herold, interview, RH Reality Check, October 20, 2009.

68   Sara Skinner, activist, in discussion with the author, May 17, 2010.

69   Alexis Zepeda, activist, in discussion with the author, July 1, 2009.

70   Kyle Marie Stock, interview, RH Reality Check, October 23, 2009.

71   Ibid.

72   Kira Baughman Jabri, social worker, in discussion with the author, 2010.

73   Angie Young, e-mail message to author, August 20, 2009.

74   Steph Herold, interview, RH Reality Check, October 20, 2009.

75   Yahel Carmon, interview, RH Reality Check, October 20, 2009.

76   Michelle Fortier, clinic director, in discussion with the author, July 7, 2009.

77   Melissa Bird, e-mail message to author, September 10, 2009.

Chapter Four: (Mis)Representations of Reality

1   "A Timeline of Abortion Stories in Popular US Media," The Abortion Diaries, accessed April 10, 2012, http://theabortiondiaries.com/archive.htm.

2   *Waitress*, directed by Adrienne Shelley (2007; Century City, CA: Fox Searchlight, 2007), accessed April 10, 2012, http://www.imdb.com/video/hulu/vi1127284761/.

3   Ibid.

4   *Juno*, directed by Jason Reitman (2007; Century City, CA: Fox Searchlight, 2007), accessed August 24, 2012, 2012, http://www.hulu.com/watch/17414.

5   Ibid.

6   Matt Berry, "Being Alive," *Desperate Housewives*, season 6, episode 2, directed by David Grossman, aired October 4, 2009, accessed April 10, 2012, http://www.hulu.com/watch/99991/desperate-housewives-being-alive#s-p5-n6-so-i0.

7   Lawrence B. Finer and Mia R. Zolna, "Unintended Pregnancy in the United States: Incidence and Disparities, 2006," *Contraception* 84, no. 5 (November 2011): 478-85, accessed August 24, 2012, http://www.guttmacher.org/pubs/journals/j.contraception.2011.07.13.pdf.

8   Jennifer Armstrong, "Exclusive 'No Easy Decision' Preview: Why MTV's Special Report on Abortion is Worth Watching," *Entertainment Weekly*, December 28, 2010, accessed February 10, 2012, http://insidetv.ew.com/2010/12/28/mtv-abortion-special-preview-exclusive/.

9   "Briana," *16 & Pregnant*, season 4, episode 3, aired April 3, 2012, accessed April 10, 2012, http://www.mtv.com/videos/16-and-pregnant-season-4-ep-3-briana/1682365/playlist.jhtml#series=2211&seriesId=27285&channelId=1.

10   Ibid.

11   Ibid.

12 "Censorship and Scandals," TV Acres, accessed February 10, 2012, http://www.tvacres.com/censorship_maude.htm.

13 Lynda Waddington, "True Reality Television: Where's Abortion?", *RH Reality Check*, April 23, 2008, accessed August 24, 2012, http://www.rhrealitycheck.org/blog/2008/04/18/true-reality-television.

14 Jay Sharbutt, "'Maude' Abortion Furor in Repeat," *Pittsburgh Post Gazette*, August 22, 1973, accessed February 6, 2012, http://news.google.co.uk/newspapers?id=AUsNAAAAIBAJ&sjid=Dm0DAAAAIBAJ&dq=maude%20abortion&pg=3411%2C2835386.

15 "Censorship and Scandals," TV Acres, accessed February 10, 2012, http://www.tvacres.com/censorship_maude.htm.

16 Austin Guzman, "Have You Seen Me Lately?" *Grey's Anatomy*, season eight, episode 15, directed by Tony Phelan, aired February 16, 2012, accessed April 10, 2012, http://www.hulu.com/watch/329124/greys-anatomy-have-you-seen-me-lately#s-p1-so-i0.

17 Willa Paskin, "Shonda Rhimes on *Grey's Anatomy*'s Recent Abortion Story Line," *New York*, September 27, 2011, accessed February 6, 2012, http://nymag.com/daily/entertainment/2011/09/shonda_rhimes_talks_about_grey.html.

18 Ibid.

19 Ginia Bellafante, "Abortion in the Eyes of a Girl From Dillon," *New York Times*, July 9, 2010, accessed February 10, 2012, http://www.nytimes.com/2010/07/10/arts/television/10lights.html.

20 "Degrassi Franchise," Degrassi Wiki, accessed August 24, 2012, http://degrassi.wikia.com/wiki/Degrassi_Franchise.

21 Maddy Pumilia, "Controversial *Degrassi* Issue Finally Premieres in the USA," Blogcritics.org, August 18, 2006, accessed September 7, 2012, http://blogcritics.org/video/article/controversial-degrassi-issue-finally-premieres-in/.

22 Ibid.

23 Melissa Silverstein, "*Roe v. Wade* Anniversary: *Friday Night Lights* and *Private Practice* Tackle Abortion," Women and Hollywood, January 22, 2010, accessed February 10, 2012, http://womenandhollywood.com/2010/01/22/roe-v-wade-anniversary-friday-night-lights-and-private-practice-tackle-abortion/.

24 Noah Evslin, "Do You Abort a Baby Twice?" Researcher's Blog, *Private Practice* website, ABC.com, accessed October 26, 2012, http://abc.go.com/shows/private-practice/researchers-blog/ThemeGallery/777704.

25 Melissa Silverstein, "Private Practice Takes on Abortion Again," Women and Hollywood, May 17, 2011, accessed October 26, 2012, http://blogs.indiewire.com/womenandhollywood/private_practice_takes_on_abortion_again.

26 Dave Itzkoff, "How 'Family Guy' Tried to Talk About Abortion," *New York Times*, July 19, 2010, accessed February 6, 2012, http://artsbeat.blogs.nytimes.com/2010/07/19/how-family-guy-tried-to-talk-about-abortion/.

27   Dave Itzkoff, "Banned TV Episode Has Its Day on DVD," *New York Times*. July 19, 2010, accessed February 6, 2012, http://www.nytimes.com/2010/07/20/arts/television/20family.html?_r=1&adxnnl=1&adxnnlx=1326813294-lO+PQwZy9obMIZ4Z1YSS+w.

28   *The Big Chill*, directed by Lawrence Kasdan (1983; Culver City, CA: Sony Home Pictures Entertainment, 1999), DVD.

29   Carrie Nelson, "An Interview with Eleanor Bergstein: On *Dirty Dancing*, Feminism and the Film Industry," Gender Without Borders, May 25, 2010, accessed January 28, 2012, http://www.genderacrossborders.com/2010/05/25/an-interview-with-eleanor-bergstein-on-dirty-dancing-feminism-and-the-film-industry/.

30   "1987 Domestic Grosses," Box Office Mojo, accessed September 12, 2012, http://boxofficemojo.com/yearly/chart/?yr=1987&p=.htm.

31   "Dirty Dancing," Box Office Mojo, accessed September 12, 2012, http://boxofficemojo.com/movies/?id=dirtydancing.htm.

Chapter Five: The Amazing Talking Fetus of Ohio

1   Michelle Goldberg, "The Latest Abortion Outrage," *The Daily Beast*, March 2, 2011, accessed February 10, 2012, http://www.thedailybeast.com/articles/2011/03/02/ohio-heartbeat-bill-abortion-outrage-the-religious-rights-grip-on-republican-party.html.

2   Kyle Mantyla, "Porter's Fetus Stunt Falls Flat," *Right Wing Watch*, March 2, 2011, accessed January 19, 2012, http://www.rightwingwatch.org/content/porters-fetus-stunt-falls-flat.

3   Catherine Candisky, "Ohio House Approves Anti-Abortion Bills," *The Columbus Dispatch*, June 28, 2011, accessed August 29, 2012, http://www.dispatch.com/content/stories/local/2011/06/28/ohio-house-approves-heartbeat-bill.html.

4   Tanya Somanader, "Ohio GOP Brings In 9-Week-Old Baby To 'Testify' For Anti-Abortion 'Heartbeat' Bill," *Think Progress*. December 8, 2011, accessed January 19, 2012, http://thinkprogress.org/health/2011/12/08/385096/ohio-gop-brings-in-9-week-old-baby-to-testify-for-anti-abortion-heartbeat-bill/.

5   Jim Siegel, "Ohio House Passes $55.8 Billion 'Reform-Oriented' Budget," *The Columbus Dispatch*, June 30, 2011, accessed April 13, 2012, http://www.dispatch.com/content/stories/local/2011/06/30/ohio-house-passes-55-8-billion-reform-oriented-budget.html.

6   Mary Kuhlman and Deb Courson Smith, "Ohio Budget: Cuts 'Sudden, Swift, and Difficult,'" Public News Service, July 20, 2011, accessed April 13, 2012, http://www.publicnewsservice.org/index.php?/content/article/21257-1.

7   Jim Siegel, "Ohio House Passes $55.8 Billion 'Reform-Oriented' Budget."

8   Sharon Lerner, "Meet the Ohio Woman Who Would Have Testified Against the 'Heartbeat Bill'," *The Nation*, March 7, 2011, accessed January 19, 2012, http://

www.thenation.com/blog/159068/meet-ohio-woman-who-would-have-testified-against-heartbeat-bill.

9 Ibid.

10 "States Enact Record Number of Abortion Restrictions in 2011," Guttmacher Institute, January 5, 2012, accessed January 19, 2012, http://www.guttmacher.org/media/inthenews/2012/01/05/endofyear.html.

11 Ibid.

12 The Associated Press, "Gov. Brewer Signs Arizona Bill With 20-Week Abortion Ban," FoxNews.com, April 13, 2012, accessed April 13, 2012, http://www.foxnews.com/politics/2012/04/13/gov-brewer-signs-arizona-bill-with-20-week-abortion-ban/.

13 Robin Marty, "Arizona Governor Jan Brewer Signs Country's First 20 Week Gestational Ban Into Law," *RH Reality Check*, April 12, 2012, accessed April 13, 2012, http://www.rhrealitycheck.org/article/2012/04/12/arizona-governor-jan-brewer-signs-countrys-first-20-week-gestational-ban-into-law.

14 "Calculating Your Dates: Gestation, Conception & Due Date," American Pregnancy Association, accessed August 29, 2012, http://www.americanpregnancy.org/during-pregnancy/calculatingdates.html.

15 The Associated Press, "Study: Fetus Feels No Pain Until Third Trimester," MSNBC, August 24, 2005, accessed February 6, 2012, http://www.msnbc.msn.com/id/9053416/#.Tr64tYDHDeg.

16 Branwen Jeffreys, "No Foetal Pain Before 24 Weeks," BBC News, June 24, 2010, accessed February 6, 2012, http://www.bbc.co.uk/news/10403496.

17 "State Policies in Brief: Counseling and Waiting Periods for Abortion," Guttmacher Institute, April 1, 2012, accessed April 13, 2012, http://www.guttmacher.org/statecenter/spibs/spib_MWPA.pdf.

18 Ibid.

19 Kira Baughman Jabri, social worker, in discussion with the author, 2010.

20 "Press Release: Federal Court Blocks Demeaning North Carolina Ultrasound Law," Center for Reproductive Rights, October 25, 2011, accessed April 13, 2012, http://reproductiverights.org/en/press-room/federal-court-blocks-demeaning-north-carolina-ultrasound-law.

21 Michael Avok, "South Dakota Law Requires 3-Day Abortion Wait," Reuters, March 22, 2011, accessed April 13, 2012, http://www.reuters.com/article/2011/03/22/us-s-dakota-abortion-idUSTRE72L6UR20110322.

22 Zach Zagger, "Federal Judge Blocks South Dakota Abortion Law with 72-hour Waiting Period," *Jurist*, July 1, 2011, accessed April 13, 2012, http://jurist.org/paperchase/2011/07/federal-judge-blocks-south-dakota-abortion-law-with-72-hour-waiting-period.php.

23 James Eng, "Texas Begins Enforcing Strict Anti-Abortion Sonogram Law," MSNBC.com, February 8, 2012, accessed April 13, 2012, http://usnews.msnbc.msn.com/_

news/2012/02/08/10355099-texas-begins-enforcing-strict-anti-abortion-sono-gram-law.

24 Jodi Jacobson, "Texas Sonogram Law Found to Violate First Amendment," *RH Reality Check*, August 30, 2011, accessed April 13, 2012, http://www.rhrealitycheck.org/blog/2011/08/30/texas-sonogram-found-violate-first-amendment.

25 Patrick Michels, "Texas Gets Pass to Enforce 'Empowering' Pre-Abortion Sonogram Law," *Texas Observer*, January 10, 2012, accessed April 13, 2012, http://www.texasobserver.org/snakeoil/appeals-court-texas-can-start-empowering-women-by-enforc-ing-pre-abortion-sonogram-law.

26 Ibid.

27 Rachel K. Jones, Lawrence B. Finer, and Susheela Singh, "Characteristics of US Abortion Patients, 2008," Guttmacher Institute, accessed April 24, 2012, http://www.guttmacher.org/pubs/US-Abortion-Patients.pdf.

28 "State Facts About Abortion: Texas," Guttmacher Institute, 2011, accessed April 13, 2012, http://www.guttmacher.org/pubs/sfaa/pdf/texas.pdf.

29 Laura Bassett, "Bob McDonnell, Va. Governor, Signs Mandatory Ultrasound Bill Into Law," *The Huffington Post*, March 7, 2012, accessed April 13, 2012, http://www.huffingtonpost.com/2012/03/07/bob-mcdonnell-virginia-mandatory-ultrasound-bill_n_1327707.html/.

30 Emily Ramshaw, "In Texas and Va., Different Reactions to Sonogram Bills," *The Texas Tribune*, February 23, 2012, accessed April 13, 2012, http://www.texastribune.org/texas-legislature/2011-abortion-sonogram-bill/tx-and-va-sonogram-bills-faced-different-challenge/.

31 Beverly McPhail, "Mandatory Ultrasound Bill Giant Step Back for Women," *Houston Chronicle*, May 7, 2011, accessed April 13, 2012, http://www.chron.com/opinion/outlook/article/Mandatory-ultrasound-bill-giant-step-back-for-1688395.php.

32 Andrea Grimes, "Forced Ultrasound, 'Informed Consent,' and Women's Health in Texas: The Sad State of State," *RH Reality Check*, March 7, 2012, accessed April 13, 2012, http://www.rhrealitycheck.org/article/2012/03/01/womens-health-in-texas-state-state.

33 Editorial Board, "Virginia Gov. Bob McDonnell's Abortion Crucible," *The Washington Post*, February 22, 2012, accessed April 13, 2012, http://www.washingtonpost.com/opinions/virginia-gov-mcdonnells-abortion-crucible/2012/02/22/gIQAONOBUR_story.html.

34 Laura Bassett, "Bob McDonnell, Va. Governor, Signs Mandatory Ultrasound Bill Into Law." .

35 Judith Lichtman, in a telephone conversation with the author, April 17, 2012.

36 Dahlia Lithwick, "No Cause for Celebration," *Slate*. February 29, 2012, accessed April 13, 2012, http://www.slate.com/articles/news_and_politics/jurispru-dence/2012/02/virginia_governor_bob_mcdonnell_will_sign_a_revised_ultra-sound_law_that_is_as_bad_as_the_old_one_.html.

37 Ibid.

38 Tyler Kingkade, "Wisconsin Doctors: Scott Walker Should Veto Abortion Legislation," Campus Progress, April 9, 2012, accessed April 19, 2012, http://campusprogress.org/articles/wisconsin_doctors_scott_walker_should_veto_abortion_legislation/.

39 Samhita, "Wisconsin's Coercive and Web Cam Abortion Prevention Act," Feministing.com, April 23, 2012, accessed August 29, 2012, http://feministing.com/2012/04/23/wisconsins-coercive-and-web-cam-abortion-prevention-act/.

40 Robin Marty, "Wisconsin Planned Parenthood to Immediately Stop Offering Medical Abortions Due to New, Medically-Unsupported, Regulations," RH Reality Check, April 20, 2012, accessed August 29, 2012, http://www.rhrealitycheck.org/article/2012/04/20/wisconsin-planned-parenthood-to-immediately-stop-offering-medication-abortions-du.

41 "New Law Infringes on Patient-Physician Relationship," Wisconsin Medical Society, April 6, 2012, accessed April 19, 2012, http://www.wisconsinmedicalsociety.org/.

42 Harris v. McRae, 448 US 297; 100 S. Ct. 2671 (1980).

43 Mark Egerman, attorney, in discussion with the author, June 4, 2010.

44 "Harris v. McRae," Center for Constitutional Rights, accessed August 29, 2012, http://ccrjustice.org/ourcases/past-cases/harris-v.-mcrae.

45 "Harris v. McRae," The Oyez Project, accessed August 29, 2012, http://www.oyez.org/cases/1970-1979/1979/1979_79_1268.

46 Griswold v. Connecticut, 381 US 479, 484; 85 S. Ct. 1678, 1681 (1965).

47 Griswold, 381 US at 497; 85 S. Ct. at 1688.

48 Eisenstadt v. Baird, 405 US 438; 92 S. Ct. 1029 (1972).

49 Doe v. Bolton, 410 US 179, 200-201; 93 S. Ct. 739, 751-752 (1973).

50 Jeffery Toobin, The Nine (New York: Doubleday, 2007), 59.

51 Roe v. Wade, 410 US 113, 93 S. Ct. 705, 35 L. Ed. 2d 147 (1973) (on appeal from 314 F. Supp. 1217 (N.D. Tex. 1970); probable jurisdiction noted, 402 US 941 (1971); set for reargument, 408 US 919 (1972)).

52 Noah Schabacker, interview, RH Reality Check, October 21, 2009.

53 Toobin, The Nine, 58.

54 Roe v. Wade, 410 US 113, 164; 93 S. Ct. 705, 732 (1973).

55 Ibid.

56 18 Pa. Cons. Stat. §§ 3203-3220 (1990). More information about the Act and how it affects women today can be found at http://www.plannedparenthood.org/ppsp/pa-abortion-control-act-18387.htm

57 Planned Parenthood of Southeastern Pa. v. Casey, Case No. 91-744, 744 F.Supp. 1323 (ED Pa. 1990).

58 Emily Bazelon, "Alito v. O'Connor," *Slate*, October 31, 2005, accessed April 24, 2012, http://www.slate.com/articles/news_and_politics/jurisprudence/2005/10/alito_v_oconnor.html.

59 *Planned Parenthood of Southeastern Pa. v. Casey*, 947 F.2d 682, 722-723 (3d Cir. 1991) (Alito, concurring in part and dissenting in part).

60 *Planned Parenthood of Southeastern Pa. v. Casey*, 947 F.2d 682, 722-723 (3d Cir. 1991) (Alito, concurring in part and dissenting in part). As discussed in this chapter, on appeal in 1992 the Supreme Court partly reversed but partly affirmed then-Judge Alito's reasoning.

61 "Statistics," American Pregnancy Association, accessed August 29, 2012, http://www.americanpregnancy.org/main/statistics.html.

62 *Casey*, 505 US at 872; 112 S. Ct. at 2818.

63 Ibid.

64 Noah Schabacker, interview, RH Reality Check, October 21, 2009..

65 *Stenberg v. Carhart*, 530 US 914; 120 S. Ct. 2597 (2000).

66 Lawrence B. Finer and Stanley K. Henshaw, "Abortion Incidence and Services in the United States in 2000," *Perspectives on Sexual and Reproductive Health* 35, no. 1 (2003): 6-15, accessed February 6, 2012, http://www.guttmacher.org/pubs/journals/3500603.html.

67 Ibid.

68 "Facts on Induced Abortion in the United States," Guttmacher Institute, August 2011, accessed August 29, 2012, http://www.guttmacher.org/pubs/fb_induced_abortion.html

69 Julie Rovner, "'Partial-Birth Abortion:' Separating Fact from Spin," National Public Radio, February 21, 2006, accessed February 10, 2012, http://www.npr.org/templates/story/story.php?storyId=5168163.

70 Pub.L. 108-105, codified at 18 USC. § 1531.

71 Nina Tottenberg, "High Court Takes Up Partial-Birth Abortion Case," National Public Radio, February 21, 2006, accessed February 10, 2012, http://www.npr.org/templates/story/story.php?storyId=5227039&ps=rs.

72 413 F.3d 791 (8th Cir. 2005).

73 Toobin, *The Nine*, 348.

74 *Gonzales v. Carhart*, 550 US 124; 127 S. Ct. 1610 (2007).

75 Ibid.

76 *Gonzales v. Carhart*, 550 US 124; 127 S. Ct. 1610 (2007).

77 Courtney Lewis, e-mail message to author, August 16, 2009.

78 Keely Monroe, e-mail message to author, September 4, 2009.

79 Denise Ross, "Why Won't South Dakota Ban Abortions?" CBS News, September 22, 2009, accessed April 14, 2012, http://www.cbsnews.com/2100-215_162-4643908.html.

80 Kathy Lohr, "Abortion Debate Likely to Heat Up in 2012," National Public Radio, February 1, 2012, accessed February 2, 2012, http://www.npr.org/2012/02/01/145980360/abortion-debate-likely-to-heat-up-in-2012.

81 Terry Baynes, "Oklahoma 'Personhood' Bill Poses Challenge to *Roe*," Thomson Reuters, April 9, 2012, accessed April 14, 2012, http://newsandinsight.thomson-reuters.com/Legal/News/2012/04_-_April/Oklahoma__personhood__bill_poses_challenge_to_Roe/.

82 Wayne Green, "'Personhood Bill' Won't be Heard This Session," *Tulsa World*, April 19, 2012, accessed August 30, 2012, http://www.tulsaworld.com/news/article.aspx?subjectid=504&articleid=20120419_504_0_OKLAHO818222&utm_source=twitter&utm_medium=tweet&utm_content=oklahoma&utm_campaign=ppact.

83 Ibid.

84 John M. Glionna, "New Arizona Law Bans Most Abortions After 20 Weeks," *The Seattle Times*, April 13, 2012, accessed April 19, 2012, http://seattletimes.nwsource.com/html/health/2017977758_azabortion14.html.

85 Mark Egerman, attorney, in discussion with the author, June 4, 2010.

86 Christine Vestal, "States Probe Limits of Abortion Policy," *Stateline*, June 22, 2006, accessed April 14, 2012, http://www.stateline.org/live/ViewPage.action?siteNodeId=136&languageId=1&contentId=121780.

87 Rachel Benson Gold, "Lessons From Before *Roe*: Will Past be Prologue?" *The Guttmacher Report on Public Policy* 6, no. 1 (2003) 8-11, accessed April 14, 2012, http://www.guttmacher.org/pubs/tgr/06/1/gr060108.html#box.

88 Ibid.

89 Ibid.

90 Ibid.

91 Christine Vestal, "States Probe Limits of Abortion Policy."

92 Rachel Benson Gold, "Lessons From Before *Roe*: Will Past be Prologue?"

93 David Crary, "Ruth Bader Ginsberg Questions Timing of *Roe v. Wade*, Gives Hint on Same-Sex Marriage Issue," *The Huffington Post*, February 10, 2012, accessed April 14, 2012, http://www.huffingtonpost.com/2012/02/10/ruth-bader-ginsburg-roe-v-wade-gay-marriage_n_1269399.html.

94 Ibid.

95 Christine Vestal, "States Probe Limits of Abortion Policy."

96 Ibid.

97 Ibid.

98 Ibid.

99   Courtney Lewis, e-mail message to author, August 16, 2009.

100 "State Policies in Brief: Parental Involvement in Minors' Abortions as of February 1, 2012," Guttmacher Institute, accessed February 2, 2012, http://www.guttmacher.org/statecenter/spibs/spib_PIMA.pdf

101 "Mandatory Parental Consent and Notification Laws," Center for Reproductive Rights, March 1, 2001, accessed April 15, 2012, http://reproductiverights.org/en/document/parental-involvement-for-abortion-mandatory-parental-consent-and-notification-laws.

102 Kyle Marie Stock, interview, RH Reality Check, October 23, 2009.

103 "NAF Violence and Disruption Statistics," The National Abortion Federation, accessed April 14, 2012, http://www.prochoice.org/pubs_research/publications/downloads/about_abortion/stats_table2011.pdf.

104 Ibid.

105 Ibid.

106 Ibid.

107 "2010 National Clinic Violence Survey," Feminist Majority Foundation, September 2010, accessed April 14, 2012, http://feminist.org/research/cvsurveys/2010/survey2010.pdf.

108 Ibid., 2.

109 Ibid., 3.

110 Ibid., 5.

111 Ibid., 6-7.

112 Ibid., 8.

113 Ibid.

114 "Clinic Violence: Freedom of Access to Clinic Entrances Act," The National Abortion Federation, accessed February 6, 2012, http://www.prochoice.org/about_abortion/violence/FACE_act.html.

115 "NAF Violence and Disruption Statistics," The National Abortion Federation, accessed April 14, 2012, http://www.prochoice.org/pubs_research/publications/downloads/about_abortion/stats_table2011.pdf.

116 Ibid.

117 Rebecca A. Hart and Dana Sussman, "About FACE: Using Legal Tools to Protect Abortion Providers, Clinics, and Their Patients," American Constitution Society Blog, July 7, 2009, accessed April 14, 2012, http://reproductiverights.org/en/pressroom/about-face-using-legal-tools-to-protect-abortion-providers-clinics-and-their-patients.

118 "NAF Violence and Disruption Statistics."

119 Rebecca A. Hart and Dana Sussman, "About FACE: Using Legal Tools to Protect Abortion Providers, Clinics, and Their Patients."

120 "Protection From Clinic Violence," NARAL Pro-Choice America, accessed April 14, 2012, http://www.prochoiceamerica.org/what-is-choice/fast-facts/clinic-violence.html.

121 Ibid.

122 June Ayers, clinic director, in discussion with the author, July 8, 2009.

123 Dr. David Gunn was shot and killed by an anti-choice extremist in Pensacola, Florida in 1993.

124 Emily Lyons, in discussion with the author, July 8, 2009.

125 "Rudolph Reveals Motives," CNN, April 19, 2005, accessed February 10, 2012, http://articles.cnn.com/2005-04-13/justice/eric.rudolph_1_emily-lyons-pipe-bomb-attack-eric-robert-rudolph?_s=PM:LAW.

126 Abbey Marr, activist, in discussion with the author, June 19, 2009.

127 Melinda Henneberger, "Rick Santorum: 'The Idea I'm Coming After Your Birth Control is Absurd,'" *The Washington Post*, January 6, 2012, accessed April 14, 2012, http://www.washingtonpost.com/blogs/she-the-people/post/rick-santorum-the-idea-im-coming-after-your-birth-control-is-absurd/2012/01/06/gIQAOVy0fP_blog.html?tid=sm_btn_tw.

128 "Rush Limbaugh vs. Sandra Fluke: A Timeline," *The Week*, March 9, 2012, accessed April 14, 2012, http://theweek.com/article/index/225214/rush-limbaugh-vs-sandra-fluke-a-timeline.

129 Judith Lichtman, in a telephone conversation with the author, April 17, 2012.

Chapter Six: Defending Choice One Generation at a Time

1   Willie Parker, physician, in discussion with the author, July 7, 2010.

2   Melissa Bird, e-mail message to author, September 10, 2009.

3   Michelle Fortier, clinic director, in discussion with the author, July 7, 2009.

4   Adrienne Kimmell, e-mail message to author, August 20, 2009.

5   Katie Groke Ellis, e-mail messages to author, August 19 and 27, 2009.

6   Kelsey Collier-Wise, e-mail message to author, August 12, 2009.

7   Mary Ann Sorrentino, "The Right to Hate Angie Jackson's Choice," *Salon*, March 9, 2010, accessed February 6, 2012, http://www.salon.com/2010/03/09/sorrentino_on_jackson/.

8   Alexa Kolbi-Molinas, e-mail message to author, July 21, 2009.

9   Megan Evans, medical student, in discussion with the author, June 30, 2009.

10 Ayesha Chatterjee, e-mail message to author, August 24, 2009.

11 Michael Winerip, "Where to Pass the Torch," *New York Times*, March 6, 2009, accessed February 6, 2012, http://www.nytimes.com/2009/03/08/fashion/08generationb.html?pagewanted=all.

12 Roula, activist, in discussion with the author, June 13, 2009.

13 Shannon Connolly, in a telephone conversation with the author, June 27, 2009.

14 Melissa Weston, e-mail message to author, August 28, 2009.

15 Anti-Anti, activist, e-mail message to the author, December 12, 2009.

16 The Associated Press, "South Dakota's Abortion Ban Rejected," *USA Today*, November 8, 2006, accessed February 6, 2012, http://www.usatoday.com/news/politicselections/vote2006/SD/2006-11-08-abortion-ban_x.htm.

17 Kyle Marie Stock, interview, RH Reality Check, October 23, 2009.

18 Rebecca Hart, e-mail message to author, September 1, 2009.

19 "Women in County Without Abortion Provider (%)," National Women's Law Center, accessed October 26, 2012, http://hrc.nwlc.org/status-indicators/women-county-without-abortion-provider.

20 Courtney Lewis, e-mail message to author, August 16, 2009.

21 "In-Clinic Abortion Procedures," Planned Parenthood, accessed April 15, 2012, http://www.plannedparenthood.org/health-topics/abortion/in-clinic-abortion-procedures-4359.asp.

22 According to Dana, although she and her husband had health insurance when she was diagnosed, their plan would only cover $1,250 because she had to use an out-of-network provider. After months of work, Dana was able to convince her insurance company to cover the procedure. The amount Dana quoted in her interview did not include travel or hotel costs.

23 Dana Weinstein, in discussion with the author, April 8, 2010.

24 Melissa Bird, e-mail message to author, conducted September 10, 2009.

25 Wayne Goldner, in telephone conversations with the author, July 2009.

26 June Ayers, clinic director, in discussion with the author, June 8, 2009.

27 Rozalyn Love, in telephone conversations with author, August 2009.

28 Alexis Zepeda, activist, in discussion with the author, July 1, 2009.

29 Kyle Marie Stock, interview, RH Reality Check, October 23, 2009.

30 Anti-Anti, activist, e-mail message to the author, December 12, 2009.

31 Alexis Zepeda, activist, in discussion with the author, July 1, 2009.

32 Steph Herold, interview, RH Reality Check, October 20, 2009.

Chapter Seven: I Went to the March for Life and
All I Got Was this Fear of Choice

1   Shaundell Hall, in a telephone conversation with the author, June 24, 2009.

2   "2008 Republican Platform," GOP.com, accessed July 12, 2012, http://www.gop.
    com/2008Platform/Values.htm#5.

3   Emily Bazelon, "Is There a Post-Abortion Syndrome?", *The New York Times Maga-
    zine*, January 21, 2007, http://www.nytimes.com/2007/01/21/magazine/21abortion.t
    .html?pagewanted=all, accessed July 18, 2012.

4   "About Us," Rachel's Vineyard, http://www.rachelsvineyard.org/aboutus/theresa.
    htm, accessed July 18, 2012.

5   "About Us," Silent No More, http://www.silentnomoreawareness.org/about-us/
    index.aspx, accessed July 18, 2012.

6   "Priests for Life," Charity Navigator, accessed August 30, 2012, http://www.chari-
    tynavigator.org/index.cfm?bay=search.summary&orgid=6438.

7   "Condoms: What's Still at Risk?" The Medical Institute, Austin TX, © 2003.

8   The Medical Institute, accessed March 3, 2012, http://www.medinstitute.org/.

9   "Testimony Before Congress on the American STD Epidemic," Joe S. McIlhaney
    Jr., MD, April 23, 2002, accessed March 3, 2012. http://energycommerce.house.
    gov/107/hearings/04232002Hearing541/McIlhaney932print.htm

10 "Comprehensive Sex Education: Research and Results," Advocates for Youth, Sep-
    tember 2009, accessed August 30, 2012, http://www.advocatesforyouth.org/compo-
    nent/content/article/1487-publications.

11 "Breaking the Contraceptive Barrier: Techniques for Effective Contraceptive Con-
    sultations," Association of Reproductive Health Professionals, September 2008,
    accessed March 3, 2012, http://www.arhp.org/Publications-and-Resources/Clinical-
    Proceedings/Breaking-the-Contraceptive-Barrier/Use-Knowledge.

12 "Facts on Contraceptive Use in the United States," Guttmacher Institute, June 2010,
    accessed March 3, 2012. http://www.guttmacher.org/pubs/fb_contr_use.html.

13 "Sex Was Never Meant to Kill You," Why kNOw Abstinence Education, Inc., Chat-
    tanooga, TN. © 2005.

14 Ibid.

15 Ibid.

16 "WHY KNOW?: *A Fear-Based Abstinence-Only-Until-Marriage Curriculum
    for Grades 6-12*," Curricula and Speaker Reviews, SIECUS, © 2008, accessed
    March 3, 2012, http://www.communityactionkit.org/index.cfm?fuseaction=page.
    viewpage&pageid=994#_ednref5.

17 "The Content of Federally Funded Abstinence-Only Education Programs," prepared
    for Rep. Henry A. Waxman, United States House of Representatives, Committee
    on Government Reform—Minority Staff Special Investigations Division, page 19,

December 2004, accessed March 3, 2012, http://www.apha.org/apha/PDFs/HIV/The_Waxman_Report.pdf.

18   "Mission/Vision," Care Net, accessed March 3, 2012,https://www.care-net.org/aboutus/mission.php.

19   Vincent Rue, PhD., "Forgotten Fathers: Men and Abortion," Life Cycle Books, Fort Collins, CO. © 2006.

20   Teri K. Reisser, M.S., M.F.T., and Paul C Reisser, M.D., "Healing the Hurt," Focus on the Family © 2010.

21   Ibid.

22   "Information from Focus on the Family: How to Help Others Who are Struggling with a Past Abortion," Focus on the Family, revised August 30, 2000.

23   Teri K. Reisser, M.S., M.F.T., and Paul C Reisser, M.D., "Healing the Hurt," Focus on the Family © 2010.

24   "The Care of Women Requesting Induced Abortion," Evidence-based Clinical Guideline Number 7, Royal College of Obstetricians and Gynaecologists, September 2004, accessed March 3, 2012, http://www.rcog.org.uk/files/rcog-corp/uploaded-files/NEBInducedAbortionfull.pdf.

25   "Summary Report: Early Reproductive Events and Breast Cancer Workshop," National Cancer Institute, posted March 4, 2003, updated January 12, 2010, accessed March 3, 2012, http://www.cancer.gov/cancertopics/causes/ere/workshop-report

26   "Patient Rights for the Woman Who is Seeking a Legal Abortion," Life Dynamics Incorporated, Denton, TX.

27   Sarah Coppola, "Crisis Pregnancy Centers that Don't Offer Abortions, Birth Control Will Have to Post Signs, Council Says," *American-Statesman*, April 8, 2010, accessed March 3, 2012, http://www.statesman.com/news/local/crisis-pregnancy-centers-that-dont-offer-abortions-birth-540483.html.

28   David W. Chen, "Judge Blocks City's Crisis Pregnancy Center Law," *New York Times*, July 13, 2011, accessed March 3, 2012, http://www.nytimes.com/2011/07/14/nyre-gion/judge-blocks-law-requiring-disclosure-at-pregnancy-centers.html?_r=0.

29   "2010 National Clinic Violence Survey," Feminist Majority Foundation, September 2010, accessed April 16, 2012, http://feminist.org/research/cvsurveys/2010/survey2010.pdf.

30   Kathryn Joyce, "The Clinic Across the Street," *Ms.*, Fall 2010, 27-29.

31   Ibid., 28.

32   Sara B., "The Truth About Anti-Abortion Pictures of Alleged Aborted Fetuses," Life and Liberty for Women, accessed August 30, 2012, http://www.lifeandlibertyfor-women.org/truth_about_photos.html.

33   Damien Cave, "Behind the Scenes: Picturing Fetal Remains," *New York Times*, October 9, 2009, accessed February 11, 2012, http://lens.blogs.nytimes.com/2009/10/09/behind-19/.

34 Loretta J. Ross, "Fighting the Black Anti-Abortion Campaign: Trusting Black Women," *On the Issues*, Winter 2011, accessed April 17, 2012, http://www.global-sisterhood-network.org/content/view/2524/59/.

35 Sara Rubin, "The New Push for Abortion Restrictions, *The Atlantic*, March 18, 2010, accessed April 17, 2012, http://www.theatlantic.com/politics/archive/2010/03/the-new-push-for-abortion-restrictions/37656/.

36 Loretta J. Ross, "Fighting the Black Anti-Abortion Campaign: Trusting Black Women."

37 Ibid.

38 Ibid.

39 Aaron Gould Sheinin, "Exclusive: Ralston Scraps 'Special Interest' Abortion Bill; Crafts His Own," *The Atlanta Journal-Constitution*, April 27, 2010, accessed April 17, 2012, http://www.ajc.com/news/georgia-politics-elections/exclusive-ralston-scraps-special-499723.html.

40 "SISTERSONG, SPARK, and SisterLove Defeat SB 529," INCITE! Women of Color Against Violence, July 11, 2010, accessed April 17, 2012, http://inciteblog.wordpress.com/2010/07/11/sistersong-spark-and-sisterlove-defeat-sb-529/.

41 Nadra Kareem Nittle, "Race Card: Anti-Abortion Billboards Target Black Women," *Bitch* Media, February 25, 2011, accessed April 17, 2012, http://bitchmagazine.org/post/race-card-anti-abortion-billboards-targeting-black-women.

42 The Associated Press, "Anti-Abortion Ad Provokes Lawsuit," *New York Times*, April 27, 2011, accessed April 17, 2012, http://www.nytimes.com/2011/04/27/nyregion/anti-abortion-group-is-sued-over-girls-photo-in-ad.html?_r=2&src=recg.

43 Laura Bassett, "Racially-Charged Anti-Abortion Bill Angers Civil Rights Community," *The Huffington Post*, December 6, 2011, accessed April 17, 2012, http://www.huffingtonpost.com/2011/12/06/racially-charged-anti-abortion-bill-angers-civil-rights-community_n_1132734.html.

44 Ibid.

45 "Facts on Induced Abortion in the United States," Guttmacher Institute, August 2011, accessed February 6, 2012, http://www.guttmacher.org/pubs/fb_induced_abortion.html.

46 "Prenatal Testing: Ultrasound," American Pregnancy Association, last updated March, 2006, accessed April 17, 2012, http://www.americanpregnancy.org/prenatal-testing/ultrasound.html.

47 Debra Ness and Andrea D. Friedman, "Susan B. Anthony and Frederick Douglass Prenatal Nondiscrimination Act of 2011" (H.R. 3541), submitted to the US House of Representatives Committee on the Judiciary, Subcommittee on the Constitution, December 6, 2011.

48 "Reading Between the Lines: How H.R. 3541, the Prenatal Nondiscrimination Act, Discriminates Against Women of Color," The National Partnership for Women &

Families, April 2012, accessed April 24, 2012, http://www.nationalpartnership.org/site/DocServer/PRENDA_fact_sheet.pdf?docID=10181.

49   Ibid.

50   Ibid.

51   "Facts on Induced Abortion in the United States" Guttmacher Institute, August 2011, accessed February 6, 2012, http://www.guttmacher.org/pubs/fb_induced_abortion.html.

52   Ibid.

53   Susan A. Cohen, "Abortion and Women of Color: The Bigger Picture," *Guttmacher Policy Review* 11, no. 3 (Summer 2008): 2-5, 12, accessed February 6, 2012, http://www.guttmacher.org/pubs/gpr/11/3/gpr110302.html.

54   Willie Parker, physician, in discussion with the author, July 7, 2010.

55   "A Disgrace," Press Release, National Partnership for Women & Families, February 16, 2012, accessed April 17, 2012, http://www.nationalpartnership.org/site/News2?page=NewsArticle&id=32067&security=2141&news_iv_ctrl=2103.

56   *Gonzales v. Carhart*, 550 US 124; 127 S. Ct. 1610 (2007).

57   Alexis Zepeda, activist, in discussion with the author, July 1, 2009.

Chapter Eight: On Demand and Without Apology

1   Bess, activist, e-mail messages to the author, November 1 and 8, 2011.

2   Kelsey Collier-Wise, e-mail message to author, August 12, 2009.

3   Daniel Nasaw, "Obama Reverses 'Global Gag Rule' on Family Planning Organisations," *The Guardian*, January 23, 2009, accessed February 11, 2012, http://www.guardian.co.uk/world/2009/jan/23/barack-obama-foreign-abortion-aid.

4   "In the Spirit of Abigail Allen," *Alphadelphian*, Vol. 13, Issue 1 (2009), accessed February 2, 2012 http://www.alfred.edu/wmst/current.cfm#WLA.

5   Angie Young, e-mail message to author, August 20, 2009.

6   Steph Herold, in a telephone conversation with the author, January 16, 2012.

7   Steph Herold, "Why is the Gay Rights Movement So Far Ahead of the Abortion Rights Movement?" Feministe, March 22, 2011, accessed February 6, 2012, http://www.feministe.us/blog/archives/2011/03/22/why-is-the-gay-rights-movement-is-so-far-ahead-of-the-abortion-rights-movement/.

8   Steph Herold, "When the Movement Disappoints," Feministe. March 25, 2011, accessed February 6, 2012, http://www.feministe.us/blog/archives/2011/03/25/when-the-movement-disappoints/

9   Ibid.

10 Stan, e-mail message to the author, November 5, 2011.

11 Serena Freewomyn, e-mail message to author, November 4, 2011.

12 "Structures," Medical Students for Choice, accessed April 24, 2012, http://www. medicalstudentsforchoice.org/index.php?page=structures.

13 Steph Herold, in a telephone conversation with the author, January 16, 2012.

14 Serena Freewomyn, e-mail message to author, November 4, 2011.

15 Sarah Kliff, "Mississippi Personhood Amendment Poised to Pass," *The Washington Post*, November 7, 2011, accessed January 29, 2012, http://www. washingtonpost.com/blogs/ezra-klein/post/mississippi-personhood-amendment-poised-to-pass/2011/11/07/gIQA3xlYvM_blog.html.

16 Tanya Somanader, "Gov. Barbour May Vote Against Mississippi's Personhood Abortion Ban: It 'Concerns Me, I Have To Just Say It'," ThinkProgress. org, November 2, 2011, accessed January 29, 2012, http://thinkprogress.org/ health/2011/11/02/359104/gov-barbour-may-vote-against-mississippis-personhood-abortion-ban-it-concerns-me-i-have-to-just-say-it/?mobile=nc.

17 Irin Carmon, "How Mississippi Beat Personhood," *Salon*, November 9, 2011, accessed February 11, 2012, http://www.salon.com/2011/11/09/how_mississippi_beat_personhood/.

18 Pam Belluck, "Cancer Group Halts Financing to Planned Parenthood," *New York Times*, January 31, 2012, accessed April 20, 2012, http://www.nytimes. com/2012/02/01/us/cancer-group-halts-financing-to-planned-parenthood. html?ref=us.

19 Ibid.

20 "'Alarmed and Saddened' by Komen Foundation Succumbing to Political Pressure, Planned Parenthood Launches Fund for Breast Cancer Services," Planned Parenthood Federation of America, January 31, 2012, accessed August 31, 2012, http://www.plannedparenthood.org/about-us/newsroom/press-releases/alarmed-saddened-komen-foundation-succumbing-political-pressure-planned-parenthood-launches-fun-38629.htm?__utma=1.1703199279.1346419554.1346419554.134 6419554.1&__utmb=1.23.10.1346419554&__utmc=1&__utmx=-&__utmz=1.1 346419554.1.1.utmcsr=(direct)|utmccn=(direct)|utmcmd=(none)&__utmv=-&__ utmk=193183277.

21 Raven Brooks, "How Komen Flushed Their Brand in 24 Hours," *RH Reality Check*, February 3, 2012, accessed August 31, 2012, http://www.rhrealitycheck.org/ article/2012/02/03/how-komen-flushed-their-brand-in-24-hours.

22 Michael Paulson and Kate Taylor, "Mayor to Give $250,000 to Planned Parenthood," *The New York Times*, February 2, 2012, accessed August 31, 2012, http://cityroom. blogs.nytimes.com/2012/02/02/bloomberg-to-give-250000-to-planned-parenthood/.

23 Greg Sargent, "Breaking: Two Dozen Senators Call on Komen to Reverse Planned Parenthood Decision," *The Washington Post*, February 2, 2012, accessed August 31, 2012, http://www.washingtonpost.com/blogs/plum-line/post/breaking-two-dozen-

senators-call-on-komen-to-reverse-planned-parenthood-decision/2012/02/02/
gIQA5EPnkQ_blog.html.

24 Raven Brooks, "How Komen Flushed Their Brand in 24 Hours," *RH Reality Check*, February 3, 2012, accessed August 31, 2012, http://www.rhrealitycheck.org/article/2012/02/03/how-komen-flushed-their-brand-in-24-hours.

25 Pam Belluck, Jennifer Preston, and Gardiner Harris, "Cancer Group Backs Down on Cutting Off Planned Parenthood," *The New York Times*, February 3, 2012, http://www.nytimes.com/2012/02/04/health/policy/komen-breast-cancer-group-reverses-decision-that-cut-off-planned-parenthood.html.

26 Ibid.

27 Amina Khan, "Karen Handel Explains Komen Resignation, Blasts Planned Parenthood," *Los Angeles Times*, February 7, 2012, accessed April 20, 2012, http://articles.latimes.com/2012/feb/07/news/la-heb-karen-handel-susan-komen-planned-parenthood-fox-20120207.

28 Brett Smiley, "Komen Foundation President Resigns, CEO Brinker Will Transition to Management Role," *New York Magazine*, August 8, 2012, accessed August 31, 2012, http://nymag.com/daily/intel/2012/08/komen-foundation-president-resigns-ceo-changes.html.

29 Judith Lichtman, in a telephone conversation with the author, April 17, 2012.

30 Petula Dvorak, "A Clinic's Landlord Turns the Tables on Anti-Choice Protestors," *The Washington Post*, March 29, 2012, accessed April 20, 2012, http://www.washingtonpost.com/local/a-clinics-landlord-turns-the-tables-on-anti-abortion-protesters/2012/03/29/gIQAThgwiS_story.html.

31 *The Rachel Maddow Show*, September 23, 2011, accessed August 30, 2012, http://www.msnbc.msn.com/id/26315908/#44648901.

32 Petula Dvorak, "A Clinic's Landlord Turns the Tables on Anti-Choice Protestors," *The Washington Post*, March 29, 2012, accessed April 20, 2012, http://www.washingtonpost.com/local/a-clinics-landlord-turns-the-tables-on-anti-abortion-protesters/2012/03/29/gIQAThgwiS_story.html.

33 Steph Herold, in a telephone conversation with the author, January 16, 2012.

34 June Ayers, clinic director, in discussion with the author, July 8, 2009.

35 Norman, activist, in discussion with the author, December 31, 2011.

36 Judith Lichtman, in a telephone conversation with the author, April 17, 2012.

37 Steph Herold, "Why is the Gay Rights Movement is So Far Ahead of the Abortion Rights Movement?" Feministe, March 22, 2011, accessed February 6, 2012, http://www.feministe.us/blog/archives/2011/03/22/why-is-the-gay-rights-movement-is-so-far-ahead-of-the-abortion-rights-movement/.

38 Raina Aronowitz, activist, in conversation with the author, April 6, 2010.

About the Author

Women's health advocate and writer Sarah Erdreich has been identified as a leading pro-choice activist by *Newsweek*, and her incisive writings on abortion rights have been noted by *Jezebel*, *Feministing*, and the National Partnership for Women & Families. She has worked for several prominent pro-choice organizations and has been published in *On The Issues*, *Lilith*, *Feminists For Choice*, and *RH Reality Check*. She has also worked editorially with the magazines *HUES* and *Teen Voices*. *Generation Roe* is her first book.

About Seven Stories Press

SEVEN STORIES PRESS is an independent book publisher based in New York City. We publish works of the imagination by such writers as Nelson Algren, Russell Banks, Octavia E. Butler, Ani DiFranco, Assia Djebar, Ariel Dorfman, Coco Fusco, Barry Gifford, Martha Long, Luis Negrón, Hwang Sok-yong, Lee Stringer, and Kurt Vonnegut, to name a few, together with political titles by voices of conscience, including Subhankar Banerjee, the Boston Women's Health Collective, Noam Chomsky, Angela Y. Davis, Human Rights Watch, Derrick Jensen, Ralph Nader, Loretta Napoleoni, Gary Null, Greg Palast, Project Censored, Barbara Seaman, Alice Walker, Gary Webb, and Howard Zinn, among many others. Seven Stories Press believes publishers have a special responsibility to defend free speech and human rights, and to celebrate the gifts of the human imagination, wherever we can. In 2012 we launched Triangle Square *books for young readers* with strong social justice and narrative components, telling personal stories of courage and commitment. For additional information, visit www.sevenstories.com.